ɔl Ann Duffy was born in Glasgow and grew up in
ford. She won the 1993 Whitbread Award for Poetry and
Forward Prize for Best Collection for *Mean Time*. *The
ʻld's Wife* received the E. M. Forster Award in America,
e *Rapture* won the T. S. Eliot Prize 2005. She is currently
essor of Contemporary Poetry at Manchester Metro-
an University. Her most recent volumes are *New and
ʻected Poems for Children* (2009) and *The Bees* (2011),
ʻh won the Costa Poetry Award. Her *Collected Poems*
published in 2015. She is Poet Laureate.

ʻian Clarke was born in Cardiff, Wales. National Poet
ʻWales 2008–2016, winner of the Queen's Gold Medal
Poetry (2010) and the Wilfred Owen Association
try Award (2012), she is one of the best-known names in
poetry today, as well as one of the most popular poets
ʻhe school curriculum. Poet, playwright, editor, trans-
ʻ, she is president of Tŷ Newydd Writers' Centre in
ʻh Wales which she co-founded in 1990. Her collections
de *Ice* (2012) and *Zoology* (2017); her *Selected Poems*
ʻared in 2016.

D1628317

I2803135

THE MAP AND THE CLOCK

A Laureate's Choice of the Poetry
of Britain and Ireland

edited by

Carol Ann Duffy

and

Gillian Clarke

ff

FABER & FABER

First published in 2016
by Faber & Faber Ltd
Bloomsbury House
74–77 Great Russell Street
London WC1B 3DA
This paperback edition first published in 2017

Typeset by Reality Premedia Services Pvt. Ltd.
Printed in England by CPI Group (UK) Ltd, Croydon, CRO 4YY

A CIP record for this book
is available from the British Library

ISBN 978-0-571-27709-4

CONTENTS

Preface by CAROL ANN DUFFY xxiii

I

I sing my own true story, tell my travels . . .
(600–1300)

II

Bring us in good ale . . .
(1300–1500)

III

Fair rocks, goodly rivers, sweet woods . . .
(1500–1600)

IV
Church-bells beyond the stars heard . . .
(1600–1700)

[ix]

V

Till a' the seas gang dry, my dear . . .
(1700–1800)

[x]

VI

Silent icicles, quietly shining to the quiet moon . . .
(1800–1850)

VII

Our days were a joy, and our paths
through flowers . . .
(1850–1900)

[xiii]

VIII

All the birds of Oxfordshire and Gloucestershire . . .
(1900–1918)

IX

I think we are in rats' alley
where the dead men lost their bones . . .
(1918–1945)

XI

The shadows, the meadows, the lanes,
the guildhalls, the carved choirs . . .
(1970–2000)

XII

if a toktaboot thi trooth lik wanna yoo scruff
yi widny thingk it wuz troo . . .

(2000–)

[xxi]

PREFACE

When my editor Matthew Hollis first invited me to assemble an anthology to appear during my time as Poet Laureate, I began to imagine a poetry treasure-hunt using a map and a clock to travel, and time-travel, these islands. As my ideal companion on this scavenging, I chose Gillian Clarke – the National Poet of Wales (2008–16) – who is one of the most fervent advocates of the art I know. Our journey was one of shared enthusiasms in poetry's loved landscape, lone wanderings off the beaten track to forage, return and share, or an enthralled standing-still to listen to the diverse sounds of poets, past and present, from England, Ireland, Scotland and Wales. 'Be not afeard. The isle is full of noises.'

We were clear that the magical properties of our map and clock were not to be used to assert or to reflect a British or Irish canon, but rather that they bestowed a freedom to tour and to celebrate the music, accents, surprises, variousness and fierce independence of poets from the earliest times to our own 21st century, from Anon to the emerging Zaffar Kunial. As on any journey, we spent time visiting great landmarks, but we also made sure to explore the hamlets, the backwaters, the local bars and the wrong side of the tracks – often the places where poets are to be found. It is not the destiny of every poet to outlast their own map and clock, but sometimes, perhaps, one of their poems might. With all our wanderings, foragings and listenings, we tried to find as many delights as we could to cram into our poetry backpacks and smuggle through Customs. Poetry should always be duty-free.

Although the earliest poems of these islands were orally composed, we chose to begin with the earliest acknowledged written poem, 'Caedmon's Hymn', beautifully translated here by Paul Muldoon; and where we intuit that the clock ticks significantly forward for poetry, we indicate this by a brief section marker. There are poets who write across these markers, and our placements may reflect a context or theme as much as a rigid chronology. Some great poets from the past, even the recent past, rightly claim more time from the clock, more space from the map. In the case of living poets, we restricted ourselves to one poem from each, and have taken great pleasure in including as diverse and generous a range of voices as possible within the spirit of this journey.

We would like to thank Tŷ Newydd, the Writers' Centre of Wales, and Adam Horovitz, for hospitality, poem sourcing, and photocopying help in the initial stages of this book, and Bernard O'Donoghue for his wise and generous advice on the early texts. Our warm thanks to Stephen Raw for the textual illustrations.

CAROL ANN DUFFY

I

I SING MY OWN TRUE STORY, TELL MY TRAVELS...

Caedmon's Hymn

Now we must praise to the skies,   the Keeper of the
   heavenly kingdom,
The might of the Measurer,   all he has in mind,
The work of the Father of Glory,   of all manner of marvel,

Our eternal Master,   the main mover.
It was he who first summoned up,   on our behalf,
Heaven as a roof,   the holy Maker.

Then this middle-earth,   the Watcher over humankind,
Our eternal Master,   would later assign
The precinct of men,   the Lord Almighty.

CAEDMON
translated from the Anglo-Saxon by Paul Muldoon

Song to a Child

Dinogad's smock is pied, pied –
Made it out of marten hide.
Whit, whit, whistle along,
Eight slaves with you sing the song.

When your dad went to hunt,
Spear on his shoulder, cudgel in hand,
He called his quick dogs, 'Giff, you wretch,
Gaff, catch her, catch her, fetch, fetch!'

From a coracle he'd spear
Fish as a lion strikes a deer.
When your dad went to the crag
He brought down roebuck, boar and stag,
Speckled grouse from the mountain tall,
Fish from Derwent waterfall.

Whatever your dad found with his spear,
Boar or wild cat, fox or deer,
Unless it flew, would never get clear.

ANON
translated from the Welsh by Tony Conran

Jesus and the Sparrows

The little lad, five years of age
– Son of the living God –
Blessed twelve puddles he'd just then coaxed
From water and from mud.

Twelve statuettes he made next;
'Sparrows shall you be named'
He whispered to those perfect shapes
That Sabbath in his game.

'Who plays with toys this holy day?'
A Jew scowled at the scene
And marched the culprit straight to Joseph
To scold his foster-son.

'What sort of brat have you brought up
That wastes his sacred time
Scrabbling in mud on the Sabbath Day
To make bird-dolls from slime?'

At that the lad clapped two small hands
And with sweet piping words
Called on the dolls before their eyes
To rise as living birds.

No music ever heard was sweeter
Than the music from his mouth
When he told those birds 'Fly to your homes
To east and west and south.'

The story spread throughout the land
And is heard down to this day
And all who hear it still can hear
The sparrows' voices pray.

ANON
translated from the Irish by Patrick Crotty

from Beowulf

These were hard times, heart-breaking
for the prince of the Shieldings; powerful counsellors,
the highest in the land, would lend advice,
plotting how best the bold defenders
might resist and beat off sudden attacks.
Sometimes at pagan shrines they vowed
offerings to idols, swore oaths
that the killer of souls might come to their aid
and save the people. That was their way,
their heathenish hope; deep in their hearts
they remembered hell. The Almighty Judge
of good deeds and bad, the Lord God,
Head of the Heavens and High King of the World,
was unknown to them. Oh, cursed is he
who in time of trouble has to thrust his soul
in the fire's embrace, forfeiting help;
he has nowhere to turn. But blessed is he
who after death can approach the Lord
and find friendship in the Father's embrace.

So that troubled time continued, woe
that never stopped, steady affliction
for Halfdane's son, too hard an ordeal.
There was panic after dark, people endured
raids in the night, riven by the terror.

When he heard about Grendel, Hygelac's thane
was on home ground, over in Geatland.
There was no one else like him alive.
In his day, he was the mightiest man on earth,

high-born and powerful. He ordered a boat
that would ply the waves. He announced his plan:
to sail the swan's road and search out that king,
the famous prince who needed defenders.
Nobody tried to keep him from going,
no elder denied him, dear as he was to them.
Instead, they inspected omens and spurred
his ambition to go, whilst he moved about
like the leader he was, enlisting men,
the best he could find; with fourteen others
the warrior boarded the boat as captain,
a canny pilot along coast and currents.

Time went by, the boat was on water,
in close under the cliffs.
Men climbed eagerly up the gangplank,
sand churned in surf, warriors loaded
a cargo of weapons, shining war-gear
in the vessel's hold, then heaved out,
away with a will in their wood-wreathed ship.
Over the waves, with the wind behind her
and foam at her neck, she flew like a bird
until her curved prow had covered the distance
and on the following day, at the due hour,
those seafarers sighted land,
sunlit cliffs, sheer crags
and looming headlands, the landfall they sought.
It was the end of their voyage and the Geats vaulted
over the side, out on to the sand,
and moored their ship. There was a clash of mail
and a thresh of gear. They thanked God
for that easy crossing on a calm sea.

When the watchman on the wall, the Shieldings' lookout
whose job it was to guard the sea-cliffs,
saw shields glittering on the gangplank
and battle-equipment being unloaded
he had to find out who and what
the arrivals were. So he rode to the shore,
this horseman of Hrothgar's, and challenged them
in formal terms, flourishing his spear:

'What kind of men are you who arrive
rigged out for combat in coats of mail,
sailing here over the sea-lanes
in your steep-hulled boat? I have been stationed
as lookout on this coast for a long time.
My job is to watch the waves for raiders,
any danger to the Danish shore.
Never before has a force under arms
disembarked so openly – not bothering to ask
if the sentries allowed them safe passage
or the clan had consented. Nor have I seen
a mightier man-at-arms on this earth
than the one standing here: unless I am mistaken,
he is truly noble. This is no mere
hanger-on in a hero's armour.
So now, before you fare inland
as interlopers, I have to be informed
about who you are and where you hail from.
Outsiders from across the water,
I say it again: the sooner you tell
where you come from and why, the better.'

ANON

translated from the Anglo-Saxon by Seamus Heaney

from The Gododdin

Men went to Catraeth, keen their war-band.
Pale mead their portion, it was poison.
Three hundred under orders to fight.
And after celebration, silence.
Though they went to churches for shriving,
True is the tale, death confronted them.

*

Men went to Catraeth at dawn:
All their fears had been put to flight.
Three hundred clashed with ten thousand.
They stained their spears ruddy with blood.
He held firm, bravest in battle,
Before Mynyddawg Mwynfawr's men.

*

Men went to Catraeth at dawn:
Their high spirits lessened their life-spans.
They drank mead, gold and sweet, ensnaring;
For a year the minstrels were merry.
Red their swords, let the blades remain
Uncleansed, white shields and four-sided spearheads,
Before Mynyddawg Mwynfawr's men.

*

Men went to Catraeth at morn.
He made certain the shame of armies;
They made sure that a bier was needed.
The most savage blades in Christendom,
He contrived, no request for a truce,
A blood-path and death for his foeman.
When he was before Gododdin's band
Neirthiad's deeds showed a hero's bold heart.

*

No cowards could bear the hall's uproar.
Before battle a battle broke out
Like a fire that rages when kindled.
On Tuesday they donned their dark armour,
On Wednesday, bitter their meeting,
On Thursday, terms were agreed on,
On Friday, dead men without number,
On Saturday, fearless, they worked as one,
On Sunday, crimson blades were their lot,
On Monday, men were seen waist-deep in blood.
After defeat, the Gododdin say,
Before Madawg's tent on his return
There came but one man in a hundred.

ANEIRIN
translated from the Welsh by Joseph P. Clancy

Bede's Death Song

Before the journey that awaits us all,
No man becomes so wise that he does not
Need to think out, before his going hence,
What judgment will be given to his soul
After his death, of evil or of good.

BEDE
translated from the Anglo-Saxon by Richard Hamer

Death Song for Owain ab Urien

God, consider the soul's need
    Of Owain son of Urien!
Rheged's prince, secret in loam:
    No shallow work, to praise him!

A strait grave, a man much praised,
    His whetted spear the wings of dawn:
That lord of bright Llwyfenydd,
    Where is his peer?

Reaper of enemies; strong of grip;
    One kind with his fathers;
Owain, to slay Fflamddwyn,
    Thought it no more than sleep.

Sleepeth the wide host of England
   With light in their eyes,
And those that had not fled
   Were braver than were wise.

Owain dealt them doom
   As the wolves devour sheep;
That warrior, bright of harness,
   Gave stallions for the bard.

Though he hoarded wealth like a miser,
   For his soul's sake he gave it.
God, consider the soul's need
   Of Owain son of Urien.

TALIESIN
translated from the Welsh by Tony Conran

'Birdsong from a willow tree'

Birdsong from a willow tree.
Whet-note music, clear, airy;
Inky treble, yellow bill –
Blackbird, practising his scale.

ANON
translated from the Irish by Seamus Heaney

The Battle of Brunanburh

Æthelstan, the King, ruler of earls
and ring-giver to men, and Prince Eadmund
his brother, earned this year fame everlasting
with the blades of their swords in battle
at Brunanburh; with their well-wrought weapons
both Eadweard's sons cleaved the linden shields,
cut through the shield-wall; as was only fitting
for men of their lineage, they often carried arms
against some foe in defence of their land,
their treasure, their homes. The enemy perished,
fated Scots and seafarers
fell in the fight; from the hour when that great
constellation the sun, the burning candle
of God eternal, first glides above the earth
until at last that lordly creation
sinks into its bower, the battlefield flowed
with dark blood. Many a warrior lay there,
spreadeagled by spears, many a Norse seafarer
stabbed above his shield and many a weary Scot,
surfeited by war. All day,
in troops together, the West Saxons
pursued those hateful people,
hewed down the fugitives fiercely from behind
with their sharpened swords. The Mercians did not stint
hard handplay to any of the heroes
who, fated to fight, sought this land
with Anlaf, sailed in the ship's hold
over the surging sea. Five young kings
sprawled on that field of battle,
put to sleep by swords; likewise seven

of Anlaf's earls and countless in the host,
seafarers and Scots. There, the Norse king
was forced to flee, driven to the ship's prow
with a small bodyguard; the little ship
scurried out to sea, the king sped
over the dark waves and so saved his life.
Constantine, too, (a man of discretion)
fled north to the comforts of his own country;
deprived of kinsmen and comrades cut down
in the strife, that old warrior
had no reason whatsoever to relish
the swordplay; he left his son
savaged by weapons on that field of slaughter,
a mere boy in battle. That wily, grizzled warrior
had no grounds at all to boast about the fight,
and neither did Anlaf; with their leavings
of an army, they could scarcely exult
that things went their own way
in the thick of battle – at the crash of standards
and the clash of spears, at the conflict of weapons
and struggle of men – when they grappled
on that slaughter-field with Eadweard's sons.
Then the Norsemen made off in their nailed boats,
sad survivors shamed in battle,
they crossed the deep water from Dingesmere
to the shelter of Dublin, Ireland once more.
Likewise both brothers together,
king and prince, returned to Wessex,
their own country, exulting in war.
They left behind them to devour the corpses,
relish the carrion, the horny-beaked raven
garbed in black, and the grey-coated
eagle (a greedy war-hawk)

with its white tail, and that grey beast,
the wolf in the wood. Never, before this,
were more men in this island slain
by the sword's edge – as books and aged sages
confirm – since Angles and Saxons sailed here
from the east, sought the Britons over the wide seas,
since those warsmiths hammered the Welsh,
and earls, eager for glory, overran the land.

ANON
translated from the Anglo-Saxon by Kevin Crossley-Holland

The King of Connacht

'Have you seen Hugh,
The Connacht king in the field?'
'All that we saw
Was his shadow under his shield.'

ANON
translated from the Irish by Frank O'Connor

Wulf

The men of my people will hunt him as game.
They will kill him if he comes with force.

    It is different with us.

Wulf is on one shore, I on another,
fast is that island, thickened with fens;
fierce are the men who guard it:
they will kill him if he comes with force.

    It is different with us.

It was rainy weather, and I sat down and wept,
and grieved for my Wulf, his far wanderings,
when a battle-quick captain laid me down;
that was peace for a moment, but only a moment.

Wulf, my Wulf, it was wanting you
that made me sick, your never coming,
the unanswered heart, no mere starvation.

Do you hear, Eadwacer? Wulf will carry
our whelp to the woods.

Men easily break what is never bound.
Our song, for one.

ANON
translated from the Anglo-Saxon by Matthew Hollis

'Wind fierce to-night'

Wind fierce to-night.
Mane of the sea whipped white.
I am not afraid. No ravening Norse
On course through quiet waters.

ANON
translated from the Irish by Seamus Heaney

The Wife's Lament

I sing this poem full of grief.
                Full of sorrow about my life.
Ready to say the cruel state
                I have endured, early and late,
And never more I will tell
                Than now – now that exile
Has fallen to me with all its pain.
                My lord had gone, had fled away
Over the sea. The break of day
                Found me grieving for a prince
Who had left his people. Then at once
                I set out on my journey,
Little more than a refugee,
                Lacking a retinue and friends,
With needy means and needy ends.
                They plotted together, his kith and kin.
They met in secret, they made a plan
                To keep us as far apart, away

From each other, night and day
                    As ever they could while making sure
I would feel anguish and desire.
                    My lord and master made his will
Plain to me: He said, be still:
                    Stay right here, in this place.
And here I am – penniless, friendless,
                    Lacking him, my heart's companion
And sad indeed because our union
                    Suited me so well, so well
And for so long. And yet the real
                    State of his heart, the actual weakness
Of his mind, the true darkness
                    Of murderous sin was hidden away.
And yet I well remember the day,
                    Our singular joy on this earth
When we two vowed that only death
                    Could separate us. Now I see
Love itself has deserted me:
                    Love that was so true, so trusted
Is now as if it never existed.
                    Wherever I go, far or near,
Enmity springs from what is dear.
                    I was commanded to this grove
Under an oak tree, to this cave –
                    An ancient cave – and I am filled
With longing here where hedges, wild
                    With briars, valleys, rolling,
Steep hills make a joyless dwelling.
                    Often here, the fact of his leaving
Seizes my heart. There are lovers living
                    On this earth who keep their beds

While I am walking in the woods
                    Through these caves alone at dawn.
Here I sit. Here I mourn,
                    Through the summer hours, all my woes,
My exiled state. I can't compose
                    My careworn heart nor ease the strife
Of that desire which is my life.
                    Let a young man be sober, tough
And sunny withal however weighed
                    Down his soul, however sad.
May his self be its only source.
                    My lost lord, my lover-felon –
Let him be cast from his land alone
                    By an icy cliff in a cold storm.
Let his own mind bedevil him
                    With weariness as the water flows
Far below his makeshift house.
                    Let my weary friend beside the sea
Suffer his cruel anxiety.
                    Let him be reminded in this place
Of another dwelling: all its grace,
                    And all the affliction, all the cost
Of longing for a love that's lost.

ANON
translated from the Anglo-Saxon by Eavan Boland

Exile

What happier fortune can one find
Than with the girl who pleased one's mind
To leave one's home and friends behind
And sail on the first favouring wind?

ANON
translated from the Irish by Frank O'Connor

from The Seafarer

I sing my own true story, tell my travels,
How I have often suffered times of hardship
In days of labour, and have undergone
Bitter anxiety, my troubled home
On many a ship has been the heaving waves,
Where grim night-watch has often been my lot
At the ship's prow as it beat past the cliffs.
Oppressed by cold my feet were bound by frost
In icy bonds, while worries simmered hot
About my heart, and hunger from within
Tore the sea-weary spirit. He who lives
Most easily on land knows not how I
Have spent my winter on the ice-cold sea,
Wretched and anxious on the paths of exile,
Lacking dear friends, hung round by icicles,
While hail flew past in showers. There I heard nothing
But the resounding sea, the ice-cold waves.
Sometimes I made the song of the wild swan

My pleasure, or the gannet's call, the cry
Of curlews for the missing mirth of men,
The singing gull instead of mead in hall.
Storms beat the rocky cliffs, and icy-winged
The tern replied, the horn-beaked eagle shrieked.
I had no patron there who might have soothed
My desolate spirit. He can little know
Who, proud and flushed with wine, has spent his time
With all the joys of life among the cities
Rather than baleful wanderings, how I,
Weary, have often suffered on the seas.
Night's shadow darkened, snow came from the north,
Frost bound the ground and hail fell on the earth,
Coldest of corns. And yet the heart's desires
Incite me now that I myself should go
On towering seas among the salt waves' play;
And all the time the heartfelt wishes urge
The spirit to venture, that I should go forth
To find the lands of strangers far away.

ANON
translated from the Anglo-Saxon by Richard Hamer

'There's a lady in these parts'

There's a lady in these parts
whose name I'm slow to divulge
but she's known to let off farts
like stones from a catapult

ANON
translated from the Irish by Maurice Riordan

The Wish of Manchán of Liath

I wish, O son of the Living God, ancient eternal King, for a secret hut in the wilderness that it may be my dwelling.

A very blue shallow well to be beside it, a clear pool for washing away sins through the grace of the Holy Ghost.

A beautiful wood close by around it on every side, for the nurture of many-voiced birds, to shelter and hide it.

Facing the south for warmth, a little stream across its enclosure, a choice ground with abundant bounties which would be good for every plant.

A few sage disciples, I will tell their number, humble and obedient, to pray to the King.

Four threes, three fours, fit for every need, two sixes in the church, both south and north.

Six couples in addition to me myself, praying through the long ages to the King who moves the sun.

A lovely church decked with linen, a dwelling for God of Heaven; then, bright candles over the holy white Scriptures.

One room to go to for the care of the body, without wantonness, without voluptuousness, without meditation of evil.

This is the housekeeping I would undertake, I would choose it without concealing; fragrant fresh leeks, hens, speckled salmon, bees.

My fill of clothing and of food from the King of good fame, and for me to be sitting for a while praying to God in every place.

ANON
translated from the Irish by Kenneth Hurlstone Jackson

The Praises of God

How foolish the man
Who does not raise
His voice and praise
With joyful words,
As he alone can,
Heaven's High King.
To Whom the light birds

With no soul but air,
All day, everywhere
Laudation sing.

ANON
translated from the Irish by W. H. Auden

The End of Clonmacnois

'Whence are you, learning's son?'
'From Clonmacnois I come
My course of studies done,
I'm off to Swords again.'
'How are things keeping there?'
'Oh, things are shaping fair –
Foxes round churchyards bare
Gnawing the guts of men.'

ANON
translated from the Irish by Frank O'Connor

Winter Cold

Cold, cold, chill tonight is wide Moylurg; the snow is higher than a mountain, the deer cannot get at its food.

Eternal cold! The storm has spread on every side; each sloping furrow is a river and every ford is a full mere.

Each full lake is a great sea and each mere is a full lake; horses cannot get across the ford of Ross, no more can two feet get there.

The fishes of Ireland are roving, there is not a strand where the wave does not dash, there is not a town left in the land, not a bell is heard, no crane calls.

The wolves of Cuan Wood do not get repose or sleep in the lair of wolves; the little wren does not find shelter for her nest on the slope of Lon.

Woe to the company of little birds for the keen wind and the cold ice! The blackbird with its dusky back does not find a bank it would like, shelter for its side in the Woods of Cuan.

Snug is our cauldron on its hook, restless the blackbird on Leitir Cró; snow has crushed the wood here, it is difficult to climb up Benn Bó.

The eagle of brown Glen Rye gets affliction from the bitter wind; great is its misery and its suffering, the ice will get into its beak.

It is foolish for you – take heed of it – to rise from quilt and feather bed; there is much ice on every ford; that is why I say 'Cold!'

ANON

translated from the Irish by Kenneth Hurlstone Jackson

Durham

Known throughout Britain this noble city.
Its steep slopes and stone buildings
are thought a wonder; weirs contain
its fast river; fish of all kinds
thrive here in the thrusting waters.
A great forest has grown up here,
thickets throng with wild creatures;
deer drowse in the deep dales.
Everyone knows this renowned town
holds the body of blessèd Cuthbert,
also the holy head of Oswald,
lion of England, Eadberch and Eadfrith,
brothers in battle, the bishop Aidan
and here besides the bishop Athelwold,
learnèd Bede and the abbot Basil,
inspiring tutor to Cuthbert in youth
who gladly took his grave instruction.
Together with these tombs in the minster

numerous recognised relics remain
that work wonders, as records say,
where worthy men await Judgment Day.

ANON
translated from the Anglo-Saxon by Derek Mahon

Advice to Lovers

The way to get on with a girl
Is to drift like a man in a mist,
Happy enough to be caught,
Happy to be dismissed.

Glad to be out of her way,
Glad to rejoin her in bed,
Equally grieved or gay
To learn that she's living or dead.

ANON
translated from the Irish by Frank O'Connor

from Sweeney Astray

The Mournes are cold tonight,
my quarters are desolate:
no milk or honey in this land
of snowdrift and gusting wind.

In a sharp-branched holly tree
I shiver and waste away,
chilled to the bone, camped out
up here on the naked summit.

The pools are ice, frost hardens on me.
Then I shake and break free,
coming alive like a fanned ember
in winds sweeping north from Leinster,

dreaming dreams of autumn days
round Hallowe'en and All Hallows,
longing for my old ground –
the clear waters of Glen Bolcain.

Astray no more then east or west,
blizzards whipping my bare face,
atremble no more in some den,
a starved, pinched, raving madman,

but sheltered in that dappled arbour,
my haven, my winter harbour,
my refuge from the bare heath,
my royal fort, my king's rath.

Every night I glean and raid
and comb the floor of the oak wood.
My bands work into leaf and rind,
roots, windfalls on the ground,

they rake through matted watercress
and grope among the bog-berries,
cool brooklime, sorrel, damp moss,
wild garlic and raspberries,

apples, hazel-nuts, acorns,
the haws of sharp, jaggy hawthorns,
blackberries, the floating weed,
the whole store of the oak wood.

Keep me here, Christ, far away
from open ground and flat country.
Let me suffer the cold of glens.
I dread the cold of open plains.

ANON
translated from the Irish by Seamus Heaney

Writing Out of Doors

A wall of forest looms above
   and sweetly the blackbird sings;
all the birds make melody
   over me and my books and things.

There sings to me the cuckoo
   from bush-citadels in grey hood.
God's doom! May the Lord protect me
   writing well, under the great wood.

ANON
translated from the Irish by James Carney

from The Mabinogi: Rhiannon

It's little more than a bump in the land, a footnote
in the catalogue of hills, crags and ridges,
felt as an ache in the thighs, the heart's
flip and gulp, by those heavy
with mutton and wine,

then a subtle sense of arrival, a breeze
scurrying up to attend to you,
the green swell of crown, the fields
gathering below.

They say if you sit on the summit
you'll see a sight more chilling
than the greys of rain,

or something more brilliant than
lightning's snazzy gold.

*

From up here, everything is cloud: the grass, forest, corn,
even the rocks, are nuances of weather.
The road's a white line through the billows.
Pwyll watches with his men as
a figure grows there:

a horse with a lick of sunlight on its back,
a horse with a knight in gilt armour,
a horse with a splash of silk
horsewoman riding,

not so much moving as sharpening.
Will she ever be real?
The boy he sends down

finds the road silent, her back
already dwindling.

*

She is woman and horse. She rides slower than daydreams.
She is what you've forgotten, where the time went.
Singleminded as the sun, she rides
always one way, and the air's
warmed by her passing.

The man he sends after her, the second day,
tries slowing down; she rides slower still
and the road grows between them.
He gallops again –

always she dawdles away from him
till she's as small as a gnat,
and his horse gasping.

She slips into yesterday
without being now.

*

On the third day he rides himself, on his sleekest horse,
till it's yeasty with sweat. She is a brushstroke
on the stillness of the facing page,
illuminated in gold
on a green background

and there is always a white space between them.
At last he calls out to her to stop.
There's a wispy sound, the sense
of a veil lifting,

and they are side-by-side, flank to flank,
He should have asked her sooner –
better for the horse.

They talk in time to the hoofs:
saddle-courtesies.

*

Later he will ask himself how she knew who he was
and why she chose him out of all the princes
who hunt under these lumbering clouds.

Now he is watching her smile
as it comes and goes,

a slip of candlelight seen under a door,
listening to the cluck of laughter
that nestles in the depths of her throat,
hearing himself talk back

in the silences she leaves for him.
Later they will feast and dance
and climb the long stairs.

Later he'll wonder. Today
there's wonder enough.

ANON
translated from the Welsh by Matthew Francis

'Derry I cherish ever'

Derry I cherish ever.
It is calm, it is clear.
Crowds of white angels on their rounds
At every corner.

ANON
translated from the Irish by Seamus Heaney

I am Taliesin

Taliesin. I sing perfect metre,
Which will last to the end of the world.
My patron is Elphin . . .

I know why there is an echo in a hollow;
Why silver gleams; why breath is black; why liver is bloody;
Why a cow has horns; why a woman is affectionate;
Why milk is white; why holly is green;
Why a kid is bearded; why the cow-parsnip is hollow;
Why brine is salt; why ale is bitter;
Why the linnet is green and berries red;
Why a cuckoo complains; why it sings;
I know where the cuckoos of summer are in winter.
I know what beasts there are at the bottom of the sea;
How many spears in battle; how many drops in a shower;
Why a river drowned Pharaoh's people;
Why fishes have scales.
Why a white swan has black feet . . .

I have been a blue salmon,
I have been a dog, a stag, a roebuck on the mountain,
A stock, a spade, an axe in the hand,
A stallion, a bull, a buck,
I was reaped and placed in an oven;
I fell to the ground when I was being roasted
And a hen swallowed me.

For nine nights was I in her crop.
I have been dead, I have been alive.
I am Taliesin.

ANON
translated from the Welsh by Gwyn Jones

The Heart of the Wood

My hope and my love,
we will go for a while into the wood,
scattering the dew,
where we will see the trout,
we will see the blackbird on its nest;
the deer and the buck calling,
the little bird that is sweetest singing on the branches;
the cuckoo on the top of the fresh green;
and death will never come near us
for ever in the sweet wood.

ANON
translated from the Irish by Lady Augusta Gregory

This ae Night

This ae night, this ae night,
    Everie night and alle,
Fire and salt and candle light
    And Christ receive thy sawle!

When thou from here away hast past,
    Everie night and alle,
To Whinny moor thou com'st at last,
    And Christ receive thy sawle!

If ever thou gavest hosen and shoon,
    Everie night and alle,
Sit thee down and put them on:
    And Christ receive they sawle!

If hosen and shoon thou never gav't nane
    Everie night and alle,
The whins shall prick thee to the bare bane:
    And Christ receive thy sawle!

From Whinny moor when thou may'st pass,
    Everie night and alle,
To Brig o'Dread thou com'st at last:
    And Christ receive thy sawle!

From Brig o'Dread when thou may'st pass
    Everie night and alle,
To Purgatory fire thou com'st at last,
    And Christ receive thy sawle!

If ever thou gavest meat or drink,
    Everie night and alle,
The fire shall never make thee shrink:
    And Christ receive thy sawle!

If meat and drink thou ne'er gav't nane,
    Everie night and alle,
The fire will burn thee to the bare bane,
    And Christ receive thy sawle!

This ae night, this ae night,
    Everie night and alle,
Fire and salt and candle light,
    And Christ receive thy sawle!

ANON

II

1300–1500

from The Parliament of Fowls

I saw a garden, full of blossoming trees,
In a green mead through which a river goes,
Where sweetness everlasting fills the breeze,
Of flowers blue and yellow, white and rose,
And cold wellsprings whose water deathless flows,
Teeming with little fishes quick and light,
With fins of red and scales of silver bright.

On every bough were birds; I heard them sing
With voice angelic in their harmony,
And some were busy hatchlings forth to bring;
The little rabbits came to play nearby,
And further off I then began to spy
The timid roe, the buck, the hart and hind,
Squirrels, and other beasts of gentle kind.

Of stringed instruments playing in accord
I heard the sound so ravishing that day
That God himself, maker of all and Lord,
Might never have heard better, I dare say.
Therewith a wind that scarce could gentler play
Made in the leafage green a murmur soft,
Harmonious with the sound of birds aloft.

And of that place the air so temperate was,
No hurt was known of either heat or cold;
There goodly spices grew, and wholesome grass,
And no man there grew ever sick or old.

Still was there joy above a thousand-fold
More than man's telling, nor was it ever night,
But day for ever in all people's sight.

GEOFFREY CHAUCER
translated from the Middle English by E. B. Richmond

from The General Prologue

When in April the sweet showers fall
And pierce the drought of March to the root, and all
The veins are bathed in liquor of such power
As brings about the engendering of the flower,
When also Zephyrus with his sweet breath
Exhales an air in every grove and heath
Upon the tender shoots, and the young sun
His half-course in the sign of the *Ram* has run,
And the small fowl are making melody
That sleep away the night with open eye
(So nature pricks them and their heart engages)
Then people long to go on pilgrimages
And palmers long to seek the stranger strands
Of far-off saints, hallowed in sundry lands,
And specially, from every shire's end
Of England, down to Canterbury they wend
To seek the holy blissful martyr, quick
To give his help to them when they were sick.

GEOFFREY CHAUCER
translated from the Middle English by Nevill Coghill

from The Nun's Priest's Tale

Now let me turn again to tell my tale;
This blessed widow and her daughters two
Heard all these hens in clamour and halloo
And, rushing to the door at all this shrieking,
They saw the fox towards the covert streaking
And, on his shoulder, Chanticleer stretched flat.
'Look, look!' they cried, 'O mercy, look at that!
Ha! Ha! the fox!' and after him they ran,
And stick in hand ran many a serving man,
Ran Coll our dog, ran Talbot, Bran and Shaggy,
And with a distaff in her hand ran Maggie,
Ran cow and calf and ran the very hogs
In terror at the barking of the dogs;
The men and women shouted, ran and cursed,
They ran so hard they thought their hearts would burst,
They yelled like fiends in Hell, ducks left the water
Quacking and flapping as on point of slaughter,
Up flew the geese in terror over the trees,
Out of the hive came forth the swarm of bees
So hideous was the noise – God bless us all,
Jack Straw and all his followers in their brawl
Were never half so shrill, for all their noise,
When they were murdering those Flemish boys,
As that day's hue and cry upon the fox.
They grabbed up trumpets made of brass and box,

Of horn and bone, on which they blew and pooped,
And therewithal they shouted and they whooped
So that it seemed the very heavens would fall.

GEOFFREY CHAUCER
translated from the Middle English by Nevill Coghill

The Seagull

Smooth gull on the sea's lagoon,
White as snow or the white moon,
Sun shard, gauntlet of the sea,
Untroubled is your beauty.
Buoyant you ride the rough tide,
A swift, proud, fish-eating bird.
Come to me, anchored on land,
Sea-lily, come to my hand.
White-robed, whiter than paper,
You're a sea-nun, sleek and pure.

Wide praise is for you and her;
Circle that castle tower,
Search till you see her, seagull,
Bright as Eigr on that wall.
Take all my pleading to her,
Tell her my life I offer.
Tell her, should she be alone –
Gently with that gentle one –
If she will not take me, I,
Losing her, must surely die.

I completely worship her.
Friends, no man ever loved more –
Taliesin's nor Merlin's eye
Saw a woman as lovely.
Copper-curled, curved as Venus,
How beautiful the girl is.
O seagull, but see her face,
Loveliest on the world's surface,
Then bring me her sweet greeting,
Or my certain death you bring.

DAFYDD AP GWILYM
translated from the Welsh by Leslie Norris

The Thrush

Music of a thrush, clearbright
Lovable language of light,
Heard I under a birchtree
Yesterday, all grace and glee –
Was ever so sweet a thing
Fine-plaited as his whistling?

Matins, he reads the lesson,
A chasuble of plumage on.
His cry from a grove, his brightshout
Over countrysides rings out,
Hill prophet, maker of moods,
Passion's bright bard of glenwoods.
Every voice of the brookside
Sings he, in his darling pride,

Every sweet-metred love-ode,
Every song and organ mode,
Competing for a truelove,
Every catch for woman's love.
Preacher and reader of lore,
Sweet and clear, inspired rapture,
Bard of Ovid's faultless rhyme,
Chief prelate mild of Springtime.

From his birch, where lovers throng,
Author of the wood's birdsong,
Merrily the glade re-echoes –
Rhymes and metres of love he knows.
He on hazel sings so well
Through cloistered trees (winged angel)
Hardly a bird of Eden
Had by rote remembered then
How to recite what headlong
Passion made him do with song.

DAFYDD AP GWILYM
translated from the Welsh by Tony Conran

from Piers Plowman

In the season of summer   with the sun at its highest
I dressed in my work-clothes   like any poor shepherd,
in the garb of a hermit   but for worldly work
and set off through the country   to find what I'd find.
I met many wonders   and uncommon sights,
till one morning in May   on the hills behind Malvern
I fell sound asleep,   worn out by the walking.
As I lay on the ground,   resting and slumbering,
I'd this marvellous dream   I'll describe to you now.
I saw all the good   that live in the world
and the bad just as busy,   be certain of that:
loyalty, betrayal,   let-down and cunning –
I saw them all in my sleep: that's what I'm saying.
I looked to the East,   in the track of the sun
and saw a great tower –   Truth's home, I imagined.
Then to the westward   I looked shortly after
and saw a deep valley.   Death lived down there,
I'd no doubt in my mind,   with all evil spirits.
I saw in the middle   between these two points
a beautiful meadow,   thronging with people
of every station,   the poor and the needful
who slaved at their labours   as this hard world requires them.
Some trudged behind ploughs   with no chance of a respite,
sowing and seeding.   They worked without ceasing
to win for the people   what the greedy would waste.
Others grew proud   and dressed up accordingly,
their faces and get-up   a sight for sore eyes.
But many more,   it has to be said,
lived in penance and prayer   for the love of Our Lord,
in the confident hope   of ascending to Heaven.

As monks and nuns   they remained in their cells,
never wishing   to dash round the country
on the lookout for luxuries   to pamper their whims.
Some took to business   and did very well –
at least as we see it –   'getting on in the world'.
More had a fine time,   acting the clown
With dancing and singing   and swearing their heads off,
inventing daft stories,   making fools of themselves.
Such people imagine   that work's a poor option.

                              *

While I was dreaming,   Nature enlightened me,
Calling my name   and saying to take notice
While she led me on   through all the world's marvels.
And on this great mountain named Earth,   I imagined,
I was first led away   to find out in practice
How God might be loved   through observing his creatures.
The sun I saw, and the sea, and the sand by the shore;
I saw how the birds   make their nests in the trees;
No man has the skill   to equal the least of them.
Who on earth, then I wondered,   tutored the magpie
To arrange all the sticks   that she lays on to breed?
No joiner, I'm certain,   could make a dome like it.
What kind of a builder   might follow that blueprint?
There were visions besides   that I marvelled at further:
Other bird pairs   that sheltered their eggs
In the deepest seclusion on moor and in marsh, in swamp
     or on water,
So no-one could find them   but the two of themselves.
Then I looked out to sea   and beyond to the stars.
Such marvels I saw   I can hardly describe them:
Flowers in the wood   of beautiful colours,

And all shining through   the green grass and brown earth.
Some were rank and some scented: a magical world
That I haven't the time   or the skill to describe.
There's provision enough here,   faith has no doubt,
For no life ever given   lacked the means of survival,
An element to live in   and a reason for living.
First the wild worm   lives in wet earth;
The fish lives in water,   the cricket in fire.
The curlew by nature   lives on the air,
So of any bird   its meat is the cleanest.
Animals live   on grass, grain and rootcrops:
This shows that man too   has a natural food
Which is not only bread   but sustained faith and love.

WILLIAM LANGLAND
translated from the Middle English by Bernard O'Donoghue

In Defence of Women

Woe to him who speaks ill of women! it is not right to abuse them. They have not deserved, that I know, all the blame they have always had.

Sweet are their words, exquisite their voice, that sex for which my love is great; woe to him who does not scruple to revile them, woe to him who speaks ill of women!

They do no murder nor treachery, nor any grim or hateful deed, they do no sacrilege to church nor bell; woe to him who speaks ill of women!

Certain it is, there has never been born bishop nor king nor
great prophet without fault, but from a woman; woe to him
who speaks ill of women!

They are thrall to their own hearts, they love a man slender
and sound – it would be long before they would dislike him.
Woe to him who speaks ill of women!

An old fat greybeard, they do not desire a tryst with him –
dearer to them is a young lad, though poor. Woe to him who
speaks ill of women!

EARL GERALD FITZGERALD
translated from the Irish by Kenneth Hurlstone Jackson

from Sir Gawain and the Green Knight

So the morning dawns when man remembers
the day our redeemer was born to die,
and every house on earth is joyful for Lord Jesus.
Their day was no different, being a diary of delights:
banquets and buffets were beautifully cooked
and dutifully served to diners at the dais.
The ancient elder sat highest at the table
with the lord, I believe, in the chair to her left;
the sweeter one and Gawain took seats in the centre
and were first at the feast to dine, then food
was carried around as custom decrees
and served to each man as his status deserved.
There was feasting, there was fun, and such feelings of joy
as could not be conveyed by quick description,

yet to tell it in detail would take too much time.
But I'm aware that Gawain and the beautiful woman
found such comfort and closeness in each other's company
through warm exchanges of whispered words
and refined conversation free from foulness
that their pleasure surpassed all princely sports
                    by far.
            Beneath the din of drums
            men followed their affairs,
            and trumpets thrilled and thrummed
            as those two tended theirs.

They drank and danced all day and the next
and danced and drank the day after that,
then St John's Day passed with a gentler joy
as the Christmas feasting came to a close.
Guests were to go in the greyness of dawn,
so they laughed and dined as the dusk darkened,
swaying and swirling to music and song.
Then at last, in the lateness, they upped and left
towards distant parts along different paths.
Gawain offered his goodbyes, but was ushered by his host
to his host's own chamber and the heat of its chimney,
waylaid by the lord so the lord might thank him
profoundly and profusely for the favour he had shown
in honouring his house at that hallowed season
and lighting every corner of the castle with his character.
'For as long as I live my life shall be better
that Gawain was my guest at God's own feast.'
'By God,' said Gawain, 'but the gratitude goes to you.
May the High King of Heaven repay your honour.
Your requests are now this knight's commands.
I am bound by your bidding, no boon is too high

to say.'
At length his lordship tried
to get his guest to stay.
But proud Gawain replied
he must now make his way.

ANON
*translated from the Middle English
by Simon Armitage*

from Pearl

One thing I know for certain: that she
was peerless, pearl who would have added
light to any prince's life
however bright with gold. None
could touch the way she shone
in any light, so smooth, so small –
she was a jewel above all others.
So pity me the day I lost her
in this garden where she fell
beneath the grass into the earth.
I stand bereft, struck to the heart
with love and loss. My spotless pearl.

I've gazed a hundred times at the place
she left me, grieving for that gift
which swept away all shadow, that face
which was the antidote to sorrow.
And though this watching sears my heart
and wrings the wires of sadness tighter,
still the song this silence sings me

is the sweetest I have heard –
the countless quiet hours in which
her pale face floats before me, mired
in mud and soil, a perfect jewel
spoiled, my spotless pearl.

In the place where such riches lie rotting
a carpet of spices will spring up and spread,
blossoms of blue and white and red
which fire in the full light facing the sun.
Where a pearl is planted deep in the dark
no fruit or flower could ever fade;
all grasscorn grows from dying grain
so new wheat can be carried home.
From goodness other goodness grows:
so beautiful a seed can't fail
to fruit or spices fail to flower
fed by a precious, spotless pearl.

So I came to this very same spot
in the green of an August garden, height
and heart of summer, at Lammas time
when corn is cut with curving scythes.
And I saw that the little hill where she fell
was a shaded place showered with spices:
pink gillyflower, ginger and purple gromwell,
powdered with peonies scattered like stars.
But more than their loveliness to the eye,
the sweetest fragrance seemed to float
in the air there also – I knew beyond doubt
that's where she lay, my spotless pearl.

Caught in the chill grasp of grief I stood
in that place clasping my hands, seized
by the grip on my heart of longing and loss.
Though reason told me to be still
I mourned for my poor imprisoned pearl
with all the fury and force of a quarrel.
The comfort of Christ called out to me
but still I wrestled in wilful sorrow.
Then the power and perfume of those flowers
filled up my head and felled me, slipped me
into sudden sleep in the place
where she lay beneath me. My girl.

ANON

translated from the Middle English by Jane Draycott

The Prologue

The fables told by poets in old times
Are by no means all grounded upon truth
Yet their attractive style, their craft and themes
Still make for pleasant listening; and with
Good cause, since they, from the beginning,
Aimed to reprove man's whole wrong way of living
Under the figure of another thing.

Just as through a hard unyielding ground,
If it is laboured with real diligence,
The flowers will spring and young shoots of green corn,
Wholesome and good for human sustenance,

So sweetly edifying moral lessons
Spring from the well-worked plot of poetry
For those who have ears to hear and eyes to see.

The shell upon the nut, though hard and tough,
Holds the kernel and is still delightful.
Just so there lies a doctrine of great worth
And fruitfulness beneath a made-up fable.
And scholars say it is most profitable
To mix the merry in with graver matter:
It makes the spirit lift and time go quicker.

Furthermore, a bow that's always bent
Goes weak and gives and loses all its spring.
The same is true of minds always intent
On earnest thought and constant studying.
To alleviate what's sad by adding something
Cheerful is good; Aesop expressed it thus:
Dulcius arrident seria picta iocis.

Which author's Latin, masters, by your leave,
Submitting myself here to your correction,
I would convert to mother tongue and prove
Equal to the task of a translation –
Not out of vain presumption of my own,
But at the invitation of a lord
Whose name it is not needful to record.

In homely language and rough turns of speech
I have to write, for always eloquence
And rhetoric remained beyond my reach.
Therefore I humbly pray your reverence

That if you find here through my negligence
Anything much shortened – or protracted –
By your good will and good grace you'll correct it.

My author in his fables records how
Wild animals spoke sense and understood,
Debated point for point, could argue too,
Propound a syllogism and conclude;
He shows by example and similitude
How often humans in their own behaviour
Resemble the wild animals in nature.

No wonder that a man grows like a beast!
Loving each carnal and each foul delight
Until no shame can hold or halt his lust,
He soon indulges every appetite
Which through repetition and bad habit
Roots in the mind so ineradicably
He is transformed: then bestiality.

This scholar, Aesop, as I have been telling,
Composed in verse of elegance and weight
A coded book, for he was unwilling
That readers high or low should underrate
His art; and first of a cock he wrote,
Hunting for food, that found a brilliant stone.
His is the fable you shall hear anon.

ROBERT HENRYSON
translated from the Middle Scots by Seamus Heaney

The Toad and the Mouse

Upon a time, as Aesop makes report,
A little mouse came to a riverside.
She couldn't wade, her mouse-shanks were so short,
She couldn't swim, she had no horse to ride,
So willy-nilly there she had to bide
And to and fro beside that river deep
She ran and cried with many a piteous *peep*.

'Help, help me over,' cried the poor wee mouse,
'For love of God, someone, across this stream.'
With that a toad, in water nearby, rose
(For toads by nature nimbly duck and swim),
And showed her head to mount the bank and come
Croaking ashore, then gave her greetings thus:
'Good morning! And what brings you here, Miss Mouse?'

'The corn', she said, 'in yon field, do you see it?
The ripened oats, the barley, peas and wheat?
I'm hungry and I'd love to get to it
But the water here's too wide, so here I sit
And on this side get not a thing to eat
But hard nuts that I have to gnaw and bore.
Over beyond, I'd feast on better fare.

'I have no boat, there is no ferryman,
And if there were, I have no coin to pay.'
'Sister,' said toad, 'would you stop worrying.
Do what I tell you and I shall find a way

Without horse, bridge or boat or any ferry
To get you over safely, never fear –
And not wet once a whisker or a hair.'

'I greatly wonder', said the little mouse,
'How you can, without fin or feather, float.
This river is so deep and dangerous
I think you'd drown as soon as you'd wade out.
Tell me, therefore, what is the gift or secret
You own to bring you over this dark flood?'
And thus in explanation spoke the toad:

'With my two feet for oars, webbed and broad,
I row the stream,' she said, 'and quietly pull,
And though it's deep and dangerous to wade,
I swim it to and fro at my own will
And cannot sink, because my open gill
Vents and voids the water I breathe in.
So truly, I am not afraid to drown.'

The mouse gazed up into her furrowed face,
Her wrinkled cheeks, her ridged lips like a lid
Hasped shut on her hoarse voice, her hanging brows,
Her lanky wobbly legs and wattled hide;
Then, taken aback, she faced the toad and cried,
'If I know any physiognomy,
The signs on you are of untruth and envy.

'For scholars say the main inclination
Of a man's thought will usually proceed
According to the corporal complexion,
The good or evil prompting in the blood.

A thrawn feature means a nature twisted.
The Latin tag affords a proof of this –
Mores, it says, are mirrored in the face.'

'No,' said the toad, 'that proverb isn't true,
For what looks good is often a false showing.
The bilberry may have a dreary hue
But will be picked while primrose is left growing.
The face may fail to be the heart's true token.
Therefore I find this judgement still applies:
'You shouldn't judge a man just by his face.'

ROBERT HENRYSON
translated from the Middle Scots by Seamus Heaney

A Girl's Hair

Shall I have the girl I love,
The grove of light, my truelove,
With her silk top like a star
And her head's golden pillar?
Dragon fire lights a doorway,
Three chains, like the Milky Way.
A heaven of hair she'll set fire
In one bush, like a bonfire.
Broom or great birchtree's sweetness,
Maelor's yellow-headed lass,
An angel host, a legion,
Breastplate many links are on,
Pennon of peacock feather,

Tall bush like a golden door,
All this lively-looking hair,
Virtue's sun, maiden's fetter,
Were she a goldsmith, we'd guess
Who owned its splendid brightness.
There's something round her head then
Like summer on Rhiw Felen.
Round her, growing raiment springs,
Tent of the sun, like harpstrings,
Rush peelings, tips of harvest,
Fur upon a pinemart's chest,
Peahen that wears, from custom,
Head to foot, the hair of broom,
Tough amber, like a twig-chain,
All inwoven, golden grain.
As tall as trees are those locks,
A crown of twigs, new beeswax.
Labour of bees brought ripeness,
Shoots of sunshine from her flesh,
Saffron on herbs of eye-bright,
Gold cherries, stars of the night.
Good was the growing harvest,
Water grasses, golden-tressed.
Pure herbs, with the lye rinsed wet,
Yellow hammer, silk thicket.
Mass of Mary Maudlen's broom
Round her head, golden besom,
And ruddy, if it's loosened,
Like a gold gown she has donned.
Her two breasts are overall
Roofed in gold, each a marvel.
Her skull is weighed with tresses,

Flax upon the yellow trees,
And if it's left unravelled
Was there ever a bush so gold?

That the mark on her be patent
Of faith's chrism from the font
And this bush hold life's sunshine,
No bush under sun's so fine.

DAFYDD AB EDMWND
translated from the Welsh by Tony Conran

To a Ladye

Sweit rois of vertew and of gentilnes,
Delytsum lyllie of everie lustynes,
   Richest in bontie and in bewtie cleir,
   And everie vertew that is held most deir,
Except onlie that ye ar mercyles.

In to your garthe this day I did persew,
Thair saw I flowris that fresche were of hew;
   Baith whyte and reid moist lusty wer to seyne,
   And halsum herbis upone stalkis grene;
Yit leif nor flour fynd could I nane of rew.

I dout that Merche, with his caild blastis keyne,
Hes slane this gentill herbe that I of mene,
   Whois petewous deithe dois to my hart sic pane
   That I wald mak to plant his rute agane,
So confortand his levis unto me bene.

WILLIAM DUNBAR

'I sing of a maiden'

I sing of a maiden   beyond compare:
King of all kings   she chose to bear.

He came all so still   where his mother was
As dew in April   that falleth on the grass.

He came all so still   to his mother's bower
As dew in April   that falleth on the flower.

He came all so still   where his mother lay
As dew in April   that falleth on the spray.

Mother and maiden   was never none but she:
Well may such a lady   God's mother be.

ANON

translated from the Middle English by Seamus Heaney

Shirt of a Lad

As I did the washing one day
Under the bridge at Aberteifi,
  And a golden stick to drub it,
And my sweetheart's shirt beneath it –
  A knight came by upon a charger,
Proud and swift and broad of shoulder,
And he asked if I would sell
The shirt of the lad that I loved well.

No, I said, I will not trade –
Not if a hundred pounds were paid;
Not if two hillsides I could keep
Full with wethers and white sheep;
Not if two fields full of oxen
  Under yoke were in the bargain;
Not if the herbs of all Llanddewi,
Trodden and pressed, were offered to me –
Not for the likes of that, I'd sell
The shirt of the lad that I love well.

ANON
translated from the Welsh by Tony Conran

'The silver swan, who living had no note'

The silver swan, who living had no note,
When death approached unlocked her silent throat,
Leaning her breast against the reedy shore,
Thus sung her first and last, and sung no more:
Farewell all joys, O death come close mine eyes,
More geese than swans now live, more fools than wise.

ANON

The Blackbird of Derrycairn

Stop, stop and listen for the bough top
Is whistling and the sun is brighter
Than God's own shadow in the cup now!
Forget the hour-bell. Mournful matins
Will sound, Patric, as well at nightfall.

Faintly through mist of broken water
Fionn heard my melody in Norway.
He found the forest track, he brought back
This beak to gild the branch and tell, there,
Why men must welcome in the daylight.

He loved the breeze that warns the black grouse,
The shout of gillies in the morning
When packs are counted and the swans cloud
Loch Erne, but more than all those voices
My throat rejoicing from the hawthorn.

In little cells behind a cashel,
Patric, no handbell gives a glad sound.
But knowledge is found among the branches.
Listen! That song that shakes my feathers
Will thong the leather of your satchels.

ANON
translated from the Irish by Austin Clarke

'Dear, if you change, I'll never choose again'

Dear, if you change, I'll never choose again,
Sweet, if you shrink, I'll never think of love;
Fair, if you fail, I'll judge all beauty vain,
Wise, if too weak, my wits I'll never prove.
  Dear, sweet, fair, wise; change, shrink nor be not weak,
  And on my faith, my faith shall never break.

Earth with her flowers shall sooner heaven adorn,
Heaven her bright stars through earth's dim globe shall move,
Fire heat shall lose and frosts of flames be born,
Air made to shine as black as hell shall prove:
  Earth, heaven, fire, air, the world transformed shall view,
  Ere I prove false to faith, or strange to you.

ANON

May Poem

O lusty May, with Flora queen!
The balmy dropis from Phoebus sheen
Preluciand beams before the day:
By that Diana growis green
Through gladness of this lusty May.

Then Esperus, that is so bricht,
Til woful hairtis castis his light,
With bankis that bloomis on every brae;
And schouris are shed forth of their sicht
Through gladness of this lusty May.

Birdis on bewis of every birth,
Rejoicing notis makand their mirth
Richt plesantly upon the spray,
With flourishingis o'er field and firth
Through gladness of this lusty May.

All luvaris that are in care
To their ladies they do repair
In fresh morningis before the day,
And are in mirth ay mair and mair
Through gladness of this lusty May.

ANON

The Wife Who Would a Wanton Be

All night I clatter upon my creed,
Prayand to God that I were dead;
   Or else out of this world he were:
Then should I see for some remeid.
   Wo worth marriage for evermair!

Ye should hear tell (an *he* were gane)
That I should be a wanton ane.
   To learn the law of lovis layr
In our town like me should be nane.
   Wo worth marriage for evermair!

I should put on my russet gown,
My red kirtill, my hose of brown.
   And let them see my yellow hair
Under my kerchief hingand down.
   Wo worth marriage for evermair!

Lovers both should hear and see,
I should love them that would love me;
   Their hearts for me should ne'er be sair:
But aye unweddit should I be.
   Wo worth marriage for evermair!

ANON

Bring Us in Good Ale

Bring us in good ale, and bring us in good ale;
For our blessèd Lady sake bring us in good ale!

Bring us in no browne bred, for that is made of brane,
Nor bring us in no white bred, for therein is no gane,
   But bring us in good ale!

Bring us in no befe, for there is many bones,
But bring us in good ale, for that goth downe at ones,
   And bring us in good ale!

Bring us in no bacon, for that is passing fate,
But bring us in good ale, and gife us enought of that;
   And bring us in good ale!

Bring us in no mutton, for that is often lene,
Nor bring us in no tripes, for they be seldom clene,
   But bring us in good ale!

Bring us in no egges, for there are many schelles,
But bring us in good ale, and gife us nothing elles;
   And bring us in good ale!

Bring us in no butter, for therein are many heres,
Nor bring us in no pigges flesch, for that will make us bores,
   But bring us in good ale!

Bring us in no podinges, for therein is all Godes good,
Nor bring us in no venesen, for that is not for our blod;
  But bring us in good ale!

Bring us in no capons flesch, for that is ofte dere,
Nor bring us in no dokes flesch, for they slober in the mere,
  But bring us in good ale!

ANON

III

1500–1600

fair rocks,
Goodly
Rivers,
Sweet
woods...

'Western wind, when wilt thou blow?'

Western wind, when wilt thou blow,
The small rain down can rain?
Christ, if my love were in my arms,
And I in my bed again.

ANON

The Breach in the Wall

Alas, my love, they knocked you down,
Alas, my love, they knocked you down,
Alas, my love, they knocked you down,
In the breach in the wall.

It is a shame I was not there,
It is a shame I was not there,
It is a shame I was not there,
   With four men at either hand.

The ale they brought to your wedding,
The ale they brought to your wedding,
The ale they brought to your wedding,
   Was drunk at your wake.

I was a bride and a maiden,
A bride and a maiden,
A bride and a maiden
   And a widow all at once.

You had no fault to speak of,
You had no fault to speak of,
You had no fault to speak of,
But that you did not betoken a long life.

translated from the Scots Gaelic by Meg Bateman

This is the House That Jack Built

This is the farmer sowing his corn,
That kept the cock that crowed in the morn,
That waked the priest all shaven and shorn,
That married the man all tattered and torn,
That kissed the maiden all forlorn,
That milked the cow with the crumpled horn,
That tossed the dog,
That worried the cat,
That killed the rat,
That ate the malt
That lay in the house that Jack built.

ANON

'They flee from me that sometime did me seek'

They flee from me that sometime did me seek
  With naked foot stalking in my chamber.
I have seen them gentle tame and meek
  That now are wild and do not remember
  That sometime they put themselves in danger
To take bread at my hand; and now they range
Busily seeking with a continual change.

Thanked be fortune, it hath been otherwise
  Twenty times better; but once in special,
In thin array after a pleasant guise,
  When her loose gown from her shoulders did fall,
  And she me caught in her arms long and small;
And therewithal sweetly did me kiss,
And softly said, *Dear heart, how like you this?*

It was no dream: I lay broad waking.
  But all is turned thorough my gentleness
Into a strange fashion of forsaking;
  And I have leave to go of her goodness
  And she also to use newfangleness.
But since that I so kindly am served,
I would fain know what she hath deserved.

THOMAS WYATT

The Ballad which Anne Askew Made and Sang when She was in Newgate

Like as the armed knight
Appointed to the field,
With this world will I fight,
And faith shall be my shield.

Faith is that weapon strong,
Which will not fail at need;
My foes, therefore, among
Therewith will I proceed.

Thou sayst, lord, whoso knock,
To them wilt thou attend,
Undo, therefore, the lock,
And thy strong power send.

More enemies now I have
Than hairs upon my head;
Let them not me deprave,
But fight thou in my stead.

Not oft I used to write
In prose, nor yet in rhyme;
Yet will I show one sight,
That I saw in my time:

I saw a royal throne,
Where Justice should have sit;
But in her stead was one
Of moody, cruel wit.

Absorpt was rightwiseness,
As by the raging flood;
Satan, in his excess,
Sucked up the guiltless blood.

Then thought, I – Jesus, Lord,
When thou shalt judge us all,
Hard is it to record
On these men what will fall!

Yet, Lord, I thee desire,
For that they do to me,
Let them not taste the hire
Of their iniquity.

ANNE ASKEW

Satyr upon Sir Niel Laing

Canker'd, cursed creature, crabbed, corbit kittle,
Buntin-ars'd, beugle-back'd, bodied like a beetle;
Sarie shitten, shell-padock, ill shapen shit,
Kid-bearded gennet, all alike great:
Fiddle-douped, flindrikin, fart of a man,
Wa worth the, wanwordie, wanshapen wran!

SIR THOMAS MAITLAND

A— B— on the learned Bartholo Sylva

By this title, the book declares itself, and the amount of riches
  that it conceals,
    itself trusting in its own name, it shows forth.
It promises the world, it promises the stars: what man
    do such names not attact to it?
Heaven does not abhor darkness, nor the world thorns,
    For thus each perceives the hand of the maker.
There was first a WOOD, but now, a still lovelier garden, so
  that you,
    whoever you are, may attain the roses at its centre.

ANNE BACON

The Doubt of Future Foes

The doubt of future foes exiles my present joy,
And wit me warns to shun such snares as threaten mine
  annoy;
For falsehood now doth flow, and subjects' faith doth ebb,
Which should not be if reason ruled or wisdom weaved the
  web.
But clouds of joys untried do cloak aspiring minds,
Which turn to rain of late repent by changed course of winds.
The top of hope supposed the root upreared shall be,
And fruitless all their grafted guile, as shortly ye shall see.
The dazzled eyes with pride, which great ambition blinds,
Shall be unsealed by worthy wights whose foresight
  falsehood finds.

The daughter of debate that discord aye doth sow
Shall reap no gain where former rule still peace hath taught
  to know.
No foreign banished wight shall anchor in this port;
Our realm brooks not seditious sects, let them elsewhere resort.
My rusty sword through rest shall first his edge employ
To poll their tops that seek such change or gape for future joy.

QUEEN ELIZABETH I

When I Was Fair and Young

When I was fair and young, then favour graced me.
Of many was I sought their mistress for to be.
But I did scorn them all and answered them therefore:
Go, go, go, seek some other where; importune me no more.

How many weeping eyes I made to pine in woe,
How many sighing hearts I have not skill to show,
But I the prouder grew and still this spake therefore:
Go, go, go, seek some other where, importune me no more.

Then spake fair Venus' son, that proud victorious boy,
Saying: You dainty dame, for that you be so coy,
I will so pluck your plumes as you shall say no more:
Go, go, go, seek some other where, importune me no more.

As soon as he had said, such change grew in my breast
That neither night nor day I could take any rest.
Wherefore I did repent that I had said before:
Go, go, go, seek some other where, importune me no more.

QUEEN ELIZABETH I

To Queen Elizabeth

Lo thus in brief (most sacred Majesty)
I have set down whence all these Sibyls were
What they foretold, or saw, we see, and hear
And profit reap by all their prophesy
Would God I wear a Sibyl to divine
In worthy verse your lasting happiness
Then only I should be characteress
Of that, which worlds with wonder might define
But what need I to wish, when you are such,
Of whose perfections none can write too much.

JANE SEAGER

A Communication Which the Author Had to London, Before She Made Her Will

The time is come, I must depart
    from thee, ah famous city;
I never yet to rue my smart,
    did find that thou had'st pity.
Wherefore small cause there is, that I
    should grieve from thee to go;
But many women foolishly,
    like me, and other moe,
Do such a fixèd fancy set,
    on those which least deserve,
That long it is ere wit we get
    away from them to swerve.
But time with pity oft will tell
    to those that will her try,
Whether it best be more to mell,
    or utterly defy.
And now hath time me put in mind
    of thy great cruelness,
That never once a help would find,
    to ease me in distress.
Thou never yet would'st credit give
    to board me for a year;
Nor with apparel me relieve,
    except thou payèd were.
No, no, thou never did'st me good,
    nor ever wilt, I know.
Yet am I in no angry mood,
    but will, or ere I go,

In perfect love and charity,
    my testament here write,
And leave to thee such treasury,
    as I in it recite.
Now stand aside and give me leave
    to write my latest will;
And see that none you do deceive
    of that I leave them till.

ISABELLA WHITNEY

Verses in Italian and French, written by the Queen of Scots to the Queen of England

A single thought which benefits and harms me
Bitter and sweet alternate endlessly in my heart.
Between hope and fear this thought weighs down on me
So much that peace and rest flee from me

So, dear sister, if this paper reiterates
My pressing desire to see you;
It is because I see in pain and sorrow
The immediate outcome if this request should fail.

I have seen the ship blown by contrary winds
On the high seas, near to the harbour mouth
And the calm turning to troubled water

Likewise [sister] I live in fear and terror
Not on account of you, but because there are times
When Fortune can destroy sail and rigging at once.

MARY STUART, QUEEN OF SCOTS

God send euerie Preist ane wyfe

God send euerie Preist ane wyfe.
And euerie Nunne ane man.
That thay mycht leue that haly lyfe
As first the Kirk began

Sanct Peter, quhome nane can reprufe,
His lyfe in Mariage led
All guide Preistis, quhome God did lufe
Thair maryit wyffis had

Greit causis than, I grant, had thay
Fra wyffis to refraine
Bot greiter causis half thay may,
Now wyffis to wed againe

For than suld nocht sa mony hure
Be vp and downe this land:
Nor zit sa mony beggeris pure,
In Kirk and mercat stand

And nocht sa mekle bastard seid,
Throw out this cuntrie sawin:
Nor gude men vncouth fry suld feid,
And all the suitli war knawin

Sen Christis law, and commoun law.
And Doctouris will admit,
That Prestis in that zock suld draw,
Quha dar say contrair it?

JAMES, JOHN AND ROBERT WEDDERBURN

from The Faerie Queene

So forth issued the Seasons of the year;
First lusty Spring, all dight in leaves of flowers
That freshly budded, and new blooms did bear,
In which a thousand birds had built their bowers,
That sweetly sung to call forth paramours;
And in his hand a javelin he did bear,
And on his head (as fit for warlike stoures)
A gilt engraven morion he did wear,
That as some did him love, so others did him fear.

Then came the jolly Summer, being dight
In a thin silken cassock, coloured green,
That was unlined all, to be more light,
And on his head a garland well beseen,
He wore, from which, as he had chauffed been,
The sweat did drop, and in his hand he bore

A bow and shafts, as he in forest green
Had hunted late the libbard or the boar,
And now would bathe his limbs with labour heated sore.

Then came the Autumn, all in yellow clad,
As though he joyed in his plenteous store,
Laden with fruits that made him laugh, full glad
That he had banished Hunger, which to-fore
Had by the belly oft him pinched sore;
Upon his head a wreath, that was enroll'd
With ears of corn of every sort, he bore,
And in his hand a sickle he did hold,
To reap the ripen'd fruits the which the earth had yold.

Lastly came Winter, clothed all in frieze,
Chattering his teeth for cold that did him chill,
Whilst on his hoary beard his breath did freeze,
And the dull drops that from his purpled bill
As from a limbeck did adown distill;
In his right hand a tipped staff he held
With which his feeble steps he stayed still,
For he was faint with cold and weak with eld,
That scarce his loosed limbs he able was to weld.

These, marching; softly, thus in order went,
And after them the Months all riding came;
First sturdy March, with brows full sternly bent,
And armed strongly, rode upon a Ram,
The same which over Hellespontus swam;
Yet in his hand a spade be also hent,
And in a bag all sorts of seeds ysame,
Which on the earth he strewed as he went,
And fill'd her womb with fruitful hope of nourishment.

Next came fresh April, full of lustyhed,
And wanton as a kid, whose horn new buds;
Upon a Bull he rode, the same which led
Europa floating through the Argolic floods;
His horns were gilden all with golden studs.
And garnished with garlands goodly dight
Of all the fairest flowers and freshest buds
Which th'earth brings forth, and wet he seemed in sight
With waves, through which he waded for his love's delight.

Then came fair May, the fairest maid on ground
Decked all with dainties of her season's pride,
And throwing flowers out of her lap around;
Upon two brethren's shoulders she did ride
The Twins of Leda, which on either side
Supported her like to their sovereign queen;
Lord! how all creatures laugh'd when her they spied,
And leaped and danced as they had ravished been!
And Cupid's self about her fluttered all in green.

And after her came jolly June, arrayed
All in green leaves, as he a player were,
Yet in his time he wrought as well as played
That by his plough-irons might right well appear;
Upon a Crab he rode, that did him bear
With crooked crawling steps an uncouth pace,
And backward yode, as bargemen wont to fare,
Bending their force contrary to their face;
Like that ungracious crew which feigns demurest grace.

Then came hot July, boiling like to fire,
That all his garments he had cast away;
Upon a Lion, raging; yet with ire,
He boldly rode, and made him to obey;
It was the beast that whilome did forray
The Nemæan forest, till th' Amphytrionide
Him slew, and with his hide did him array;
Behind his back a scythe, and by his side,
Under his belt, he bore a sickle circling wide.

The sixth was August, being rich arrayed
In garment all of gold down to the ground;
Yet rode he not, but led a lovely maid
Forth by the lily hand, the which was crowned
With ears of corn, and full her hand was found;
That was the righteous Virgin, which of old
Lived here on earth, and plenty made abound,
But after wrong was loved, and justice sold,
She left the unrighteous world, and was to heaven extolled.

Next him September marched, eke on foot;
Yet was he heavy laden with the spoil
Of harvest's riches, which he made his boot,
And him enriched with bounty of the soil;
In his one hand, as fit for harvest's toil,
He held a knife-hook, and in the other hand
A pair of Weights, with which he did assoyle
Both more and less, where it in doubt did stand,
And equal gave to each, as justice duly scanned.

Then came October, full of merry glee,
For yet his noule was totty of the must,
Which he was treading in the wine-fat's see,
And of the joyous ale, whose gentle gust
Made him so frolick, and so full of lust;
Upon a dreadful Scorpion he did ride,
The same which, by Diana's doom unjust,
Slew great Orion; and eke by his side
He had his ploughing-share and coulter ready tied.

Next was November; he full gross and fat,
As fed with lard, and that right well might seem,
For he had been a fatting hogs of late,
That yet his brows with sweat did reek and steem,
And yet the season was full sharp and breem;
In planting eke he took no small delight:
Whereon he rode, not easy was to deem,
For it a dreadful Centaur was in sight,
The seed of Saturn and fair Nais, Chiron hight.

And after him came next the chill December,
Yet he, through merry feasting which he made,
And great boofires, did not the cold remember,
His Saviour's birth his mind so much did glad;
Upon a shaggy, bearded Goat he rode,
The same wherewith Dan Jove in tender years,
They say, was nourished by the Iæan maid;
And in his hand a broad deep bowl he bears,
Of which he freely drinks a health to all his peers.

Then came old January, wrapped well
In many weeds, to keep the cold away,
Yet did he quake and quiver like to quell,
And blow his nails to warm them if he may,
For they were numb'd with holding all the day
A hatchet keen, with which he felled wood,
And from the trees did lop the needless spray;
Upon a huge great earth-pot steane he stood,
From whose wide mouth there flowed forth the Roman flood.

And lastly came old February, sitting
In an old waggon, for he could not ride,
Drawn of two Fishes, for the season fitting,
Which through the flood before did softly slide
And swim away; yet had he by his side
His plough and harness fit to till the ground,
And tools to prune the trees, before the pride
Of hasting prime did make them burgeon round;
So passed the Twelve Months forth, and their due places found.

EDMUND SPENSER

Echo

Fair rocks, goodly rivers, sweet woods, when shall I see peace?
   Peace.
Peace! what bars me my tongue? who is it that comes me so
   nigh? *I.*
Oh, I do know what guest I have met, it is Echo. *'Tis Echo.*
Well met, Echo, approach; then tell me thy will too. *I will too.*
Echo, what do I get yielding my sprite to my grieves? *Grieves.*
What medicine may I find for a grief that draws me to death?
   Death.
O poisonous medicine! what worse to me can be than it? *It.*
In what state was I then, when I took this deadly disease?
   Ease.
And what manner a mind which had to that humour a vein?
   Vain.
Hath not reason enough vehemence the desire to reprove?
   Prove.
Oft prove I: but what salve, when reason seeks to be gone?
   One.
Oh, what is it? what is it that may be a salve to my love?
   Love.
What do lovers seek for, long seeking for to enjoy? *Joy.*
What be the joys which for to enjoy they went to the pains?
   Pains.
Then to an earnest love what doth best victory lend? *End.*
End! but I can never end, Love will not give me leave? *Leave.*
How be the minds dispos'd that cannot taste thy physick?
   Sick.
Yet say again thy advice for the evils that I told thee?
   I told thee.

Doth the infected wretch of his harm the extremity know?
  No.
But if he know not his harms, what guides hath he whilst he
  be blind? *Blind.*
What blind guides can he have that leans to a fancy? *A fancy.*
Can fancies want eyes, or he fall that steppeth aloft? *Oft.*
What causes first made these torments on me to light? *Light.*
Can then a cause be so light that forceth a man to go die? *Ay.*
Yet tell what light thing I had in me to draw me to die? *Eye.*
Eyesight made me to yield; but what first pierced to my eyes?
  Eyes.
Eyes hurters, eyes hurt; but what from them to me falls?
  Falls.
But when I first did fall, what brought most fall to my heart?
  Art.
Art I what can be that art that thou dost mean by thy speech?
  Speech.
What be the fruits of speaking art? what grows by the words?
  Words.
O, much more than words: those words served more me to
  bless. *Less.*
Oh, when shall I be known where most to be known I do long?
  Long.
Long be thy woes for such news; but how recks she my thoughts?
  Oughts.
Then, then, what do I gain, since unto her will I do wind?
  Wind.
Wind, tempests, and storms, yet in end what gives she desire?
  Ire.
Silly reward! yet among women hath she of virtue the most.
  Most.
What great name may I give to so heav'nly a woman?
  A wo-man.

Woe but seems to me joy, that agrees to my thought so.
   I thought so.
Think so, for of my desirèd bliss it is only the course. *Curse.*
Curs'd be thyself for cursing that which leads me to joys.
   Toys.
What be the sweet creatures where lowly demands be not heard?
   Hard.
What makes them be unkind? speak, for thou hast narrowly
   pried? *Pride.*
Whence can pride come there, since springs of beauty be thence?
   Thence.
Horrible is this blasphemy unto the most holy. *O lie.*
Thou liest, false Echo! their minds as virtue be just. *Just.*
Mock'st thou those diamonds which only be matcht by the
   gods? *Odds.*
Odds! what an odds is there! since them to the heavens I prefer.
   Err.
Tell yet again me the names of these fair form'd to do evils?
   Devils.
Devils! if in hell such devils do abide, to the hell I do go. *Go.*

SIR PHILIP SIDNEY

'Sweet kiss, thy sweets I fain would sweetly indite'

Sweet kiss, thy sweets I fain would sweetly indite
Which even of sweetness sweetest sweetener art,
Pleasingst consort, where each sense holds a part,
Which, coupling doves, guides Venus' chariot right;
Best charge and bravest retrait in Cupid's fight,
A double key which opens to the heart,
Most rich when most his riches it impart;
Nest of young joys, schoolmaster of delight,
Teaching the means at once to take and give;
The friendly fray, where blows both wound and heal,
The pretty death, while each in other live.
Poor hope's first wealth, hostage of promist weal,
Breakfast of love. But lo, lo, where she is,
Cease we to praise: now pray we for a kiss.

SIR PHILIP SIDNEY

The Description of Sir Geoffrey Chaucer

His stature was not very tall,
Lean he was, his legs were small,
Hosed within a stock of red,
A buttoned bonnet on his head,
From under which did hang, I ween,
Silver hairs both bright and sheen.
His beard was white, trimmed round,

His countenance blithe and merry found.
A sleeveless jacket large and wide,
With many plights and skirts side,
Of water camlet did he wear;
A whittle by his belt he bare,
His shoes were corned, broad before,
His inkhorn at his side he wore,
And in his hand he bore a book.
Thus did this ancient poet look.

ROBERT GREENE

from Poly-Olbion

When *Watling* in his words that took but small delight,
Hearing the angry Brook so cruelly to bite;
As one that fain would drive these fancies from his mind,
Quoth he, I'll tell thee things that suit thy gentler kind.
My Song is of my self, and my three sister Streets,
Which way each of us run, where each his fellow meets,
Since us, his Kingly Ways, *Mulmutius* first began,
From Sea, again to Sea, that through the Island ran.
Which that in mind to keep posterity might have,
Appointing first our course, this privilege he gave,
That no man might arrest, or debtors goods might seize
In any of us for his military Ways.
And though the Fosse in length exceed me many a mile,
That holds from shore to shore the length of all the Isle,
From where Rich *Cornwall* points, to the *Iberian* Seas,
Till colder *Cathnes* tells the scattered *Orcades*,
I measuring but the breadth, that is not half his gate;

Yet, for that I am graced with goodly *Londons* state,
And *Tames* and *Severne* both since in my course I cross,
And in much greater trade; am worthier far then *Fosse*.
But O unhappy chance! through times disastrous lot,
Our other fellow Streets lie utterly forgot:
As Icning, that set out from *Yarmouth* in the East,
By the *Iceni* then being generally possessed
Was of that people first termed Icning in her race,
Upon the *Chiltern* here that did my course embrace:
Into the dropping South and bearing then outright,
Upon the *Solent* Sea stopped on the *Ile*-of-*Wight*.

And *Rickneld*, forth that raft from *Cambria's* farther shore,
Where *South-Wales* now shoots forth *Saint David's* Promontory.
And, on his mid-way near, did me in England meet;
Then in his oblique course the lusty straggling Street
Soon overtook the *Fosse*; and toward the fall of *Tine*,
Into the *Germane* Sea dissolved at his decline.

Here *Watling* would have ceased, his tale as having told:
But now this Flood that fain the Street in talk would hold,
Those ancient things to hear, which well old *Watling* knew,
With these enticing words, her fairly forward drew.

Right Noble Street, quoth he, thou hast lived long, gone far,
Much traffic had in peace, much travailed in war;
And in thy larger course surveyed as sundry grounds
(Where I poor Flood am locked within these narrower bounds,
And like my ruined self these ruins only see,
And there remains not one to pity them or me)
On with thy former speech: I pray thee somewhat say.
For, *Watling*, as thou art a military Way,
Thy story of old Streets likes me so wondrous well,
That of the ancient folk I fain would hear thee tell.

MICHAEL DRAYTON

The Passionate Shepherd to his Love

Come live with me, and be my love,
And we will all the pleasures prove,
That valleys, groves, hills and fields,
Woods, or steepy mountain yields.

And we will sit upon the rocks,
Seeing the shepherds feed their flocks
By shallow rivers, to whose falls
Melodious birds sing madrigals.

And I will make thee beds of roses,
And a thousand fragrant posies,
A cap of flowers and a kirtle
Embroidered all with leaves of myrtle.

A gown made of the finest wool
Which from our pretty lambs we pull,
Fair lined slippers for the cold,
With buckles of the purest gold;

A belt of straw and ivy-buds,
With coral clasps and amber studs,
And if these pleasures may thee move,
Come live with me, and be my love.

The shepherd swains shall dance and sing
For thy delight each May-morning,
If these delights thy mind may move;
Then live with me, and be my love.

CHRISTOPHER MARLOWE

from The Tempest

Ye elves of hills, brooks, standing lakes and groves,
And ye that on the sands with printless foot
Do chase the ebbing Neptune, and do fly him
When he comes back; you demi-puppets that
By moonshine do the green sour ringlets make
Whereof the ewe not bites; and you whose pastime
Is to make midnight mushrooms, that rejoice
To hear the solemn curfew; by whose aid,
Weak masters though ye be, I have bedimmed
The noontide sun, called forth the mutinous winds,
And 'twixt the green sea and the azured vault
Set roaring war – to the dread rattling thunder
Have I given fire, and rifted Jove's stout oak
With his own bolt; the strong-based promontory
Have I made shake, and by the spurs plucked up
The pine and cedar; graves at my command
Have waked their sleepers, oped, and let 'em forth
By my so potent art. But this rough magic
I here abjure. And when I have required
Some heavenly music – which even now I do –
To work mine end upon their senses that

This airy charm is for, I'll break my staff,
Bury it certain fathoms in the earth,
And deeper than did ever plummet sound
I'll drown my book.

WILLIAM SHAKESPEARE

from King John

Grief fills the room up of my absent child,
Lies in his bed, walks up and down with me,
Puts on his pretty looks, repeats his words,
Remembers me of all his gracious parts,
Stuffs out his vacant garments with his form;
Then have I reason to be fond of grief.
Fare you well. Had you such a loss as I,
I could give better comfort than you do.
I will not keep this form upon my head
When there is such disorder in my wit.
O Lord, my boy, my Arthur, my fair son,
My life, my joy, my food, my all the world,
My widow-comfort, and my sorrow's cure!

WILLIAM SHAKESPEARE

'How like a winter hath my absence been'

How like a winter hath my absence been
From thee, the pleasure of the fleeting year!
What freezings have I felt, what dark days seen;
What old December's bareness everywhere!
And yet this time removed was summer's time,
The teeming autumn big with rich increase,
Bearing the wanton burden of the prime,
Like widowed wombs after their lord's decease.
Yet this abundant issue seemed to me
But hope of orphans and unfathered fruit,
For summer and his pleasures wait on thee,
And, thou away, the very birds are mute,
    Or if they sing, 'tis with so dull a cheer
    That leaves look pale, dreading the winter's near.

WILLIAM SHAKESPEARE

from Antony and Cleopatra

The barge she sat in, like a burnished throne,
Burned on the water: the poop was beaten gold;
Purple the sails, and so perfuméd that
The winds were love-sick with them; the oars were silver,
Which to the tune of flutes kept stroke, and made
The water which they beat to follow faster,
As amorous of their strokes. For her own person,
It beggar'd all description: she did lie
In her pavilion, – cloth-of-gold of tissue, –

O'er-picturing that Venus where we see
The fancy outwork nature: on each side her
Stood pretty dimpled boys, like smiling Cupids,
With divers-colour'd fans, whose wind did seem
To glow the delicate cheeks which they did cool,
And what they undid did.

WILLIAM SHAKESPEARE

from Love's Labour's Lost

SPRING

When daisies pied and violets blue,
    And lady-smocks, all silver-white,
And cuckoo-buds of yellow hue
    Do paint the meadows with delight,
The cuckoo then on every tree
Mocks married men, for thus sings he:
        Cuckoo!
Cuckoo, cuckoo – O word of fear,
Unpleasing to a married ear.

When shepherds pipe on oaten straws,
    And merry larks are ploughmen's clocks:
When turtles tread, and rooks and daws,
    And maidens bleach their summer smocks,
The cuckoo then on every tree
Mocks married men, for thus sings he:
        Cuckoo!
Cuckoo, cuckoo – O word of fear,
Unpleasing to a married ear.

When icicles hang by the wall,
  And Dick the shepherd blows his nail,
And Tom bears logs into the hall,
  And milk comes frozen home in pail;
When blood is nipped, and ways be foul,
Then nightly sings the staring owl:
Tu-whit, tu-whoo! – a merry note,
While greasy Joan doth keel the pot.

When all aloud the wind doth blow,
  And coughing drowns the parson's saw,
And birds sit brooding in the snow,
  And Marian's nose looks red and raw;
When roasted crabs hiss in the bowl,
Then nightly sings the staring owl:
        To-who;
Tu-whit, tu-whoo! – a merry note,
While greasy Joan doth keel the pot.

WILLIAM SHAKESPEARE

from Henry V

Once more unto the breach, dear friends, once more,
Or close the wall up with our English dead.
In peace there's nothing so becomes a man
As modest stillness and humility,
But when the blast of war blows in our ears,
Then imitate the action of the tiger.

Stiffen the sinews, conjure up the blood,
Disguise fair nature with hard-favoured rage.
Then lend the eye a terrible aspéct,
Let it pry through the portage of the head
Like the brass cannon, let the brow o'erwhelm it
As fearfully as doth a gallèd rock
O'erhang and jutty his confounded base,
Swilled with the wild and wasteful ocean.
Now set the teeth and stretch the nostril wide,
Hold hard the breath, and bend up every spirit
To his full height. On, on, you noblest English,
Whose blood is fet from fathers of war-proof,
Fathers that like so many Alexanders
Have in these parts from morn till even fought,
And sheathed their swords for lack of argument.
Dishonour not your mothers; now attest
That those whom you calld fathers did beget you.
Be copy now to men of grosser blood,
And teach them how to war. And you, good yeomen,
Whose limbs were made in England, show us here
The mettle of your pasture; let us swear
That you are worth your breeding – which I doubt not,
For there is none of you so mean and base
That hath not noble lustre in your eyes.
I see you stand like greyhounds in the slips,
Straining upon the start. The game's afoot.
Follow your spirit, and upon this charge
Cry 'God for Harry! England and Saint George!'

WILLIAM SHAKESPEARE

from King Richard II

This royal throne of kings, this sceptred isle,
This earth of majesty, this seat of Mars,
This other Eden, demi-paradise,
This fortress built by Nature for herself
Against infection and the hand of war,
This happy breed of men, this little world,
This precious stone set in the silver sea,
Which serves it in the office of a wall,
Or as a moat defensive to a house
Against the envy of less happier lands;
This blessèd plot, this earth, this realm, this England,
This nurse, this teeming womb of royal kings,
Feared by their breed and famous by their birth,
Renownèd for their deeds as far from home
For Christian service and true chivalry
As is the sepulchre in stubborn Jewry,
Of the world's ransom, blessèd Mary's son;
This land of such dear souls, this dear, dear land,
Dear for her reputation through the world,
Is now leas'd out – I die pronouncing it –
Like to a tenement, or pelting farm.
England, bound in with the triumphant sea,
Whose rocky shore beats back the envious siege
Of watery Neptune, is now bound in with shame,
With inky blots, and rotten parchment bonds.
That England, that was wont to conquer others
Hath made a shameful conquest of itself.

WILLIAM SHAKESPEARE

'Now winter nights enlarge'

Now winter nights enlarge
The number of their hours,
And clouds their storms discharge
Upon the airy towers.
Let now the chimneys blaze,
And cups o'erflow with wine;
Let well-tuned words amaze
With harmony divine.
Now yellow waxen lights
Shall wait on honey Love,
While youthful revels, masks, and courtly sights
Sleep's leaden spells remove.

This time doth well dispense
With lovers' long discourse.
Much speech hath some defence
Though beauty no remorse.
All do not all things well:
Some measures comely tread,
Some knotted riddles tell,
Some poems smoothly read.
The Summer hath his joys,
And Winter his delights.
Though Love and all his pleasures are but toys,
They shorten tedious nights.

THOMAS CAMPION

'There is a garden in her face'

There is a garden in her face
Where roses and white lilies grow;
  A heavenly paradise is that place
Wherein all pleasant fruits do flow.
  There cherries grow which none may buy,
  Till 'Cherry ripe' themselves do cry.

Those cherries fairly do enclose
Of orient pearl a double row,
  Which when her lovely laughter shows,
They look like rose-buds filled with snow;
  Yet them nor peer nor prince can buy,
  Till 'Cherry ripe' themselves do cry.

Her eyes like angels watch them still,
Her brows like bended bows do stand,
  Threatening with piercing frowns to kill
All that attempt with eye or hand
  Those sacred cherries to come nigh,
  Till 'Cherry ripe' themselves do cry.

THOMAS CAMPION

Inviting a Friend to Supper

Tonight, grave sir, both my poor house, and I
Do equally desire your company:
Not that we think us worthy such a guest,
But that your worth will dignify our feast,
With those that come; whose grace may make that seem
Something, which, else, could hope for no esteem.
It is the fair acceptance, sir, creates
The entertainment perfect: not the cates.
Yet shall you have, to rectify your palate,
An olive, capers, or some better salad
Ush'ring the mutton; with a short-legged hen,
If we can get her, full of eggs, and then,
Lemons, and wine for sauce: to these, a cony
Is not to be despaired of, for our money;
And, though fowl, now, be scarce, yet there are clerks,
The sky not falling, think we may have larks.
I'll tell you of more, and lie, so you will come:
Of partridge, pheasant, woodcock, of which some
May yet be there; and godwit, if we can:
Knat, rail, and ruff too. Howsoe'er, my man
Shall read a piece of Virgil, Tacitus,
Livy, or of some better hook to us,
Of which we'll speak our minds, amidst our meat;
And I'll profess no verses to repeat:
To this, if aught appear, which I not know of,
That will the pastry, not my paper, show of.
Digestive cheese, and fruit there sure will be;
But that, which most doth take my muse, and me,
Is a pure cup of rich canary wine,
Which is the Mermaid's, now, but shall be mine:

Of which had Horace, or Anacreon tasted,
Their lives, as do their lines, till now had lasted.
Tobacco, nectar, or the Thespian spring,
Are all but Luther's beer, to this I sing.
Of this we will sup free, but moderately,
And we will have no Pooly, or Parrot by;
Nor shall our cups make any guilty men:
But, at our parting, we will be, as when
We innocently met. No simple word,
That shall be uttered at our mirthful board,
Shall make us sad next morning: or affright
The liberty, that we'll enjoy tonight.

BEN JONSON

To the Memory of My Beloved, the Author
Mr William Shakespeare: And What
He Hath Left Us

To draw no envy (Shakespeare) on thy name,
Am I thus ample to thy book, and fame:
While I confess thy writings to be such,
As neither man, nor muse, can praise too much.
Tis true, and all men's suffrage. But these ways
Were not the paths I meant unto thy praise:
For seeliest ignorance on these may light,
Which, when it sounds at best, but echoes right;
Or blind affection, which doth ne'er advance
The truth, but gropes, and urgeth all by chance;
Or crafty malice, might pretend this praise,
And think to ruin, where it seemed to raise.
These are, as some infamous bawd, or whore,
Should praise a matron. What could hurt her more?
But thou art proof against them, and indeed
Above the ill fortune of them, or the need.
I therefore will begin. Soul of the age!
The applause, delight, the wonder of our stage!
My Shakespeare, rise; I will not lodge thee by
Chaucer, or Spenser, or bid Beaumont lie
A little further, to make thee a room:
Thou art a monument, without a tomb,
And art alive still, while thy book doth live,
And we have wits to read, and praise to give.
That I not mix thee so, my brain excuses;
I mean with great, but disproportioned muses:
For, if I thought my judgement were of years,

I should commit thee surely with thy peers,
And tell, how far thou didst our Lyly outshine,
Or sporting Kyd, or Marlowe's mighty line.
And though thou hadst small Latin, and less Greek,
From thence to honour thee, I would not seek
For names; but call forth thundering Aeschylus,
Euripides, and Sophocles to us,
Pacuvius, Accius, him of Cordova dead,
To life again, to hear thy buskin tread,
And shake a stage: or, when thy socks were on,
Leave thee alone, for the comparison
Of all that insolent Greece, or haughty Rome
Sent forth, or since did from their ashes come.
Triumph, my Britain, thou hast one to show,
To whom all scenes of Europe homage owe.
He was not of an age, but for all time!
And all the muses still were in their prime,
When like Apollo he came forth to warm
Our ears, or like a Mercury to charm!
Nature herself was proud of his designs,
And joyed to wear the dressing of his lines!
Which were so richly spun, and woven so fit,
As, since, she will vouchsafe no other wit.
The merry Greek, tart Aristophanes,
Neat Terence, witty Plautus, now not please;
But antiquated, and deserted lie
As they were not of nature's family.
Yet must I not give nature all: thy art,
My gentle Shakespeare, must enjoy a part.
For though the poet's matter, nature be,
His art doth give the fashion. And, that he,
Who casts to write a living line, must sweat,
(Such as thine are) and strike the second heat

Upon the muses' anvil: turn the same,
(And himself with it) that he thinks to frame;
Or for the laurel, he may gain a scorn,
For a good poet's made, as well as bom.
And such wert thou. Look how the father's face
Lives in his issue, even so, the race
Of Shakespeare's mind, and manners brightly shines
In his well-turned, and true-filéd lines:
In each of which, he seems to shake a lance,
As brandished at the eyes of ignorance.
Sweet swan of Avon, what a sight it were
To see thee in our waters yet appear,
And make those flights upon the banks of Thames,
That so did take Eliza, and our James!
But stay, I see thee in the hemisphere
Advanced, and made a constellation there!
Shine forth, thou star of poets, and with rage,
Or influence, chide, or cheer the drooping stage;
Which, since thy flight from hence, hath mourned like night.
And despairs day, but for thy volume's light.

BEN JONSON

Song to Celia

Drink to me, only, with thine eyes,
   And I will pledge with mine;
Or leave a kiss but in the cup,
   And I'll not look for wine.
The thirst, that from the soul doth rise,
   Doth ask a drink divine:
But might I of Jove's nectar sup,
   I would not change for thine.
I sent thee, late, a rosy wreath,
   Not so much honouring thee,
As giving it a hope, that there
   It could not withered be.
But thou thereon didst only breathe,
   And sent'st it back to me:
Since when it grows, and smells, I swear,
   Not of itself, but thee.

BEN JONSON

IV

1600-1700

CHURCH-
BELLS
BEYOND THE
STARS
heard...

The Flea

Mark but this flea, and mark in this,
How little that which thou deny'st me is;
Me it sucked first, and now sucks thee,
And in this flea, our two bloods mingled be;
Confess it, this cannot be said
A sin, or shame, or loss of maidenhead,
    Yet this enjoys before it woo,
    And pampered swells with one blood made of two,
    And this, alas, is more than we would do.

Oh stay, three lives in one flea spare,
Where we almost, nay more than married are.
This flea is you and I, and this
Our marriage bed, and marriage temple is;
Though parents grudge, and you, we'are met,
And cloistered in these living walls of jet
    Though use make you apt to kill me,
    Let not to this, self murder added be,
    And sacrilege, three sins in killing three.

Cruel and sudden, hast thou since
Purpled thy nail, in blood of innocence?
In what could this flea guilty be,
Except in that drop which it sucked from thee?
Yet thou triumph'st, and say'st that thou
Find'st not thyself, nor me the weaker now;

'Tis true, then learn how false, fears be;
Just so much honour, when thou yield'st to me,
Will waste, as this flea's death took life from thee.

JOHN DONNE

The Sun Rising

Busy old fool, unruly sun,
    Why dost thou thus,
Through windows, and through curtains call on us?
Must to thy motions lovers' seasons run?
    Saucy pedantic wretch, go chide
    Late school-boys, and sour prentices,
  Go tell court-huntsmen, that the King will ride,
  Call country ants to harvest offices;
Love, all alike, no season knows, nor clime,
Nor hours, days, months, which are the rags of time.

Thy beams, so reverend, and strong
    Why shouldst thou think?
I could eclipse and cloud them with a wink,
But that I would not lose her sight so long:
    If her eyes have not blinded thine,
    Look, and tomorrow late, tell me,
  Whether both th'Indias of spice and mine
  Be where thou left'st them, or lie here with me.
Ask for those kings whom thou saw'st yesterday,
And thou shalt hear, All here in one bed lay.

She'is all states, and all princes, I,
Nothing else is.
Princes do but play us; compared to this,
All honour's mimic; all wealth alchemy.
Thou sun art half as happy as we,
In that the world's contracted thus;
Thine age asks ease, and since thy duties be
To warm the world, that's done in warming us.
Shine here to us, and thou art everywhere;
This bed thy centre is, these walls, thy sphere.

JOHN DONNE

Elegy: To his Mistress Going to Bed

Come, Madam, come, all rest my powers defy,
Until I labour, I in labour lie.
The foe oft-times having the foe in sight,
Is tired with standing though they never fight.
Off with that girdle, like heaven's zone glistering,
But a far fairer world encompassing.
Unpin that spangled breastplate which you wear,
That th' eyes of busy fools may be stopped there.
Unlace yourself, for that harmonious chime
Tells me from you, that now 'tis your bed time.
Off with that happy busk, which I envy,
That still can be, and still can stand so nigh.
Your gown going off, such beauteous state reveals,
As when from flowery meads th' hill's shadow steals.

Off with that wiry coronet and show
The hairy diadem which on you doth grow;
Now off with those shoes, and then safely tread
In this love's hallowed temple, this soft bed.
In such white robes heaven's angels used to be
Received by men; thou angel bring'st with thee
A heaven like Mahomet's paradise; and though
Ill spirits walk in white, we easily know
By this these angels from an evil sprite,
Those set our hairs, but these our flesh upright.
　License my roving hands, and let them go
Before, behind, between, above, below.
O my America, my new found land,
My kingdom, safeliest when with one man manned,
My mine of precious stones, my empery,
How blessed am I in this discovering thee!
To enter in these bonds, is to be free;
Then where my hand is set, my seal shall be.
　Full nakedness, all joys are due to thee.
As souls unbodied, bodies unclothed must be,
To taste whole joys. Gems which you women use
Are like Atlanta's balls, cast in men's views,
That when a fool's eye lighteth on a gem,
His earthly soul may covet theirs, not them.
Like pictures, or like books' gay coverings made
For laymen, are all women thus arrayed;
Themselves are mystic books, which only we
Whom their imputed grace will dignify
Must see revealed. Then since I may know,
As liberally, as to a midwife, show
Thyself: cast all, yea, this white linen hence,

Here is no penance, much less innocence.
    To teach thee, I am naked first, why then
What needst thou have more covering than a man.

JOHN DONNE

Lady Greensleeves

Greensleeves was all my joy,
    Greensleeves was my delight:
Greensleeves was my heart of gold,
    And who but Lady Greensleeves.

Alas, my love, ye do me wrong,
    To cast me off discourteously:
And I have loved you so long,
    Delighting in your company.

I have been ready at your hand,
    To grant whatever you would crave.
I have both wagered life and land,
    Your love and good will for to have.

I bought thee kerchiefs to thy head,
    That were wrought fine and gallantly:
I kept thee both at board and bed,
    Which cost my purse well favouredly.

I bought thee petticoats of the best,
    The cloth so fine as fine might be:
I gave thee jewels for thy chest,
    And all this cost I spent on thee.

Thy smock of silk, both fair and white,
    With gold embroidered gorgeously:
Thy petticoat of Sendall right:
    And thus I bought thee gladly.

Thy girdle of gold so red,
    With pearls bedecked sumptuously:
The like no other lasses had,
    And yet thou wouldst not love me.

Thy purse and eke thy gay guilt knives,
    Thy pincase gallant to the eye:
No better wore the Burgesse wives,
    And yet thou wouldst not love me.

Thy crimson stockings all of silk,
    With gold all wrought above the knee,
Thy pumps as white as was the milk,
    And yet thou wouldst not love me.

Thy gown was of the grossie green,
    Thy sleeves of Satin hanging by:
Which made thee be our harvest Queen,
    And yet thou wouldst not love me.

Thy garters fringed with the gold,
   And silver aglets hanging by,
Which made thee blithe for to behold,
   And yet thou wouldst not love me.

My gayest gelding I thee gave,
   To ride where ever liked thee,
No lady ever was so brave,
   And yet thou wouldst not love me.

My men were clothed all in green,
   And they did ever wait on thee:
All this was gallant to be seen,
   And yet thou wouldst not love me.

They set thee up, they took thee down,
   They served thee with humility,
Thy foot might not once touch the ground,
   And yet thou wouldst not love me.

For every morning when thou rose,
   I sent thee dainties orderly:
To cheer thy stomach from all woes,
   And yet thou wouldst not love me.

Thou couldst desire no earthly thing.
   But still thou hadst it readily:
Thy music still to play and sing,
   And yet thou wouldst not love me.

And who did pay for all this gear,
    That thou didst spend when pleased thee?
Even I that am rejected here,
    And thou disdainst to love me.

Well, I wil pray to God on high,
    That thou my constancy maist see:
And that yet once before I die,
    Thou wilt vouchsafe to love me.

Greensleeves now farewell adieu,
    God I pray to prosper thee:
For I am stil thy lover true,
    Come once again and love me.

ANON

'Love like a juggler comes to play his prize'

Love like a juggler comes to play his prize,
    And all minds draw his wonders to admire,
    To see how cunningly he (wanting eyes)
    Can yet deceive the best sight of desire.

The wanton child, how can he fain his fire
    So prettily, as none sees his disguise,
    How finely do his tricks; while we fools hire
    The badge, and office of his tyrannies.

For in the end such juggling he doth make,
   As he our hearts instead of eyes doth take;
   For men can only by their flights abuse

The sight with nimble, and delightful skill,
   But if he play, his gain is our lost will,
   Yet childlike we cannot his sports refuse.

LADY MARY WROTH

'Come, darkest night, becoming sorrow best'

Come, darkest night, becoming sorrow best;
   Light, leave thy light, fit for a lightsome soul;
   Darkness doth truly suit with me oppressed,
   Whom absence' power doth from mirth control:
The very trees with hanging heads condole
   Sweet summer's parting, and of leaves distressed
   In dying colours make a grief-ful roll,
   So much, alas, to sorrow are they pressed.
Thus of dead leaves her farewell carpet's made:
   Their fall, their branches, all their mournings prove,
   With leafless, naked bodies, whose hues vade
   From hopeful green, to wither in their love:
If trees and leaves for absence mourners be,
No marvel that I grieve, who like want see.

LADY MARY WROTH

The Argument of His Book

I sing of brooks, of blossoms, birds, and bowers,
Of April, May, of June, and July flowers;
I sing of may-poles, hock-carts, wassails, wakes,
Of bridegrooms, brides, and of their bridal cakes;
I write of youth, of love, and have access
By these to sing of cleanly wantonness;
I sing of dews, of rains, and piece by piece
Of balm, of oil, of spice, and ambergris;
I sing of times trans-shifting, and I write
How roses first came red, and lilies white;
I write of groves, of twilights, and I sing
The court of Mab, and of the Fairy King;
I write of hell; I sing, and ever shall,
Of heaven, and hope to have it after all.

ROBERT HERRICK

Corinna's Going a-Maying

Get up, get up for shame, the blooming morn
Upon her wings presents the god unshorn.
 See how Aurora throws her fair
 Fresh-quilted colours through the air:
 Get up, sweet slug-a-bed, and see
 The dew bespangling herb and tree.
Each flower has wept and bow'd toward the east
Above an hour since: yet you not dressed;

Nay! not so much as out of bed?
When all the birds have matins said
And sung their thankful hymns, 'tis sin,
Nay, profanation to keep in,
Whereas a thousand virgins on this day
Spring, sooner than the lark, to fetch in May.

Rise and put on your foliage, and be seen
To come forth, like the spring-time, fresh and green,
    And sweet as Flora. Take no care
    For jewels for your gown or hair:
    Fear not; the leaves will strew
    Gems in abundance upon you:
Besides, the childhood of the day has kept,
Against you come, some orient pearls unwept;
    Come and receive them while the light
    Hangs on the dew-locks of the night:
    And Titan on the eastern hill
    Retires himself, or else stands still
Till you come forth. Wash, dress, be brief in praying:
Few beads are best when once we go a-Maying.

Come, my Corinna, come; and, coming, mark
How each field turns a street, each street a park
    Made green and trimmed with trees: see how
    Devotion gives each house a bough
    Or branch: each porch, each door ere this
    An ark, a tabernacle is,
Made up of white-thorn neatly interwove;
As if here were those cooler shades of love.

Can such delights be in the street
And open fields and we not see't ?
    Come, we'll abroad; and let's obey
    The proclamation made for May:
And sin no more, as we have done, by staying;
But, my Corinna, come, let's go a-Maying.

There's not a budding boy or girl this day
But is got up, and gone to bring in May.
    A deal of youth, ere this, is come
    Back, and with white-thorn laden home.
    Some have despatch'd their cakes and cream
    Before that we have left to dream:
And some have wept, and woo'd, and plighted troth,
And chose their priest, ere we can cast off sloth:
    Many a green-gown has been given;
    Many a kiss, both odd and even:
    Many a glance too has been sent
    From out the eye, love's firmament;
Many a jest told of the keys betraying
This night, and locks pick'd, yet we're not a-Maying.

Come, let us go while we are in our prime;
And take the harmless folly of the time.
    We shall grow old apace, and die
    Before we know our liberty.
    Our life is short, and our days run
    As fast away as does the sun;
And, as a vapour or a drop of rain,
Once lost, can ne'er be found again,

So when or you or I are made
A fable, song, or fleeting shade,
All love, all liking, all delight
Lies drowned with us in endless night.
Then while time serves, and we are but decaying,
Come, my Corinna, come, let's go a-Maying.

ROBERT HERRICK

Delight in Disorder

A sweet disorder in the dress
Kindles in clothes a wantonness:
A lawn about the shoulders thrown
Into a fine distraction:
An erring lace which here and there
Enthralls the crimson stomacher:
A cuff neglectful, and thereby
Ribbons to flow confusedly:
A winning wave, deserving note,
In the tempestuous petticoat:
A careless shoe-string, in whose tie
I see a wild civility:
Do more bewitch me than when art
Is too precise in every part.

ROBERT HERRICK

Julia in Silks

Whenas in silks my Julia goes,
Then, then, methinks, how sweetly flows
The liquefaction of her clothes.

Next, when I cast mine eyes and see
That brave vibration each way free;
O how that glittering taketh me!

ROBERT HERRICK

To the Virgins to Make Much of Time

Gather ye rose-buds while ye may,
   Old Time is still a-flying;
And this same flower that smiles today,
   Tomorrow will be dying.

The glorious lamp of heaven, the Sun,
   The higher he's a-getting,
The sooner will his race be run,
   And nearer he's to setting.

That age is best, which is the first,
   When youth and blood are warmer
But being spent, the worse, and worst
   Times sail succeed the former.

Then be not coy, but use your time,
　　And while you may, go marry:
For having lost but once your prime,
　　You may for ever tarry.

ROBERT HERRICK

Love

Love bade me welcome; yet my soul drew back,
　　Guilty of dust and sin.
But quick-eyed Love, observing me grow slack
　　From my first entrance in,
Drew nearer to me, sweetly questioning,
　　If I lacked anything.

'A guest', I answered, 'worthy to be here.'
　　Love said, 'You shall be he.'
'I, the unkind, ungrateful? Ah, my dear,
　　I cannot look on thee.'
Love took my hand, and smiling did reply,
　　'Who made the eyes but I?'

'Truth, Lord, but I have marred them; let my shame
        Go where it doth deserve.'
'And know you not', says Love, 'who bore the blame?'
        'My dear, then I will serve.'
'You must sit down', says Love, 'and taste my meat.'
        So I did sit and eat.

GEORGE HERBERT

Avarice

Money, thou bane of bliss, and source of woe,
    Whence com'st thou, that thou art so fresh and fine?
    I know thy parentage is base and low:
Man found thee poor and dirty in a mine.
Surely thou didst so little contribute
    To this great kingdom, which thou now hast got,
    That he was fain, when thou wert destitute,
To dig thee out of thy dark cave and grot:
Then forcing thee, by fire he made thee bright:
    Nay, thou hast got the face of man; for we
    Have with our stamp and seal transferred our right:
Thou art the man, and man but dross to thee.
    Man calleth thee his wealth, who made thee rich;
    And while he digs out thee, falls in the ditch.

GEORGE HERBERT

Prayer

Prayer the Church's banquet, Angels' age,
    God's breath in man returning to his birth,
    The soul in paraphrase, heart in pilgrimage,
The Christian plummet sounding heav'n and earth;
Engine against th' Almighty, sinners' tower,
    Reversed thunder, Christ-side-piercing spear,
    The six-days world-transposing in an hour,
A kind of tune, which all things hear and fear;
Softness, and peace, and joy, and love, and bliss,
    Exalted Manna, gladness of the best,
    Heaven in ordinary, man well dressed,
The milky way, the bird of Paradise,
    Church-bells beyond the stars heard, the soul's blood,
    The land of spices; something understood.

GEORGE HERBERT

The Glance

    When first thy sweet and gracious eye
Vouchsafed ev'n in the midst of youth and night
To look upon me, who before did lie
        Welt'ring in sin;
    I felt a sug'red strange delight,
Passing all cordials made by any art,
Bedew, embalm, and overrun my heart,
        And take it in.

Since that time many a bitter storm
My soul hath felt, ev'n able to destroy,
Had the malicious and ill-meaning harm
　　　His swing and sway:
　　But still thy sweet original joy
Sprung from thine eye, did work within my soul,
And surging griefs, when they grew bold, control,
　　　And got the day.

　　If thy first glance so powerful be,
A mirth but opened and sealed up again;
What wonders shall we feel, when we shall see
　　　Thy full-eyed love!
　　When thou shalt look us out of pain,
And one aspect of thine spend in delight
More than a thousand suns disburse in light,
　　　In heav'n above.

GEORGE HERBERT

The Battle of Inverlochy

O, I have been wounded
Na hì ri ri ri hó hò;
O, I have been wounded
Na hì ri ri ri hó hò;

by the day of Inverlochy,
Na hì ri ri ri hó hò;
Bho latha Blàr Inbhir Lòchaidh,
Na hì ri ri 's ri o ho ró.

from the charge of the grim Irish
who came to Scotland without anything
but what they had on their cloaks;
they added strength to Clan Donald.
They killed my father and my husband,
they struck down my four brothers,
they killed my four young sons
and my nine handsome foster-children;
they slaughtered my great cattle,
and my white sheep they roasted,
they burnt my oats and my barley.

O, I have been anguished by the death
of Duncan of Glen Faochan,
whom all in the land are lamenting
round about Inverary,
women beating their hands, dishevelled.

O, I have been devastated,
for the horsemen of reins and bridles
who fell with his men in the battle;
the Earl of Argyll took to the water
and let that blow fall on his kin!

ANON

'Like as the damask rose you see'

Like as the damask rose you see,
Or like the blossom on the tree,
Or like the dainty flower of May,
Or like the morning to the day,
Or like the sun, or like the shade,
Or like the gourd which Jonas had –
Even such is man, whose thread is spun,
Drawn out, and cut, and so is done.
The rose withers, the blossom blasteth,
The flower fades, the morning hasteth,
The sun sets, the shadow flies,
The gourd consumes; and man he dies.

Like to the grass that's newly sprung,
Or like a tale that's new begun,
Or like the bird that's here to-day,
Or like the pearléd dew of May,
Or like an hour, or like a span,
Or like the singing of a swan –
Even such is man, who lives by breath,
Is here, now there: so life, and death.
The grass withers, the tale is ended,
The bird is flown, the dew's ascended,
The hour is short, the span not long,
The swan's near death; man's life is done.

Like to the bubble in the brook,
Or, in a glass, much like a look,
Or like a shuttle in weaver's hand,
Or like a writing on the sand,
Or like a thought, or like a dream,
Or like the gliding of the stream –
Even such is man, who lives by breath,
Is here, now there: so life, and death.
The bubble's cut, the look's forgot,
The shuttle's flung, the writing's blot,
The thought is past, the dream is gone,
The water glides; man's life is done.

Like to an arrow from the bow,
Or like swift course of watery flow,
Or like the time 'twixt flood and ebb,
Or like the spider's tender web,
Or like a race, or like a goal,
Or like the dealing of a dole –
Even such is man, whose brittle state
Is always subject unto fate.
The arrow's shot, the flood soon spent,
The time no time, the web soon rent,
The race soon run, the goal soon won,
The dole soon dealt; man's life first done.

Like to the lightning from the sky,
Or like a post that quick doth hie,
Or like a quaver in short song,
Or like a journey three days long,
Or like the snow when summer's come,
Or like the pear, or like the plum –

Even such is man, who heaps up sorrow,
Lives but this day and dies to-morrow.
The lightning's past, the post must go,
The song is short, the journey's so,
The pear doth rot, the plum doth fall,
The snow dissolves, and so must all.

ANON

from Life and Death

Thus fared I through a frith . where flowers were many,
Bright boughs in the bank . breathéd full sweet.
The red railing roses . the richest of flowers,
Laid broad on their banks . with their bright leaves;
And a river that was rich . ran over the green,
With still stirring streams . that streamed full bright
Over the glittering ground . As I there glode,
Methought, it lengthened my life . to look on the banks!
Then, among the fair flowers . I settled me to sit
Under a huge hawthorn . that hoar was of blossoms.
I bent my back to the bole . and blenched to the streams.
Thus pressed I on apace . under the green hawthorn,
For breme of the birds . and breath of the flowers,
And what for watching and waking . and wandering about,
In my seat, where I sat. I sayéd asleep.
Lying edgelong on the ground . left all myself,
Deep dreams and dright . drove me to heart.

Methought, walking that I was . in a wood strong,
Upon a great mountain . where moors were large,
That I might see on every side . seventeen miles,
Both of woods and wastes . and walléd towns,
Comely castles and clear . with carven towers,
Parks and palaces . and pastures full many,
All the world full of wealth . viewly to behold.
I sat me down softly . and said these words,
'I will not kyre out of kith . before I know more!'
And I waited me about . wonders to know.

And it fairly befell . so fair me bethought,
I saw on the south side . a seemly sight
Of comely knights full keen . and knights full noble,
Princes in the press . proudly attired,
Dukes that were doughry . and many dear earls,
Squires and swains . that swarmed full thick,
There was neither hill nor holt . nor haunt there beside,
But it was planted full of people . the plain and the rough

There, over that host . eastward I looked
Into a boolish bank . the brightest of others,
That shimmered and shone . as the sheer heaven,
Through the light of a Lady . that longéd therein.
She came cheering full comely . with company noble,
Upon clear clothes . were all of clear gold,
Laid broad upon the bent . with broiders full rich,
Before that Fair on the field . where she forth passed.
She was brighter of her blee . than was the bright sun!
Her rudd redder than the rose . that on the rise hangeth!
Meekly smiling with her mouth . and merry in her looks,
Ever laughing for love . as she like would;

And, as she came by the banks . the boughs, each one,
They louted to that Lady . and laid forth their branches.
Blossoms and burgeons . breathéd full sweet,
Flowers flourished in the frith . where she forth stepped,
And the grass, that was grey . greened belive.

ANON

Brothers

You who opt for English ways
And crop your curls, your crowning glory,
You, my handsome specimen,
Are no true son of Donncha's.

If you were, you would not switch
To modes in favour with the English;
You, the flower of Fódla's land,
Would never end up barbered.

A full head of long, fair hair
Is not for you; it is your brother
Who scorns the foreigners' close cut.
The pair of you are opposites.

Eoghan Bán won't ape their ways,
Eoghan beloved of noble ladies
Is enemy to English fads
And lives beyond the pale of fashion.

Eoghan Bán is not like you.
Breeches aren't a thing he values.
A clout will do him for a cloak.
Leggings he won't wear, nor greatcoat.

He hates the thought of jewelled spurs
Flashing on his feet and footwear,
And stockings of the English sort,
And being all prinked up and whiskered.

He's Donncha's true son, for sure.
He won't be seen with a rapier
Angled like an awl, out arseways,
As he swanks it to the meeting place.

Sashes worked with threads of gold
And high stiff collars out of Holland
Are not for him, nor satin scarves
That sweep the ground, nor gold rings even.

He has no conceit in feather beds,
Would rather stretch himself on rushes,
Dwell in a bothy than a bawn,
And make the branch his battlement.

Horsemen in the mouth of a glen,
A savage dash, kernes skirmishing –
This man is in his element
Taking on the foreigner.

But you are not like Eoghan Bán.
You're a laughing stock on stepping stones
With your dainty foot: a sad disgrace,
You who opt for English ways.

LAOISEACH MAC AN BHAIRD
translated from the Irish by Seamus Heaney

The Twa Corbies

As I was walking all alane
I heard twa corbies making a mane;
The tane unto the t'other say,
'Where sall we gang and dine to-day?'

'– In behint yon auld fail dyke,
I wot there lies a new-slain knight;
And naebody kens that he lies there.
But his hawk, his hound, and lady fair.

'His hound is to the hunting gane,
His hawk to fetch the wild-fowl hame.
His lady's ta'en another mate,
So we may mak our dinner sweet.

'Ye'll sit on his white hause-bane,
And I'll pick out his bonnie blue een;
Wi' ae lock o' his gowden hair
We'll theek our nest when it grows bare.

'Mony a one for him makes mane,
But nane sall ken where he is gane;
O'er his white banes, when they are bare,
The wind sall blaw for evermair.'

ANON

Marriage of the Dwarfs

Design or Chance makes others wive.
But Nature did this match contrive:
Eve might as well have Adam fled,
As she denied her little bed
To him, for whom Heaven seem'd to frame
And measure out this only dame.
  Thrice happy is that humble pair,
Beneath the level of all care!
Over whose heads those arrows fly
Of sad distrust and jealousy;
Secured in as high extreme,
As if the world held none but them.
  To him the fairest nymphs do show
Like moving mountains top'd with snow;
And every man a Polypheme
Does to his Galatea seem:
None may presume her faith to prove;
He proffers death that proffers love.

Ah, Chloris! that kind Nature thus
From all the world had sever'd us;
Creating for ourselves us two,
As Love has me for only you!

EDMUND WALLER

from Paradise Lost

Sweet is the breath of Morn; her rising sweet,
With charm of earliest birds: pleasant the sun,
When first on this delightful land he spreads
His orient beams, on herb, tree, fruit, and flower,
Glistering with dew; fragrant the fertile earth
After soft showers; and sweet the coming on
Of grateful Evening mild; then silent Night,
With this her solemn bird, and this fair moon,
And these the gems of Heaven, her starry train:
But neither breath of Morn when she ascends
With charm of earliest birds; nor rising sun
On this delightful land; nor herb, fruit, flower,
Glistering with dew; nor fragrance after showers;
Nor grateful Evening mild; nor silent Night,
With this her solemn bird, nor walk by moon,
Or glittering star-light, without thee is sweet.

JOHN MILTON

Maggie Lauder

Wha wadna be in love
  Wi' bonnie Maggie Lauder?
A piper met her gaun to Fife
  And spier'd what was't they ca'd her
Richt scornfully she answered him.
  Begone, you hallanshaker!
Jog on your gate, you bladderskate!
  My name is Maggie Lauder.

Maggie! quoth he; and by my bags,
  I'm fidgin' fain to see thee!
Sit doun by me, my bonnie bird;
  In troth I winna steer thee;
For I'm a piper to my trade;
  My name is Rob the Ranter;
The lasses loup as they were daft,
  When I blaw up my chanter.

Piper, quo Meg, hae ye your bags,
  Or is your drone in order?
If ye be Rob, I've heard o' you;
  Live you upo' the Border?
The lasses a', baith far and near,
  Have heard o' Rob the Ranter;
I'll shake my foot wi' richt gude will,
  Gif ye'll blaw up your chanter.

Then to his bags he flew wi' speed:
   About the drone he twisted:
Meg up and wallop'd ower the green;
   For brawly could she frisk it!
Weel done! quo he. Play up! quo she.
   Weel bobb'd! quo Rob the Ranter;
It's worth my while to play, indeed,
   When I hae sic a dancer!

Weel hae ye play'd your part! quo Meg;
   Your cheeks are like the crimson!
There's nane in Scotland plays sae weel,
   Sin' we lost Habbie Simson.
I've lived in Fife, baith maid and wife,
   This ten years and a quarter:
Gin ye should come to Anster Fair,
   Spier ye for Maggie Lauder.

FRANCIS SEMPILL

Blue Song

made by Mary, daughter of Red Alasdair,
soon after she was left in Scarba

Hóireann o
Hoireann o

I am sad
since a week ago

Left on this island,
no grass, no shelter

If I could
I'd get back home,

Making the journey
rightaway

To Ullinish
of white-hoofed cattle

Where I grew up,
a little girl

Breast-fed there
by soft palmed women

In the house of brown-haired Flora
Lachlan's daughter

Milkmaid
among the cows

of Roderick Mor
MacLeod of the banners,

I have been happy
in his great house,

living it up
on the dancefloor,

fiddle music
making me sleepy,

pibroch
my dawn chorus

Hóireann ó ho bhì ó.
Ro hóireann ó o hao o

Say hullo for me
to Dunvegan

MARY MACLEOD
*translated from the Scots Gaelic
by Robert Crawford*

To His Coy Mistress

Had we but world enough, and time,
This coyness, Lady, were no crime.
We would sit down, and think which way
To walk, and pass our long love's day.
Thou by the Indian Ganges' side
Should'st rubies find: I by the tide
Of Humber would complain. I would
Love you ten years before the Flood:
And you should if you please refuse
Till the conversion of the Jews.
My vegetable love should grow
Vaster than empires, and more slow.
A hundred years should go to praise

[146]

Thine eyes, and on thy forehead gaze.
Two hundred to adore each breast:
But thirty thousand to the rest.
An age at least to every part,
And the last age should show your heart.
For, Lady, you deserve this state;
Nor would I love at lower rate.
  But at my back I always hear
Time's winged chariot hurrying near:
And yonder all before us lie
Deserts of vast eternity.
Thy beauty shall no more be found;
Nor, in thy marble vault, shall sound
My echoing song: then worms shall try
That long preserved virginity:
And your quaint honour turn to dust;
And into ashes all my lust.
The grave's a fine and private place,
But none I think do there embrace.
  Now therefore, while the youthful hue
Sits on thy skin like morning dew,
And while thy willing soul transpires
At every pore with instant fires,
Now let us sport us while we may;
And now, like amorous birds of prey,
Rather at once our time devour,
Than languish in his slow-chapped power.
Let us roll all our strength, and all
Our sweetness, up into one ball:
And tear our pleasures with rough strife,

Thorough the iron gates of life.
Thus, though we cannot make our sun
Stand still, yet we will make him run.

ANDREW MARVELL

The Mower to the Glow-Worms

Ye living lamps, by whose dear light
The nightingale does sit so late,
And studying all the summer night,
Her matchless songs does meditate;

Ye country comets, that portend
No war, nor prince's funeral,
Shining unto no higher end
Then to presage the grass's fall;

Ye glow-worms, whose officious flame
To wandering mowers shows the way,
That in the night have lost their aim,
And after foolish fires do stray;

Your courteous lights in vain you waste,
Since Juliana here is come,
For she my mind hath so displaced
That I shall never find my home.

ANDREW MARVELL

To my Daughter Catherine on Ashwednesday 1645, finding her weeping at prayers, because I would not consent to her fasting

My dearest, you may pray now it is Lent,
But ought not fast: nor have you to repent,
Since then in all you've thought, or said or done,
No motes appear though sifted by the sun.
Lent made for penance, then to you may be,
Since you are innocent, a jubily.
If not for others then, why don't you spare
Those tears which for yourself prophaned are.
Hymns of thanksgiving and of joy befit
Such a triumphant virtue, and for it
Not to rejoice, were as preposterous ill,
As in your vices to be merry still.
But if you reply, 'Tis fit you sigh and grone,
Since you have made my miseries your own;
You feel my faults as yours, so them lament,
And expiate those sins I should repent.
O cease this sorrow doubly now my due,
First for my self, but more for love of you.
I'll undertake what justice can exact
By any penance, if you will retract
Those sorrows you usurp, which do procure
A pain I only cannot well endure.

KATHERINE ASTON

'I saw eternity the other night'

I saw eternity the other night
Like a great ring of pure and endless light,
    All calm, as it was bright;
And round beneath it, time in hours, days, years,
    Driven by the spheres
Like a vast shadow moved, in. which the world
    And all her train were hurled.

HENRY VAUGHAN

Son-days

I

Bright shadows of true rest! some shoots of bliss,
    Heaven once a week;
The next world's gladness prepossessed in this;
    A day to seek
Eternity in time; the steps by which
We climb above all ages; lamps that light
Man through his heap of dark days; and the rich,
And full redemption of the whole week's flight.

II

The pulleys unto headlong man; time's bower;
    The narrow way;
Transplanted Paradise; God's walking hour;
    The cool o'the day;

The creatures' Jubilee; God's parle with dust;
Heaven here; man on those hills of myrrh, and flowers;
Angels descending; the returns of trust;
A gleam of glory, after six-days-showers.

III

The Church's love-feasts; time's prerogative,
                    And interest
Deducted from the whole; the combs, and hive,
                    And home of rest.

The milky way chalked out with suns; a clue
That guides through erring hours; and in full story
A taste of Heaven on earth; the pledge, and cue
Of a full feast; and the out courts of glory.

                    HENRY VAUGHAN

The Waterfall

With what deep murmurs through time's silent stealth
Doth thy transparent, cool, and watery wealth
                    Here flowing fall,
                    And chide and call,
As if his liquid loose retinue stayed
Lingering, and were of this steep place afraid,
                    The common pass
                    Where, clear as glass,
                    All must descend
                    Not to an end;

But quickened by this deep and rocky grave,
Rise to a longer course more bright and brave.

Dear stream! dear bank, where often I
Have sat, and pleased my pensive eye,
Why, since each drop of thy quick store
Runs thither, whence it flowed before,
Should poor souls fear a shade or night,
Who came, sure, from a sea of light?
Or since those drops are all sent back
So sure to thee, that none doth lack,
Why should trail flesh doubt any more
That what God takes, he'll not restore?
O useful Element and clear!
My sacred wash and cleanser here,
My first consigner unto those
Fountains of life, where the Lamb goes,
What sublime truths, and wholesome themes
Lodge in thy mystical, deep streams!
Such as dull man can never find,
Unless that Spirit lead his mind,
Which first upon thy face did move,
And hatched all with his quickening love.
As this loud brook's incessant fall
In streaming rings restagnates all,
Which reach by course the bank, and then
Are no more seen, just so pass men.
O my invisible estate,
My glorious liberty, still late!
Thou art the channel my soul seeks,
Not this with cataracts and creeks.

HENRY VAUGHAN

Friends Departed

They are all gone into the world of light!
    And I alone sit ling'ring here;
Their very memory is fair and bright,
    And my sad thoughts doth clear.

It glows and glitters in my cloudy breast,
    Like stars upon some gloomy grove,
Or those faint beams in which this hill is drest
    After the sun's remove.

I see them walking in an air of glory,
    Whose light doth trample on my days:
My days, which are at best but dull and hoary.
    Mere glimmerings and decays.

O holy Hope! and high Humility,
    High as the heavens above!
These are your walks, and you have showed them me,
    To kindle my cold love.

Dear, beauteous Death! the jewel of the Just,
    Shining nowhere, but in the dark;
What mysteries do lie beyond thy dust,
    Could man outlook that mark!

He that hath found some fledged bird's nest may know,
    At first sight, if the bird be flown;
But what fair well or grove he sings in now,
    That is to him unknown.

And yet as Angels in some brighter dreams
    Call to the soul, when man doth sleep:
So some strange thoughts transcend our wonted themes,
    And into glory peep.

If a star were confined into a tomb,
    Her captive flames must needs burn there;
But when the hand that locked her up gives room,
    She'll shine through all the sphere.

O Father of eternal life, and all
    Created glories under Thee!
Resume Thy spirit from this world of thrall
    Into true liberty.

Either disperse these mists, which blot and fill
    My perspective still as they pass:
Or else remove me hence unto that hill,
    Where I shall need no glass.

HENRY VAUGHAN

In Praise of a Girl

Slip of loveliness, slim, seemly,
freshly fashioned, modest maiden, star serene,
sage and queenly, gracious, granting heart;
paragon, look upon
this grave song, growing sign
that I pine, my constant moon.
No beauty clear so dear I'll hold,
not till I'm old, foam of the sea,
loveliest lily of the land,
soft of hand, white-breasted, brisk, bright, flower-created;
who'd not be charmed whose blood is warmed?
Moon of my nature, it was you
I viewed in my desire,
because your brow is like the snow,
able, notable, gifted, gay, flawless,
laughing, skilful, peerless pearl of girls.

If from all lands girls came in bands
and from a tree one could see
that sweet society of all loveliest ones,
the paragons of town and country,
dazzling, shapely, stately, fair, I declare,
Moon of Wales, your loveliness prevails.
Your praise and glory, peerless girl,
now impel me to applaud
your sweet looks, your subtle tongue,
dawn-sweet dearest, purest, prettiest, many-beautied,
unpolluted and reputed spotless rose,
there's none to make comparison,
wave sparkling in the darkling,

with your parabling of sweet peace,
piece of goodness, fond enchantress, blithesome dove,
lucent, laughing, blameless slip of love.

From love's curse who'll be my nurse?
Will you listen, light of dawn, to my dole?
Deal me charity, slip of beauty;
if I win not your good will
it will kill me, girl of worth; under earth
there's sad dearth of space for a person, in that prison;
low there my share of ash and loam.
That's my legacy from your beauty
unless, daybreak, for my sake
my love-ache you'll relieve, grant reprieve,
properly gentle, fluent, generous girl.
Cure my illness, dawn of sweetness,
shapely, lissom lass;
and bestow, for my woe,
a sweet lotion; maiden, listen
and endorse whilst I rehearse this true verse.

My sweetly woven, only chosen,
if my triumph makes you mine only,
life will be fine, flesh of the lily.
On this journey, soft of parley,
you'll find endless perfect heaven, morn and even,
swift mirth and soft ease on this earth :
I'm the most faithful man yet made,
eggshell maid, still to you.
Where you dwell it will be well
for me to love, luscious, lively slip, so sprightly,
following freely your trim tread;
in spire of all, I expect

to be your fellow, fine of eyebrow;
it's my aim, in God's good name,
nights and days in faithful ways to live
always in the solace of your love.

O, it's bitter, beauteous girl,
a true body can't escape from its sickness;
cruel harshness that I suffer for your sake!
You shall see, rarity,
who adores you ceaselessly; pity me,
cherish me charitably.
If kindly you'll my days extend
and send ending to my pain,
you shall be gloried till I'm buried:
come, to greet me, set me free, let there not be
open hurting of my diligent, good heart.
O, take my part in this story
of my weary, stark lament;
don't augment my suffering,
ease my unsparing, gloomy faring,
my sweet darling, with swift loving.

HUW MORUS
translated from the Welsh by Gwyn Williams

Nature's Cook

Death is the cook of nature, and we find
Creatures drest several ways to please her mind;
Some Death doth roast with fevers burning hot,
And some he boils with dropsies in a pot;
Some are consumed for jelly by degrees,
And some with ulcers, gravy out to squeeze;
Some, as with herbs, he stuffs with gouts and pains,
Others for tender meat he hangs in chains;
Some in the sea he pickles up to keep,
Others he, as soused brawn, in wine doth steep;
Some flesh and bones he with the Pox chops small,
And doth a French fricassee make withall;
Some on grid-irons of calentures are broiled,
And some are trodden down, and so quite spoiled:
But some are baked, when smothered they do die,
Some meat he doth by hectick fevers fry;
In sweat sometimes he stews with savory smell,
An hodge-podge of diseases he likes well;
Some brains he dresseth with apoplexy,
Or fawce of megrims, swimming plenteously;
And tongues he dries with smoak from stomachs ill,
Which, as the second course he sends up still;
Throats he doth cut, blood puddings for to make,
And puts them in the guts, which cholicks rack;
Some hunted are by him for deer, that's red,

And some as stall-fed oxen knocked o'th' head;
Some singed and scald for bacon, seem most rare,
When with salt rheum and phlegm they powdered are.

MARGARET CAVENDISH,
DUCHESS OF NEWCASTLE

A Song of Sorrow

O Robertson of Inverawe,
You take the road as a stranger;
Though Mary Cameron lies in front,
Young did I lose any interest in you.

God, it is I who am undone,
Going to lie with another man,
With my own man behind the house,
Hunter of the brown stags and hinds.

Darling of the men of the Dale,
You took me out of the house of plague,
Where my father and mother lay,
My dear sister and five brothers.

Darling of all men under the sun,
You built me a house in the spreading woods,
Joyful there my lying down and rising,
No wonder that – for I was new-wed.

MARY CAMERON

An Answer to another persuading
a Lady to Marriage

Forbear, bold youth, all's Heaven here,
    And what you do aver,
To others, courtship may appear,
    'Tis sacriledge to her.

She is a publick deity,
    And were't not very odd
She should depose her self to be
    A petty household god?

First make the sun in private shine,
    And bid the world adieu,
That so he may his beams confine
    In complement to you.

But if of that you do despair,
    Think how you did amiss,
To strive to fix her beams which are
    More bright and large than this.

KATHERINE PHILIPS

The Downfall of Charing Cross

Undone, undone the lawyers are,
   They wander about the towne,
Nor can find the way to Westminster,
   Now Charing-cross is downe:
At the end of the Strand, they make a stand,
   Swearing they are at a loss,
And chaffing say, that's not the way,
   They must go by Charing-cross.

The parliament to vote it down
   Conceived it very fitting,
For fear it should fall, and kill them all,
   In the house, as they were sitting.
They were told, god-wot, it had a plot,
   Which made them so hard-hearted,
To give command, it should not stand,
   But be taken down and carted.

But neither man, woman, nor child,
   Will say, I'm confident,
They ever heard it speak one word
   Against the parliament.
An informer swore, it letters bore,
   Or else it had been freed;
I'll take, in troth, my Bible oath,
   It could neither write, nor read.

The committee said, that verily
   To popery it was bent;
For ought I know, it might be so,
   For to church it never went.
What with excise, and such device,
   The kingdom doth begin
To think you'll leave them ne'er a cross,
   Without doors nor within.

Methinks the common-council should
   Of it have taken pity,
'Cause, good old cross, it always stood
   So firmly to the city.
Since crosses you so much disdain,
   Faith, if I were as you,
For fear the king should rule again,
   I'd pull down Tiburn too.

                                    ANON

'If all the world were paper'

If all the world were paper,
And all the sea were inke;
And all the trees were bread and cheese,
What should we do for drinke?

If all the world were sand 'o,
Oh, then what should we lack 'o;
If as they say there were no clay,
How should we make tobacco?

If all our vessels ran 'a,
If none but had a crack 'a;
If Spanish apes eat all the grapes,
What should we do for sack 'a?

If fryers had no bald pates,
Nor nuns had no dark cloysters,
If all the seas were beans and pease,
What should we do for oysters?

If there had been no projects,
Nor none that did great wrongs;
If fidlers shall turne players all,
What should we doe for songs ?

If all things were eternall,
And nothing their end bringing;
If this should be, then how should we
Here make an end of singing?

ANON

The Drowned Blackbird

Lovely daughter of Conn O'Neill,
    You are in shock. Sleep a long sleep.
After the loss of what was dearest,
    Don't let your people hear you weep.

The song of the quick-quick flitting bird
    Has fled, sweet girl, left you forlorn.
Always what's dearest is endangered
    So bear up now, no beating of hands.

Instead of keens and beating hands
    Be silent, girl, as dew in air.
Lovely daughter of Conn O'Neill,
    The bird is dead, don't shed a rear.

Child of that high-born kingly Ulster line,
Show what you're made of, don't let yourself go wild
Even though the loveliest bird in the leaf-and-branch scrim
Is drowned, washed white in whitewash: water and lime.

SÉAMAS DALL MAC CUARTA
translated from the Irish by Seamus Heaney

till a' the sas gang dry, my dear...

Verses Said to be Written on the Union

The Queen has lately lost a part
Of her entirely English heart,
For want of which by way of botch,
She pieced it up again with Scotch.
Blessed revolution, which creates
Divided hearts, united states.
See how the double nation lies;
Like a rich coat with skirts of frieze:
As if a man in making posies
Should bundle thistles up with roses.
Whoever yet a union saw
Of kingdoms, without faith or law.
Henceforward let no statesman dare,
A kingdom to a ship compare;
Lest he should call our commonweal,
A vessel with a double keel:
Which just like ours, new rigged and manned,
And got about a league from land,
By change of wind to leeward side
The pilot knew not how to guide
So tossing faction will o'erwhelm
Our crazy double-bottomed realm.

JONATHAN SWIFT

The Liberty

Shall I be one of those obsequious fools
That square their lives by Custom's scanty rules?
Condemned forever to the puny curse
Of precepts taught at boarding-school or nurse,
That all the business of my life must be
Foolish, dull, trifling formality?
Confined to a strict magic complaisance
And round a circle of nice visits dance,
Nor for my life beyond the chalk advance?
The devil Censure stands to guard the same;
One step awry, he tears my venturous fame,
So when my friends, in a facetious vein
With mirth and wit a while can entertain,
Though ne'er so pleasant, yet I must not stay,
If a commanding clock bids me away,
But with a sudden start, as in a fright,
'I must be gone indeed! 'Tis after eight!'
Sure these restraints with such regret we bear
That dreaded Censure can't be more severe,
Which has no terror if we did not fear,
But let the bugbear timorous infants fright.
I'll not be scared from innocent delight.
Whatever is not vicious I dare do.
I'll never to the idol Custom bow
Unless it suits with my own humour too.
Some boast their fetters of formality,
Fancy they ornamental bracelets be;
I'm sure they're gyves and manacles to me.
To their dull, fulsome rules I'll not be tied,
For all the flattery that exalts their pride.

My sex forbids I should my silence break;
I lose my jest, 'cause women must not speak.
Mysteries must not be with my search profaned;
My closet not with books but sweetmeats crammed,
A little china to advance the show,
My prayerbook and *Seven Champions* or so.
My pen, if ever used, employed must be
In lofty themes of useful housewifery,
Transcribing old receipts of cookery,
And what is necessary among the rest,
Good cures for agues and a cancered breast,
But I can't here write my *probatum est.*
My daring pen will bolder sallies make
And, like myself, an unchecked freedom take,
Not chained to the nice order of my sex,
And with restraints my wishing soul perplex.
I'll blush at sin, and not what some call shame,
Secure my virtue, slight precarious fame.
This courage speaks me brave. 'Tis surely worse
To keep those rules which privately we curse,
And I'll appeal to all the formal saints
With what reluctance they endure restraints.

SARAH FYGE

A Grey Eye Weeping

That my old bitter heart was pierced in this black doom,
That foreign devils have made our land a tomb,
That the sun that was Munster's glory has gone down
Has made me a beggar before you, Valentine Brown.

That royal Cashel is bare of house and guest,
That Brian's turreted home is the otter's nest,
That the kings of the land have neither land nor crown
Has made me a beggar before you, Valentine Brown.

Garnish away in the west with its master banned,
Hamburg the refuge of him who has lost his land,
An old grey eye, weeping for lost renown,
Have made me a beggar before you, Valentine Brown.

AODHÁGAN Ó RATHAILLE
translated from the Irish by Frank O'Connor

The Glamoured

Brightening brightness, alone on the road, she appears,
Crystalline crystal and sparkle of blue in green eyes,
Sweetness of sweetness in her unembittered young voice
And a high colour dawning behind the pearl of her face.

Ringlets and ringlets, a curl in every tress
Of her fair hair trailing and brushing the dew on the grass;
And a gem from her birthplace far in the high universe
Outglittering glass and gracing the groove of her breasts.

News that was secret she whispered to soothe her aloneness,
News of one due to return and reclaim his true place,
News of the ruin of those who had cast him in darkness,
News that was awesome, too awesome to utter in verse.

My head got lighter and lighter but still approached her,
Enthralled by her thraldom, helplessly held and bewildered,
Choking and calling Christ's name: then she fled in a
    shimmer
To Leachra Fort where only the glamoured can enter.

I hurtled and hurled myself madly following after
Over keshes and marshes and mosses and treacherous moors
And arrived at that stronghold unsure about how I had got
    there,
That earthwork of earth the orders of magic once reared.

A gang of thick louts were shouting loud insults and jeering
And a curly-haired coven in fits of sniggers and sneers:
Next thing I was taken and cruelly shackled in fetters
As the breasts of the maiden were groped by a thick-witted
      boor.

I tried then as hard as I could to make her hear truth,
How wrong she was to be linked to that lazarous swine
When the pride of the pure Scottish stock, a prince
      of the blood,
Was ardent and eager to wed her and make her his bride.

When she heard me, she started to weep, but pride was the
      cause
Of those tears that came wetting her cheeks and shone in her
      eyes;
Then she sent me a guard to guide me out of the fortress,
Who'd appeared to me, lone on the road, a brightening
      brightness.

                              *

Calamity, shock, collapse, heartbreak and grief
To think of her sweetness, her beauty, her mildness, her life
Defiled at the hands of a hornmaster sprung from riff-raff,
And no hope of redress till the lions ride back on the wave.

                    AODHÁGAN Ó RATHAILLE
                translated from the Irish by Seamus Heaney

To a very young Gentleman at a Dancing-School

So when the Queen of Love rose from the seas,
Divinely fair in such a blest amaze,
The enamoured watery deities did gaze,

As we when charming Flammin did surprise,
More heavenly bright, our whole seraglio's eyes,
And not a nymph her wonder could disguise,

Whilst with a lovely pride the graceful boy
Passed all the ladies, like a sultan, by,
Only he looked more absolute and coy.

When with a haughty air he did advance
To lead out some transported she to dance,
He gave his hand as carelessly as chance,

Attended with a universal sigh.
On her each beauty cast a jealous eye
And quite fell out with guiltless destiny.

ELIZABETH SINGER

A New Song of New Similes

My passion is as mustard strong;
   I sit all sober sad;
Drunk as a piper all day long,
   Or like a March-hare mad.

Round as a hoop the bumpers flow;
   I drink, yet can't forget her;
For, though as drunk as David's sow,
   I love her still the better.

Pert as a pear-monger I'd be,
   If Molly were but kind;
Cool as a cucumber could see
   The rest of womankind.

Like a stuck pig I gaping stare,
   And eye her o'er and o'er;
Lean as a rake with sighs and care,
   Sleek as a mouse before.

Plump as a partridge was I known,
   And soft as silk my skin,
My cheeks as fat as butter grown;
   But as a groat now thin!

I, melancholy as a cat,
   And kept awake to weep;
But she, insensible of that,
   Sound as a top can sleep.

Hard is her heart as flint or stone,
    She laughs to see me pale;
And merry as a grig is grown,
    And brisk as bottled ale.

The God of Love at her approach
    Is busy as a bee;
Hearts, sound as any bell or roach,
    Are smit and sigh like me.

Ay me! as thick as hops or hail,
    The fine men crowd about her;
But soon as dead as a door nail
    Shall I be, if without her.

Straight as my leg her shape appears,
    O were we join'd together!
My heart would be scot-free from cares,
    And lighter than a feather.

As fine as fivepence is her mien,
    No drum was ever tighter;
Her glance is as the razor keen,
    And not the sun is brighter.

As soft as pap her kisses are,
    Methinks I taste them yet;
Brown as a berry is her hair,
    Her eyes as black as jet:

As smooth as glass, as white as curds,
    Her pretty hand invites;
Sharp as a needle are her words;
    Her wit, like pepper, bites:

Brisk as a body-louse she trips,
    Clean as a penny drest;
Sweet as a rose her breath and lips,
    Round as the globe her breast.

Full as an egg was I with glee;
    And happy as a king.
Good Lord! how all men envy'd me!
    She lov'd like any thing.

But, false as hell! she, like the wind,
    Chang'd, as her sex must do;
Though seeming as the turtle kind,
    And like the gospel true.

If I and Molly could agree,
    Let who would take Peru!
Great as an emperor should I be,
    And richer than a Jew.

Till you grow tender as a chick,
    I'm dull as any post;
Let us, like burs, together stick,
    And warm as any toast.

You'll know me truer than a dye;
  And wish me better speed;
Flat as a flounder when I lie,
  And as a herring dead.

Sure as a gun, she'll drop a tear,
  And sigh, perhaps, and wish,
When I am rotten as a pear,
  And mute as any fish.

JOHN GAY

Ode on Solitude

Happy the man, whose wish and care
  A few paternal acres bound,
Content to breathe his native air,
    In his own ground.

Whose herds with milk, whose fields with bread,
  Whose flocks supply him with attire,
Whose trees in summer yield him shade,
    In winter fire.

Blest, who can unconcernedly find
  Hours, days, and years slide soft away,
In health of body, peace of mind,
    Quiet by day,

Sound sleep by night; study and ease,
   Together mixed; sweet recreation;
And innocence, which most does please,
         With meditation.

Thus let me live, unseen, unknown;
   Thus unlamented let me die;
Steal from the world, and not a stone
         Tell where I lie.

ALEXANDER POPE

from Song of Summer

to the air 'Through the Wood Laddie'

Month of plants and of honey,
warm, with grasses and shoots,
month of buds and of leafage,
rushes, flowers that are lovely,
wasps, bees and berries,
mellow mists, heavy dews,
like spangles of diamonds,
a sparkling cover for earth.

*

Lithe brisk fresh-water salmon,
lively, leaping the stones;
bunched, white-bellied, scaly,
fin-tail-flashing, red spot;

speckled skin's brilliant hue
lit with flashes of silver;
with curved gob at the ready,
catching insects with guile.

May, with soft showers and sunshine,
meadows, grass-fields I love,
milky, whey-white and creamy,
frothing, whisked up in pails,
time for crowdie and milk-curds,
time for firkins and kits,
lambs, goat-kids and roe-deer,
bucks, a rich time for flocks.

ALEXANDER MACDONALD
translated from the Scots Gaelic by Derick Thomson

Wedlock: A Satire

Thou tyrant, whom I will not name,
Whom Heaven and Hell alike disclaim,
Abhorred and shunned, for different ends,
By angels, Jesuits, beasts and fiends,
What terms to curse thee shall I find,
Thou plague peculiar to mankind?
Oh may my verse excel in spite
The wiliest, wittiest imps of night!
Then lend me for a while your rage,
You maidens old and matrons sage,
So may my terms in railing seem
As vile and hateful as my theme.

Eternal foe to soft desires,
Inflamer of forbidden fires,
Thou source of discord, pain and care,
Thou sure forerunner of despair,
Thou scorpion with a double face,
Thou lawful plague of human race,
Thou bane of freedom, ease and mirth,
Thou deep damnation upon earth,
Thou serpent which the angels fly,
Thou monster whom the beasts defy,
Whom wily Jesuits sneer at too,
And Satan, let him have his due,
Was never so confirmed a dunce
To risk damnation more than once.
That wretch, if such a wretch there be,
Who hopes for happiness from thee,
May search successfully as well
For truth in whores and ease in Hell.

MEHETABEL WRIGHT

On Inclosures

'Tis bad enough in man or woman
To steal a goose from off a common;
But surely he's without excuse
Who steals the common from the goose.

ANON

The Mother's Lament for Her Child

When they came looking for trouble I bared my body
Hoping to appeal to them. Child of the branches,
You smiled at your mother and then at your enemies
And chuckled before they wrenched you from my arms.

When the spear pierced your chest I registered the pain
And watched my own blood spurting. Suicidal now
I struggled with them, happy to die in the skirmish
And lie with you and our friends in unmarked graves.

They tied me to a tree and forced me to witness
Your death-throes, child of the tree of my heart and lungs,
Child of my crucifixion tree, child of the branches,
And then they stuck your screams on the end of a pike.

PEADAR Ó DOIRNÍN
translated from the Irish by Michael Longley

There's Nae Luck about the House

And are ye sure the news is true?
    And are ye sure he's weel?
Is this a time to think o' wark?
    Ye Jauds, fling by your wheel.
Is this a time to think o' wark,
    When Colin's at the door?
Rax me my cloak, I'll to the quay,
    And see him come ashore.

[181]

For there's nae luck about the house,
    There's nae luck at a'
There's little pleasure in the house,
    When our gudeman's awa'.

And gie to me my bigonet,
    My bishop-satin gown;
For I maun tell the baillie's wife
    That Colin's come to town.
My turkey slippers maun gae on.
    My hose o' pearl blue;
It's a' to please my ain gudeman,
    For he's' baith leal and true.

Rise up and mak a dean fireside,
    Put on the muckle pot;
Gle little Kate her Sunday gown
    And Jock his button coat;
And mak their shoon as black as slaes,
    Their hose as white as snaw;
It's a' to please my ain gudeman.
    For he's been lang awa'.

Since Colin's weel, I'm weel content,
    I hae nae mair to crave;
Could I but live to mak him blest,
    I'm blest aboon the lave;
And will I see his face again?
    And will I hear him speak?
I'm downricht dizzy wi' the thocht,
    In troth I'm like to greet.

There's twa fat hens upo' the bauk,
   They've fed this month and mair,
Mak haste and thraw their necks about,
   That Colin weel may fare;
And spread the table neat and clean,
   Gar ilka thing look braw;
For wha can tell how Colin fared
   When he was far awa'?

Sae true his heart, sae smooth his speech,
   His breath like caller air;
His very foot has music in't
   As he comes up the stair,
And will I see his face again?
   And will I hear him speak?
I'm downricht dizzy wi' the thocht,
   In troth I'm like to greet
     For there's nae luck about the house,
     There's nae luck at a'
     There's little pleasure in the house,
     When our gudeman's awa'.

JEAN ADAM

Satire upon the Heads;
or, Never a Barrel the Better Herring

O Cambridge, attend
To the Satire I've pen'd
On the Heads of thy Houses,
Thou Seat of the Muses!

Know the Master of Jesus
Does hugely displease us;
The Master of Maudlin
In the same dirt is dawdling;
The Master of Sidney
Is of the same kidney;
The Master of Trinity
To him bears affinity;
As the Master of Keys
Is as like as two pease,
So the Master of Queen's
Is as like as two beans;
The Master of King's
Copies them in all things;
The Master of Catherine
Takes them all for his pattern;
The Master of Clare
Hits them all to a hair;
The Master of Christ
By the rest is enticed;
But the Master of Emmanuel
Follows them like a spaniel;
The Master of Benet
Is of the like tenet;

The Master of Pembroke
Has from them his system took;
The Master of Peter's
Has all the same features;
The Master of St John's
Like the rest of the Dons.

P.S. – As to Trinity Hall
We say nothing at all.

THOMAS GRAY

from Jubilate Agno

For the doubling of flowers is the improvement of the
gardners talent.
For the flowers are great blessings.
For the Lord made a Nosegay in the meadow with his
disciples and preached upon the lily.
For the angels of God took it out of his hand and carried it to
the Height.
For a man cannot have publick spirit, who is void of private
benevolence.
For there is no Height in which there are not flowers.
For flowers have great virtues for all the senses.
For the flower glorifies God and the root parries the
adversary.
For the flowers have their angels even the words of God's
Creation.
For the warp and woof of flowers are worked by perpetual
moving spirits.

For flowers are good both for the living and the dead.
For there is a language of flowers.
For there is a sound reasoning upon all flowers.
For elegant phrases are nothing but flowers.
For flowers are peculiarly the poetry of Christ.
For flowers are medicinal.
For flowers are musical in ocular harmony.
For the right names of flowers are yet in heaven. God make
    gard'ners better nomenclators.
For the Poorman's nosegay is an introduction to a Prince.

CHRISTOPHER SMART

On the New Laureate

In merry old England, it once was a rule,
The king had his poet, as well as his fool;
And now we're so frugal, I'd have you to know it,
That Cibber may serve both for fool and for poet.

ANON

'Nor rural sights alone, but rural sounds'

Nor rural sights alone, but rural sounds
Exhilarate the spirit, and restore
The tone of languid nature. Mighty winds
That sweep the skirt of some far-spreading wood
Of ancient growth, make music not unlike
The dash of ocean on his winding shore,
And lull the spirit while they fill the mind,
Unnumbered branches waving in the blast,
And all their leaves fast fluttering, all at once
Nor less composure waits upon the roar
Of distant floods, or on the softer voice
Of neighbouring fountain, or of rills that slip
Through the cleft rock, and chiming as they fall
Upon loose pebbles, lose themselves at length
In matted grass, that with a livelier green
Betrays the secret of their silent course.
Nature inanimate employs sweet sounds,
But animated nature sweeter still
To soothe and satisfy the human ear.
Ten thousand warblers cheer the day, and one
The livelong night: nor these alone whose notes
Nice-fingered art must emulate in vain,
But cawing rooks, and kites that swim sublime
In still repeated circles, screaming loud,
The jay, the pie, and even the boding owl
That hails the rising moon, have charms for me.

Sounds inharmonious in themselves and harsh,
Yet heard in scenes where peace for ever reigns
And only there, please highly for their sake.

WILLIAM COWPER

The Post-Boy

Hark! 'tis the twanging horn o'er yonder bridge,
That with its wearisome but needful length
Bestrides the wintry flood, in which the moon
Sees her unwrinkled face reflected bright; –
He comes, the herald of a noisy world,
With spatter'd boots, strapp'd waist, and frozen locks;
News from all nations lumb'ring at his back.
True to his charge, the close-pack'd load behind,
Yet careless what he brings, his one concern
Is to conduct it to the destin'd inn:
And, having dropp'd th' expected bag, pass on.
He whistles as he goes, light-hearted wretch,
Cold and yet cheerful: messenger of grief
Perhaps to thousands, and of joy to some;
To him indiff'rent whether grief or joy.
Houses in ashes, and the fall of stocks,
Births, deaths, and marriages, epistles wet
With tears, that trickled down the writer's cheeks
Fast as the periods from his fluent quill,
Or charg'd with am'rous sighs of absent swains,
Or nymphs responsive, equally affect
His horse and him, unconscious of them all.
But oh th' important budget! usher'd in

With such heart-shaking music, who can say
What are its tidings? have our troops awak'd?
Or do they still, as if with opium drugg'd,
Snore to the murmurs of th' Atlantic wave?
Is India free? and does she wear her plum'd
And jewell'd turban with a smile of peace,
Or do we grind her still? The grand debate,
The popular harangue, the tart reply,
The logic, and the wisdom, and the wit,
And the loud laugh – I long to know them all;
I burn to set th' imprison'd wranglers free,
And give them voice and utt'rance once again.
     Now stir the fire, and close the shutters fast,
Let fall the curtains, wheel the sofa round,
And, while the bubbling and loud-hissing urn
Throws up a steamy column, and the cups,
That cheer but not inebriate, wait on each,
So let us welcome peaceful ev'ning in.

WILLIAM COWPER

Washing Day

The Muses are turned gossips; they have lost
The buskined step, and c lear high-sounding phrase,
Language of gods. Come, then, domestic Muse,
In slip-shod measure loosely prattling on,
Of farm or orchard, pleasant curds and cream,
Or droning flies, or shoes lost in the mire
By little whimpering boy, with rueful face –
Come, Muse, and sing the dreaded washing day.

Ye who beneath the yoke of wedlock bend,
With bowed soul, full well ye ken the day
Which week, smooth sliding after week, brings on
Too soon; for to that day nor peace belongs,
Nor comfort; ere the first grey streak of dawn,
The red-armed washers come and chase repose.
Nor pleasant smile, nor quaint device of mirth,
Ere visited that day; the very cat,
From the wet kitchen scared, and reeking hearth,
Visits the parlour, an unwonted guest.
The silent breakfast meal is soon despatched,
Uninterrupted, save by anxious looks
Cast at the louring, if sky should lour.
From that last evil, oh preserve us, heavens!
For should the skies pour down, adieu to all
Remains of quiet; then expect to hear
Of sad disasters – dirt and gravel stains
Hard to efface, and loaded lines at once
Snapped short, and linen-horse by dog thrown down,
And all the petty miseries of life.
Saints have been calm while stretched upon the rack,
And Montezuma smiled on burning coals;
But never yet did housewife notable
Greet with a smile a rainy washing day.
But grant the welkin fair, require not thou
Who callest thyself, perchance, the master there,
Or study swept, or nicely dusted coat,
Or usual 'tendence; ask not, indiscreet,
Thy stockings mended, though the yawning rents
Gape wide as Erebus; nor hope to find
Some snug recess impervious. Shouldst thou try
The 'customed garden walks, thine eye shall rue
The budding fragrance of thy tender shrubs,

Myrtle or rose, all crushed beneath the weight
Of coarse-checked apron, with impatient hand
Twitched off when showers impend; or crossing lines
Shall mar thy musings, as the wet cold sheet
Flaps in thy face abrupt. Woe to the friend
Whose evil stars have urged him forth to claim
On such a day the hospitable rites;
Looks blank at best, and stinted courtesy
Shall he receive; vainly he feeds his hopes
With dinner of roast chicken, savoury pie,
Or tart or pudding; pudding he nor tart
That day shall eat; nor, though the husband try –
Mending what can't be helped – to kindle mirth
From cheer deficient, shall his consort's brow
Clear up propitious; the unlucky guest
In silence dines, and early slinks away.
I well remember, when a child, the awe
This day struck into me; for then the maids,
I scarce knew why, looked cross, and drove me from them;
Nor soft caress could I obtain, nor hope
Usual indulgencies; jelly or creams,
Relic of costly suppers, and set by
For me their petted one; or buttered toast,
When butter was forbid; or thrilling tale
Of ghost, or witch, or murder. So I went
And sheltered me beside the parlour fire;
There my dear grandmother, eldest of forms,
Tended the little ones, and watched from harm;
Anxiously fond, though oft her spectacles
With elfin cunning hid, and oft the pins
Drawn from her ravelled stocking, might have soured
One less indulgent.
At intervals my mother's voice was heard,

Urging dispatch; briskly the work went on,
All hands employed to wash, to rinse, to wring,
Or fold, and starch, and clap, and iron, and plait.
Then would I sit me down, and ponder much
Why washings were; sometimes through hollow hole
Of pipe amused we blew, and sent aloft
The floating bubbles; little dreaming then
To see, Montgolfier, thy silken ball
Ride buoyant through the clouds, so near approach
The sports of children and the toils of men.
Earth, air, and sky, and ocean hath its bubbles,
And verse is one of them – this most of all.

ANNA LAETITIA BARBAULD

Cock Robbin

Who did kill Cock Robbin?
I, said the Sparrow,
With my bow and Arrow,
And I did kill Cock Robbin.

Who did see him die?
I, said the Fly,
With my little Eye,
And I did see him die.

And who did catch his blood?
I, said the Beetle,
With my little Dish,
And I did catch his blood.

And who did make his shroud?
I, said the Fish,
With my little Needle,
And I did make his shroud.

Who'll dig his grave?
I, said the Owl,
With my pick and shovel,
I'll dig his grave.

Who'll be the parson?
I, said the Rook,
With my little book,
I'll be the parson.

Who'll be the clerk?
I, said the Lark,
If it's not in the dark,
I'll be the clerk.

Who'll carry the link?
I, said the Linnet,
I'll fetch it in a minute,
I'll carry the link.

Who'll be chief mourner?
I, said the Dove,
I mourn for my love,
I'll be chief mourner.

Who'll carry the coffin?
I, said the Kite,
If it's not through the night,
I'll carry the coffin.

Who'll bear the pall?
We, said the Wren,
Both the cock and the hen,
We'll bear the pall.

Who'll sing a psalm?
I, said the Thrush,
As she sat on a bush,
I'll sing a psalm.

Who'll toll the bell?
I, said the Bull,
Because I can pull,
I'll toll the bell.

All the birds of the air
Fell a-sighing and a-sobbing,
When they heard the bell toll
For poor Cock Robbin.

ANON

Poet to Blacksmith

Seamus, make me a side-arm to take on the earth,
A suitable tool for digging and grubbing the ground,
Lightsome and pleasant to lean on or cut with or lift,
Tastily finished and trim and right for the hand.

No trace of the hammer to show on the sheen of the blade,
The thing to have purchase and spring and be fit for the strain,
The shaft to be socketed in dead true and dead straight,
And I'll work with the gang till I drop and never complain.

The plate and the edge of it not to be wrinkly or crooked –
I see it well shaped from the anvil and sharp from the file;
The grain of the wood and the line of the shaft nicely fitted,
And best thing of all, the ring of it, sweet as a bell.

EOGHAN RUA Ó SÚILLEABHÁIN
translated from the Irish by Seamus Heaney

Written near a port on a dark evening

Huge vapours brood above the clifted shore,
Night on the ocean settles, dark and mute,
Save where is heard the repercussive roar
Of drowsy billows, on the rugged foot
Of rocks remote; or still more distant tone
Of seamen in the anchored bark that tell
The watch relieved; or one deep voice alone
Singing the hour, and bidding 'Strike the bell.'

All is black shadow, but the lucid line
Marked by the light surf on the level sand,
Or where afar the ship-lights faintly shine
Like wandering fairy fires, that oft on land
Mislead the pilgrim – such the dubious ray
That wavering reason lends, in life's long darkling way.

CHARLOTTE SMITH

Caller Oysters

Happy the man who, free from care and strife,
In silken or the leathern purse retains
A splendid shilling. He nor hears with pain
New oysters cry'd, nor sighs for cheerful ale.
— PHILLIPS

Of a' the waters that can hobble
A fishin yole or salmon coble,
And can reward the fishers trouble,
          Or south or north,
There's nane sae spacious and sae noble
          As Firth o' Forth.

In her the skate and codlin sail.
The eil fou souple wags her tall,
Wi' herrin, fleuk, and mackerel.
          And whitens dainty;
Their spindle-shanks the labsters trail,
          Wi' partans plenty.

Auld Reikie's sons blyth faces wear.
September's merry month is near.
That brings in Neptune's caller chere.
                    New oysters fresh:
The halesomest and nicest gear
                    Of fish or flesh.

O! then we needna gie a plack
For dand'ring mountebank or quack.
Wha o' their drogs sae bauldly crack,
                    And spred sic notions.
As gar their feckless patient tak
                    Their stinkin potions.

Come prie, frail man! for gin thou art sick.
The oyster Is a rare cathartic.
As ever doctor patient gart lick
                    To cure his ails:
Whether you hae the head or heart-ake.
                    It ay prevails

Ye tiplers, open a, your poses,
Ye wha are faush'd wi' plouky noses,
Fling owr your craig sufficient doses,
                    You'll thole a hunder,
To fleg awa' your simmer roses,
                    And naething under.

Whan big as burns the gutters rin,
Gin ye hae catcht a droukit skin,
To Luckie Middlemist's loup in
       And sit fu snug
O'er oysters and a dram o' gin,
         Or haddock lug.

When auld Saunt Giles, at aught o'clock,
Gars merchant lowns their chopies lock,
There we adjourn wi' hearty fock
       To birle our bodies,
And get wharewi' to crack our joke,
        And clear our noddles.

Whan Phœbus did his windocks steek,
How aften at that ingle cheek
Did I my frosty fingers beek.
        And taste gude fare?
I trow there was nae hame to seek
        Whan steghin there.

While glakit fools, o'er rife o' cash,
Pamper their weyms wi' fousom trash.
I think a chiel may gayly pass:
        He's no ill boden
That gusts his gabb wi' oyster sauce,
        And hen weel soden.

At Musselbrough, and eke Newhaven,
The fisher wives will get top livin,
When lads gang out on Sunday's even
   To treat their joes,
And tak of fat pandours a prieven,
   Or mussel brose:

Than sometimes 'ere they flit their doup,
They'll ablins a' their siller coup
For liquor clear frae cutty stoup,
   To weet their wizen,
And swallow o'er a dainty soup,
   For fear they gizzen.

A' ye wha canna stand sae sicker,
Whan twice you've toom'd the big ars'd bicker,
Mix caller oysters wi' your liquor,
   And I'm your debtor,
If greedy priest or drouthy vicar
   Will thole it better.

ROBERT FERGUSSON

The Daft-Days

Now mirk December's dowie face
Glours our the rigs wi' sour grimace,
While, thro' his *minimum* of space,
   The bleer-ey'd sun,
Wi' blinkin light and stealing pace,
   His race doth run.

From naked groves nae birdie sings,
To shepherd's pipe nae hillock rings,
The breeze nae od'rous flavour brings
      From Borean cave,
And dwyning nature droops her wings,
      Wi' visage grave.

Mankind but scanty pleasure glean
Frae snawy hill or barren plain,
Whan Winter, 'midst his nipping train,
      Wi' frozen spear,
Sends drift owr a' his bleak domain,
      And guides the weir.

Auld Reikie! thou'rt the canty hole,
A bield for mony caldrife soul,
Wha snugly at thine ingle loll,
      Baith warm and couth;
While round they gar the bicker roll
      To weet their mouth.

When merry *Yule-day* comes, I trow
You'll scantlins find a hungry mou';
Sma' are our cares, our stamacks fou
      O' gusty gear,
And kickshaws, strangers to our view,
      Sin Fairn-year.

Ye browster wives, now busk ye bra,
And fling your sorrows far awa';
Then come and gies the tither blaw
      Of reaming ale,
Mair precious than the well of *Spa*,
      Our hearts to heal.

Then, tho' at odds wi' a' the warl',
Amang oursells we'll never quarrel;
Tho' Discord gie a canker'd snarl
      To spoil our glee,
As lang's there's pith into the barrel
      We'll drink and 'gree.

Fidlers, your pins in temper fix,
And roset weel your fiddle-sticks,
But banish vile Italian tricks
      From out your quorum:
Nor *fortes* wi' *pianos* mix,
      Gie's *Tulloch Gorum*.

For nought can cheer the heart sae weil
As can a canty Highland reel,
It even vivifies the heel
      To skip and dance:
Lifeless is he wha canna feel
      Its influence.

Let mirth abound, let social cheer
Invest the dawning of the year;
Let blithesome innocence appear
　　　　To crown our joy,
Nor envy wi' sarcastic sneer
　　　　Our bliss destroy.

And thou, great god of *Aqua Vitae*!
Wha sways the empire of this city,
When fou we're sometimes capernoity,
　　　　Be thou prepar'd
To hedge us frae that black banditti,
　　　　The City-Guard.

ROBERT FERGUSSON

The Litany for Doneraile

Alas! how dismal is my Tale,
I lost my Watch in Doneraile.
My Dublin Watch, my Chain and Seal,
Pilfered at once in Doneraile.
May Fire and Brimstone never fail
To fall in Showers on Doneraile.
May all the leading Fiends assail
The thieving Town of Doneraile.
As Light'ning's Flash across the vale,
So down to Hell with Doneraile.
The fate of Pompey at Pharsale,
Be that the Curse for Doneraile.
May Beef or Mutton, Lamb or Veal,

Be never found in Doneraile,
But Garlic Soup and scurvy Cale
Be still the food for Doneraile,
And forward as the creeping Snail
Th'Industry be of Doneraile.
May Heav'n a chosen Curse entail
On rigid, rotten Doneraile.
May Sun and Moon for ever fail
To beam their lights on Doneraile.
May every pestilential Gale
Blast that cursed spot called Doneraile.
May no Cuckoo, Thrush or Quail,
Be ever heard in Doneraile.
May Patriots, Kings, and Commonweal
Despise and harass Doneraile.
May every Post, Gazette and Mail,
Sad Tidings bring of Doneraile.
May loudest Thunders ring a Peal
To blind and deafen Doneraile.
May vengeance fall at head and tail
From North to South at Doneraile.
May Profit light and tardy Sale
Still damp the Trade of Doneraile.
May Egypt's plagues at once prevail
To thin the Knaves at Doneraile.
May Frost and Snow, and Sleet and Hail
Benumb each joint in Doneraile.
May Wolves and Bloodhounds trace and trail
The cursed Crew of Doneraile.
May Oscar with his fiery Flail
To Atoms thresh all Doneraile.
May every Mischief fresh and stale
Abide henceforth in Doneraile.

May all from Belfast to Kinsale
Scoff, curse, and damn you, Doneraile.
May neither Flour nor Oatmeal
Be found or known in Doneraile.
May Want and Woe each Joy curtail
That e'er was known in Doneraile.
May not one Coffin want a Nail
That wraps a Rogue in Doneraile.
May all the Sons of Granuwale
Blush at the thieves of Doneraile.
May Mischief big as Norway Whale
O'erwhelm the Knaves of Doneraile.
May Curses wholesale and retail
Pour with full force on Doneraile.
May every Transport wont to Sail
A Convict bring from Doneraile.
May every Churn and milking Pail
Fall dry to staves in Doneraile.
May Cold and Hunger still congeal
The stagnant Blood of Doneraile.
May every Hour new Woes reveal
That Hell reserves for Doneraile.
May every chosen Ill prevail
O'er all the Imps of Doneraile.
May not one Wish or Prayer avail
To soothe the Woes of Doneraile.
May th'Inquisition straight impale
The Rapparees of Doneraile.
May Curse of Sodom now prevail
And sink to Ashes Doneraile.
May Charon's Boat triumphant sail
Completely manned from Doneraile;
And may grim Pluto's inner Jail

Forever groan with Doneraile;
And may my Couplets never fail
To find new Curses for Doneraile!

PAT O'KELLY

from Peter Grimes

Old *Peter Grimes* made Fishing his employ,
His Wife he cabin'd with him and his Boy,
And seem'd that Life laborious to enjoy:
To Town came quiet *Peter* with his Fish,
And had of all a civil word and wish.
He left his Trade upon the Sabbath-Day,
And took young *Peter* in his hand to pray;
But soon the stubborn Boy from care broke loose,
At first refus'd, then added his abuse:
His Father's Love he scorn'd, his Power defied,
But being drunk, wept sorely when he died.

   Yes! then he wept, and to his Mind there came
Much of his Conduct, and he felt the Shame, –
How he had oft the good Old Man revil'd,
And never paid the Duty of a Child:
How, when the Father in his Bible read,
He in contempt and anger left the Shed:
'It is the Word of Life,' the Parent cried;
– 'This is the Life itself,' the Boy replied;
And while Old *Peter* in amazement stood,
Gave the hot Spirit to his boiling Blood: –
How he, with Oath and furious Speech, began

To prove his Freedom and assert the Man;
And when the Parent check'd his impious Rage,
How he had curs'd the Tyranny of Age, –
Nay, once had dealt the sacrilegious Blow
On his bare Head and laid his Parent low:
The Father groan'd – 'If thou art old,' said he,
'And hast a Son – thou wilt remember me:
Thy Mother left me in an happy Time,
Thou kill'dst not her – Heav'n spares the double Crime.'

On an Inn-settle, in his maudlin Grief,
This he revolv'd and drank for his Relief.

Now liv'd the Youth in freedom, but debarr'd
From constant Pleasure, and he thought it hard;
Hard that he could not every Wish obey,
But must awhile relinquish Ale and Play;
Hard! that he could not to his Cards attend,
But must acquire the Money he would spend.

With greedy eye he look'd on all he saw,
He knew not Justice, and he laugh'd at Law;
On all he mark'd, he stretch'd his ready Hand;
He fish'd by Water and he filch'd by Land:
Oft in the Night has *Peter* dropt his Oar,
Fled from his Boat and sought for Prey on shore;
Oft up the Hedge-row glided, on his Back
Bearing the Orchard's Produce in a Sack,
Or Farm-yard Load, tugg'd fiercely from the Stack;
And as these Wrongs to greater numbers rose,
The more he look'd on all Men as his Foes.

GEORGE CRABBE

The School Boy

I love to rise in a summer morn
When the birds sing on every tree;
The distant huntsman winds his horn,
And the sky-lark sings with me.
O! what sweet company.

But to go to school in a summer morn,
O! it drives all joy away;
Under a cruel eye outworn,
The little ones spend the day
In sighing and dismay.

Ah! then at times I drooping sit,
And spend many an anxious hour,
Nor in my book can I take delight,
Nor sit in learning's bower,
Worn thro' with the dreary shower.

How can the bird that is born for joy
Sit in a cage and sing?
How can a child, when fears annoy,
But droop his tender wing,
And forget his youthful spring?

O! father and mother, if buds are nip'd
And blossoms blown away,
And if the tender plants are strip'd
Of their joy in the springing day,
By sorrow and care's dismay,

How shall the summer arise in joy,
Or the summer fruits appear?
Or how shall we gather what griefs destroy,
Or bless the mellowing year.
When the blasts of winter appear?

WILLIAM BLAKE

Holy Thursday

Is this a holy thing to see,
In a rich and fruitful land,
Babes reducd to misery,
Fed with cold and usurous hand?

Is that trembling cry a song?
Can it be a song of joy?
And so many children poor?
It is a land of poverty!

And their sun does never shine,
And their fields are bleak & bare,
And their ways are fill'd with thorns;
It is eternal winter there.

For where-e'er the sun does shine,
And where-e'er the rain does fall,
Babe can never hunger there,
Nor poverty the mind appall.

WILLIAM BLAKE

A Question Answered

What is it men in women do require?
The lineaments of Gratified Desire.
What is it women do in men require?
The lineaments of Gratified Desire.

WILLIAM BLAKE

The Camp

Tents, *marquees*, and baggage-waggons;
Suttling-houses, beer in flagons;
Drums and trumpets, singing, firing;
Girls seducing, beaux admiring;
Country lasses gay and smiling,
City lads their hearts beguiling;
Dusty roads, and horses frisky,
Many an *Eton Boy* in whisky;
Tax'd carts full of farmers' daughters;
Brutes condemn'd, and man who slaughters!
Public-houses, booths, and castles,
Belles of fashion, serving vassals;
Lordly gen'rals fiercely staring,
Weary soldiers, sighing, swearing!
Petit-maitres always dressing,
In the glass themselves caressing;
Perfum'd, painted, patch'd, and blooming
Ladies – manly airs assuming!
Dowagers of fifty, simp'ring,

Misses for their lovers whimp'ring;
Husbands drill'd to household tameness;
Dames heart sick of wedded sameness.
Princes setting girls a-madding,
Wives for ever fond of gadding;
Princesses with lovely faces,
Beauteous children of the Graces!
Britain's pride and virtue's treasure,
Fair and gracious beyond measure!
Aid-de-camps and youthful pages,
Prudes and vestals of all ages!
Old coquets and matrons surly,
Sounds of distant hurly-burly!
Mingled voices, uncouth singing,
Carts full laden, forage bringing;
Sociables and horses weary,
Houses warm, and dresses airy;
Loads of fatten'd poultry; pleasure
Serv'd (to nobles) without measure;
Doxies, who the waggons follow;
Beer, for thirsty hinds to swallow;
Washerwomen, fruit-girls cheerful,
Ancient ladies – *chaste* and *fearful!!*
Tradesmen, leaving shops, and seeming
More of war than profit dreaming;
Martial sounds and braying asses,
Noise, that ev'ry noise surpasses!
All confusion, din, and riot,
Nothing clean – and nothing quiet.

MARY ROBINSON

A Riddle

'Twas in heaven pronounced, and 'twas muttered in hell
And echo caught faintly the sound as it fell:
On the confines of earth 'twas permitted to rest,
And the depths of the ocean its presence confest;
'Twill be found in the sphere when 'tis riven asunder,
Be seen in the lightning, and heard in the thunder.
'Twas allotted to man with his earliest breath,
Attends at his birth, and awaits him in death,
Presides o'er his happiness, honour, and health,
Is the prop of his house, and the end of his wealth.
In the heaps of the miser 'tis hoarded with care,
But is sure to be lost on his prodigal heir.
It begins every hope, every wish it must bound,
With the husbandman toils, and with monarchs is crown'd.
Without it the soldier, the seaman may roam,
But wo to the wretch who expels it from home!
In the whispers of conscience its voice will be found,
Nor e'en in the whirlwind of passion be drown'd.
'Twill not soften the heart; but though deaf be the ear,
It will make it acutely and instandy hear.
Yet in shade let it rest like a delicate flower,
Ah breathe on it softly – it dies in an hour.

CATHERINE MARIA FANSHAWE

Mary Morison

O Mary, at thy window be,
    It is the wish'd, the trysted hour;
Those smiles and glances let me see,
    That make the miser's treasure poor:
How blythly wad I bide the stoure,
    A weary slave frae sun to sun;
Could I the rich reward secure,
    The lovely Mary Morison.

Yestreen when to the trembling string
    The dance gaed thro' the lighted ha',
To thee my fancy took its wing,
    I sat, but neither heard nor saw:
Tho' this was fair, and that was braw,
    And yon the toast of a' the town,
I sigh'd, and said amang them a',
    'Ye are na Mary Morison.'

O Mary, canst thou wreck his peace,
    Wha for thy sake wad gladly die!
Or canst thou break that heart of his,
    Whase only faut is loving thee.
If love for love thou wilt na gie,
    At least be pity to me shown;
A thought ungentle canna be
    The thought o' Mary Morison.

ROBERT BURNS

A Red, Red Rose

My luve is like a red, red rose,
   That's newly sprung in June:
My luve is like the melodie,
   That's sweetly play'd in tune.
As fair art thou, my bonie lass,
   So deep in luve am I,
And I will luve thee still, my dear,
   Till a' the seas gang dry.

Till a' the seas gang dry, my dear,
   And the rocks melt wi' the sun!
And I will luve thee still, my dear,
   While the sands o' life shall run.
And fare-thee-weel, my only luve,
   And fare-thee-weel a while!
And I will come again, my luve,
   Tho' it were ten-thousand mile.

ROBERT BURNS

Ae Fond Kiss

Ae fond kiss, and then we sever;
Ae farewell and then forever!
Deep in heart-wrung tears I'll pledge thee,
Warring sighs and groans I'll wage thee.

Who shall say that fortune grieves him
While the star of hope she leaves him?
Me, nae chearfu' twinkle lights me;
Dark despair around benights me.

I'll ne'er blame my partial fancy,
Naething could resist my Nancy:
But to see her, was to love her;
Love but her, and love for ever.

Had we never lov'd sae kindly,
Had we never lov'd sae blindly,
Never met – or never parted,
We had ne'er been broken-hearted.

Fare thee weel, thou first and fairest!
Fare thee weel, thou best and dearest!
Thine be ilka joy and treasure,
Peace, Enjoyment, Love and Pleasure!

Ae fond kiss, and then we sever;
Ae fareweel, Alas! for ever!
Deep in heart-wrung tears I'll pledge thee,
Warring sighs and groans I'll wage thee.

ROBERT BURNS

Green Grow the Rashes

Green grow the rashes, O;
Green grow the rashes, O;
The sweetest hours that e'er I spend,
Are spent amang the lasses, O

There's nought but care on ev'ry han',
    In ev'ry hour that passes, O:
What signifies the life o' man,
        An' 'twere na for the lasses, O?
            Green grow, etc.

The warly race may riches chase,
    An' riches still may fly them, O;
An' tho' at last they catch them fast,
    Their hearts can ne'er enjoy them, O.

But gie me a canny hour at e'en
        My arms about my Dearie, O;
An' warly cares, an' warly men,
        May a' gae tapsalteerie, O!

For you sae douse, ye sneer at this,
        Ye're nought but senseless asses, O:
The wisest Man the warl' saw,
        He dearly lov'd the lasses, O.

Auld Nature swears, the lovely Dears
    Her noblest work she classes, O:
Her prentice han' she try'd on man,
    An' then she made the lasses, O.

ROBERT BURNS

Lament for Culloden

The lovely lass o' Inverness,
Nae joy nor pleasure can she see;
For e'en and morn she cries, Alas!
And aye the saut tear blins her ee:
Drumossie moor – Drumossie day –
A waefu' day it was to me!
For there I lost my father dear.
My father dear, and brethren three.

Their winding-sheet the bluidy clay,
Their graves are growing green to see;
And by them lies the dearest lad
That ever blest a woman's ee!
Now wae to thee, thou cruel lord,
A bluidy man I trow thou be:
For mony a heart thou hast made sair
That ne'er did wrang to thine or thee.

ROBERT BURNS

Hay Making

Upon the grass no longer hangs the dew;
Forth hies the mower, with his glittering scythe,
In snowy shirt bedight, and all unbraced,
He moves athwart the mead with sidling bend.
And lays the grass in many a swathey line:
In every field, in every lawn and meadow,
The rousing voice of industry is heard;
The haycock rises, and the frequent rake
Sweeps on the fragrant hay in heavy wreaths.
The old and young, the weak and strong, are there,
And, as they can, help on the cheerful work.
The father jeers his awkward half-grown lad,
Who trails his tawdry armful o'er the field,
Nor does he fear the jeering to repay.
The village oracle, and simple maid,
Jest in their turns and raise the ready laugh;
All are companions in the general glee;
Authority, hard-favoured, frowns not there.
Some, more advanced, raise up the lofty rick,
Whilst on its top doth stand the parish toast.
In loose attire, and swelling ruddy cheek.
With taunts and harmless mockery she receives
The tossed-up heaps from fork of simple youth,
Who, staring on her, takes his arm away,
While half the load falls back upon himself.
Loud is her laugh, her voice is heard afar:
The mower busied on the distant lawn,
The carter trudging on his dusty way,
The shrill sound know, their bonnets toss in air,
And roar across the field to catch her notice:

She waves her arm to them, and shakes her head,
And then renews her work with double spirit.
Thus do they jest and laugh away their toil
Till the bright sun, now past his middle course,
Shoots down his fiercest beams which none may brave.
The stoutest arm feels listless, and the swart
And brawny-shouldered clown begins to fail,
But to the weary, lo! there comes relief!
A troop of welcome children o'er the lawn
With slow and wary steps approach: some bear
In baskets oaten cakes or barley scones,
And gusty cheese and stoups of milk or whey.
Beneath the branches of a spreading tree,
Or by the shady side of the tall rick,
They spread their homely fare, and seated round,
Taste every pleasure that a feast can give.

JOANNA BAILLIE

Will Ye No Come Back Again?

Bonnie Charlie's now awa,
    Safely owre the friendly main:
Mony a heart will break in iwa.
    Should he ne'er come back again?

      Will ye no come back again?
      Will ye no come back again?
      Better lo'ed ye canna be,
      Will ye no come back again?

Ye trusted in your Heiland men,
    They trusted you, dear Charlie;
They kent you hiding in the glen.
    You cleedin was but barely.
    Will ye no, etc.

English bribes were a' in vain.
    An' e'en tho' pulrer we may be
Siller canna buy the heart
    That beats aye for thine and three.

We watched thee in the gloaming hour.
    We watched thee in the morning grey;
Tho' thirty thousand pounds they'd gie.
    Oh there is nane that wed betray.

Sweet's the laverock's note and lang,
    Lifting wildly up the glen;
But aye to me he sings ae sang,
    Will ye no come back again?

Will ye no come back again?
Will ye no come back again?
Better lo'ed ye canna
Will ye no come back again?

CAROLINE OLIPHANT

The Land o' the Leal

I'm wearin' awa', John,
Like snaw-wreaths in thaw, John,
I'm wearin' awa'
To the land o' the leal.
There's nae sorrow there, John,
There's neither cauld nor care, John,
The day's aye fair
  In the land o' the leal.

Our bonnie bairn's there, John,
She was baith gude and fair, John,
And oh! we grudged her sair
To the land o' the leal.
But sorrow's sel' wears past, John,
And joy's a-comin' fast, John,
The joy that's aye to last,
  In the land o' the leal.

Sae dear's that joy was bought, John,
Sae free the battle fought, John,
That sinfu' man e'er brought
To the land o' the leal.

Oh! dry your glist'ning e'e, John,
My saul langs to be free, John,
And angels beckon me
  To the land o' the leal.

Oh! haud ye leal and true, John,
Your day it's wearin' through, John,
And I'll welcome you
To the land o' the leal.
Now fare-ye-weel, my ain John,
This warld's cares are vain, John,
We'll meet, and we'll be fain,
  In the land o' the leal.

CAROLINE OLIPHANT

Love is like a dizziness

  O, love, love, love!
  Love is like a dizziness;
  It winna let a puir body
  Gang about his biziness!

JAMES HOGG

The Village of Balmaquhapple

D'ye ken the big village of Balmaquhapple,
The great muckle village of Balmaquhapple?
'Tis steep'd in iniquity up to the thrapple,
An' what's to become o' poor Balmaquhapple?
Fling a' aff your bannets, an' kneel for your life, fo'ks,
And pray to St Andrew, the god o' the Fife fo'ks;
Gar a' the hills yout wi' sheer vociferation,
And thus you may cry on sic needfu' occasion:

'O, blessed St Andrew, if e'er ye could pity fo'k,
Men fo'k or women fo'k, country or city fo'k,
Come for this aince wi' the auld thief to grapple,
An' save the great village of Balmaquhapple
Frae drinking an' leeing, an' flyting an' swearing,
An' sins that ye wad be affrontit at hearing,
An' cheating an' stealing; O, grant them redemption,
All save an' except the few after to mention:

'There's Johnny the elder, wha hopes ne'er to need ye,
Sae pawkie, sae holy, sae gruff, an' sae greedy;
Wha prays every hour as the wayfarer passes,
But aye at a hole where he watches the lasses;
He's cheated a thousand, an' e'en to this day yet,
Can cheat a young lass, or they're leears that say it
Then gie him his gate; he's sae slee an' sae civil,
Perhaps in the end he may wheedle the devil.

'There's Cappie the cobbler, an' Tammie the tinman,
 An' Dickie the brewer, an' Peter the skinman,
 An' Geordie our deacon, for want of a better,
An' Bess, wha delights in the sins that beset her.
O, worthy St Andrew, we canna compel ye,
But ye ken as well as a body can tell ye,
If these gang to heaven, we'll a' be sae shockit,
Your garret o' blue will but thinly be stockit.

'But for a' the rest, for the women's sake, save them,
Their bodies at least, an' their sauls, if they have them;
But it puzzles Jock Lesly, an' sma' it avails,
If they dwell in their stamocks, their heads, or their tails;
An' save, without word of confession auricular,
The clerk's bonny daughters, an' Bell in particular,
For ye ken that their beauty's the pride an' the staple
Of the great wicked village of Balmaquhapple!'

JAMES HOGG

VI

1800–1850

SILENT ICICLES, QUIETLY SHINING TO THE QUIET MOON...

Composed upon Westminster Bridge,
September 3, 1802

Earth has not anything to show more fair:
   Dull would he be of soul who could pass by
   A sight so touching in its majesty:
This City now doth, like a garment, wear
The beauty of the morning; silent, bare,
   Ships, towers, domes, theatres, and temples lie
   Open unto the fields, and to the sky;
All bright and glittering in the smokeless air.
Never did sun more beautifully steep
   In his first splendour, valley, rock, or hill;
Ne'er saw I, never felt, a calm so deep!
   The river glideth at his own sweet will:
Dear God! the very houses seem asleep;
   And all that mighty heart is lying still!

WILLIAM WORDSWORTH

from The Prelude

O pleasant exercise of hope and joy!
For mighty were the auxiliars which then stood
Upon our side, us who were strong in love!
Bliss was it in that dawn to be alive,
But to be young was very Heaven! O times,
In which the meagre, stale, forbidding ways
Of custom, law, and statute, took at once
The attraction of a country in romance!

When Reason seemed the most to assert her rights
When most intent on making of herself
A prime enchantress – to assist the work,
Which then was going forward in her name!
Not favoured spots alone, but the whole Earth,
The beauty wore of promise – that which sets
(As at some moments might not be unfelt
Among the bowers of Paradise itself)
The budding rose above the rose full blown.
What temper at the prospect did not wake
To happiness unthought of? The inert
Were roused, and lively natures rapt away!
They who had fed their childhood upon dreams,
The play-fellows of fancy, who had made
All powers of swiftness, subtilty, and strength
Their ministers, – who in lordly wise had stirred
Among the grandest objects of the sense,
And dealt with whatsoever they found there
As if they had within some lurking right
To wield it; – they, too, who of gentle mood
Had watched all gentle motions, and to these
Had fitted their own thoughts, schemers more mild,
And in the region of their peaceful selves; –
Now was it that both found, the meek and lofty
Did both find, helpers to their hearts' desire,
And stuff at hand, plastic as they could wish, –
Were called upon to exercise their skill,
Not in Utopia, – subterranean fields, –
Or some secreted island, Heaven knows where!

But in the very world, which is the world
Of all of us, – the place where, in the end,
We find our happiness, or not at all!

WILLIAM WORDSWORTH

from Lines Composed a Few Miles Above
Tintern Abbey

On revisiting the banks of the Wye during a tour

Five years have past; five summers, with the length
Of five long winters! and again I hear
These waters, rolling from their mountain-springs
With a soft inland murmur. – Once again
Do I behold these steep and lofty cliffs,
That on a wild secluded scene impress
Thoughts of more deep seclusion; and connect
The landscape with the quiet of the sky.
The day is come when I again repose
Here, under this dark sycamore, and view
These plots of cottage-ground, these orchard-tufts,
Which at this season, with their unripe fruits,
Are clad in one green hue, and lose themselves
'Mid groves and copses. Once again I see
These hedge-rows, hardly hedge-rows, little lines
Of sportive wood run wild: these pastoral farms,
Green to the very door; and wreaths of smoke
Sent up, in silence from among the trees!
With some uncertain notice, as might seem

Of vagrant dwellers in the houseless woods,
Or of some Hermit's cave, where by his fire
The Hermit sits alone.

                        These beauteous forms
Through a long absence, have not been to me
As is a landscape to a blind man's eye;
But oft, in lonely rooms, and 'mid the din
Of towns and cities, I have owed to them
In hours of weariness, sensations sweet,
Felt in the blood, and felt along the heart;
And passing even into my purer mind,
With tranquil restoration: – feelings too
Of unremembered pleasure: such, perhaps,
As have no slight or trivial influence
On that best portion of a good man's life.
His little, nameless, unremembered acts
Of kindness and of love. Nor less, I trust,
To them I may have owed another gift,
Of aspect more sublime; that blessed mood,
In which the burthen of the mystery,
In which the heavy and the weary weight
Of all this unintelligible world,
Is lightened: – that serene and blessed mood,
In which the affections gently lead us on, –
Until, the breath of this corporeal frame
And even the motion of our human blood
Almost suspended, we are laid asleep
In body, and become a living soul:
While with an eye made quiet by the power
Of harmony, and the deep power of joy,
We see into the life of things.

                              If this
Be but a vain belief, yet, oh! how oft
In darkness and amid the many shapes
Of joyless daylight; when the fretful stir
Unprofitable, and the fever of the world,
Have hung upon the bearings of my heart –
How oft, in spirit, have I turned to thee,
O sylvan Wye! thou wanderer thro' the woods,
How often has my spirit turned to thee!

                    WILLIAM WORDSWORTH

                    Floating Island

Harmonious powers with nature work
On sky, earth, river, lake and sea
Sunshine and cloud, whirlwind and breeze,
All in one duteous task agree.

Once did I see a slip of earth
By throbbing waves long undermined,
Loosed from its hold – how, no one knew,
But all might see it float, obedient to the wind,

Might see it from the mossy shore
Dissevered, float upon the lake,
Float with its crest of trees adorned
On which the warbling birds their pastime take.

Food, shelter, safety, there they find;
There berries ripen, flowerets bloom;
There insects live their lives – and die:
A peopled world it is, in size a tiny room.

And thus through many seasons' space
This little island may survive,
But nature (though we mark her not)
Will take away, may cease to give.

Perchance when you are wandering forth
Upon some vacant sunny day
Without an object, hope, or fear,
Thither your eyes may turn – the isle is passed away,

Buried beneath the glittering lake,
Its place no longer to be found.
Yet the lost fragments shall remain
To fertilise some other ground.

DOROTHY WORDSWORTH

Frost at Midnight

The Frost performs its secret ministry,
Unhelped by any wind. The owlet's cry
Came loud – and hark, again! loud as before.
The inmates of my cottage, all at rest,
Have left me to that solitude, which suits
Abstruser musings: save that at my side
My cradled infant slumbers peacefully.

'Tis calm indeed! so calm, that it disturbs
And vexes meditation with its strange
And extreme silentness. Sea, hill, and wood,
This populous village! Sea, and hill, and wood,
With all the numberless goings-on of life,
Inaudible as dreams! the thin blue flame
Lies on my low-burnt fire, and quivers not;
Only that film, which fluttered on the grate,
Still flutters there, the sole unquiet thing.
Methinks, its motion in this hush of nature
Gives it dim sympathies with me who live,
Making it a companionable form,
Whose puny flaps and freaks the idling Spirit
By its own moods interprets, every where
Echo or mirror seeking of itself,
And makes a toy of Thought.

                          But O! how oft,
How oft, at school, with most believing mind,
Presageful, have I gazed upon the bars,
To watch that fluttering *stranger*! and as oft
With unclosed lids, already had I dreamt
Of my sweet birth-place, and the old church-tower,
Whose bells, the poor man's only music, rang
From morn to evening, all the hot Fair-day,
So sweetly, that they stirred and haunted me
With a wild pleasure, falling on mine ear
Most like articulate sounds of things to come!
So gazed I, till the soothing things I dreamt,
Lulled me to sleep, and sleep prolonged my dreams!
And so I brooded all the following morn,
Awed by the stern preceptor's face, mine eye
Fixed with mock study on my swimming book:

Save if the door half opened, and I snatched
A hasty glance, and still my heart leaped up,
For still I hoped to see the *stranger's* face,
Townsman, or aunt, or sister more beloved,
My play-mate when we both were clothed alike!

Dear Babe, that sleepest cradled by my side,
Whose gentle breathings, heard in thus deep calm,
Fill up the interspersed vacancies
And momentary pauses of the thought!
My babe so beautiful! it thrills my heart
With tender gladness, thus to look at thee,
And think that thou shalt learn far other lore,
And in far other scenes! For I was reared
In the great city, pent 'mid cloisters dim,
And saw nought lovely but the sky and stars.
But *thou*, my babe! shalt wander like a breeze
By lakes and sandy shores, beneath the crags
Of ancient mountain, and beneath the clouds,
Which image in their bulk both lakes and shores
And mountain crags: so shalt thou see and hear
The lovely shapes and sounds intelligible
Of that eternal language, which thy God
Utters, who from eternity doth teach
Himself in all, and all things in himself.
Great universal Teacher! he shall mould
Thy spirit, and by giving make it ask.

Therefore all seasons shall be sweet to thee,
Whether the summer clothe the general earth
With greenness, or the redbreast sit and sing
Betwixt the tufts of snow on the bare branch
Of mossy apple-tree, while the nigh thatch

Smokes in the sun-thaw; whether the eave-drops fall
Heard only in the trances of the blast,
Or if the secret ministry of frost
Shall hang them up in silent icicles,
Quietly shining to the quiet Moon.

SAMUEL TAYLOR COLERIDGE

A Soliloquy of the full Moon,
She being in a Mad Passion –

Now as Heaven is my Lot, they're the Pests of the Nation!
Wherever they can come
With clankum and blankum
'Tis all Botheration, & Hell & Damnation,
With fun, jeering
Conjuring
Sky-staring,
Loungering,
And still to the tune of Transmogrification –
Those muttering
Spluttering
Ventriloquogusty
Poets
With no Hats
Or Hats that are rusty.
They're my Torment and Curse
And harass me worse
And bait me and bay me, far sorer I vow
Than the Screech of the Owl

Or the witch-wolf's long howl,
Or sheep-killing Butcher-dog's inward Bow wow
For me they all spite – an unfortunate Wight.
And the very first moment that I came to Light
A Rascal call'd Voss the more to his scandal,
Turn'd me into a sickle with never a handle.
A Night or two after a worse Rogue there came,
The head of the Gang, one Wordsworth by name –
'Ho! What's in the wind?' 'Tis the voice of a Wizzard!
I saw him look at me most terribly blue!
He was hunting for witch-rhymes from great A to Izzard,
And soon as he'd found them made no more ado
But chang'd me at once to a little Canoe.
From this strange Enchantment uncharm'd by degrees
I began to take courage & hop'd for some Ease,
When one Coleridge, a Raff of the self-same Banditti
Passed by – & intending no doubt to be witty,
Because I'd th' ill-fortune his taste to displease,
  He turn'd up his nose,
  And in pitiful Prose
Made me into the half of a small Cheshire Cheese.
Well, a night or two past – it was wind, rain & hail –
And I ventur'd abroad in a thick Cloak & veil –
But the very first Evening he saw me again
The last mentioned Ruffian popp'd out of his Den –
I was resting a moment on the bare edge of Naddle
I fancy the sight of me turn'd his Brains addle –
  For what was I now?
  A complete Barley-mow
And when I climb'd higher he made a long leg,
And chang'd me at once to an Ostrich's Egg –
But now Heaven be praised in contempt of the Loon,
I am I myself I, the jolly full Moon.

Yet my heart is still fluttering –
For I heard the Rogue muttering –
He was hulking and skulking at the skirt of a Wood
When lightly & brightly on tip-toe I stood
On the long level Line of a motionless Cloud
And ho! what a Skittle-ground! quoth he aloud
And wish'd from his heart nine-pins to see
In brightness & size just proportion'd to me.
So I fear'd from my soul,
That he'd make me a Bowl,
But in spite of his spite
This was more than his might
And still Heaven be prais'd! in contempt of the Loon
I am I myself I, the jolly full Moon.

SAMUEL TAYLOR COLERIDGE

Written in Winter

The green warl's awa, but the white ane can charm them
　　What skait on the burn, or wi' settin' dogs rin:
The hind's dinlin' han's, numb't wi' snaw-baws, to warm them,
　　He claps on his hard sides, whase doublets are thin.

How dark the hail show'r mak's yon vale, aince sae pleasing!
　　How laigh stoops the bush that's ower-burden't wi' drift!
The icicles dreep at the half-thow't house-easin',
　　When blunt the sun beams frae the verge o' the lift.

JAMES ORR

'She walks in beauty, like the night'

She walks in beauty, like the night
   Of cloudless climes and starry skies;
And all that's best of dark and bright
   Meet in her aspect and her eyes:
Thus mellowed to that tender light
   Which heaven to gaudy day denies.

One shade the more, one ray the less,
   Had half impaired the nameless grace
Which waves in every raven tress,
   Or softly lightens o'er her face;
Where thoughts serenely sweet express,
   How pure, how dear their dwelling-place.

And on that cheek, and o'er that brow,
   So soft, so calm, yet eloquent,
The smiles that win, the tints that glow,
   But tell of days in goodness spent,
A mind at peace with all below,
   A heart whose love is innocent!

LORD BYRON

'So, we'll go no more a roving'

So, we'll go no more a roving
   So late into the night,
Though the heart be still as loving,
   And the moon be still as bright.

For the sword outwears its sheath,
   And the soul wears out the breast,
And the heart must pause to breathe,
   And love itself have rest.

Though the night was made for loving,
   And the day returns too soon,
Yet we'll go no more a roving
   By the light of the moon.

LORD BYRON

England in 1819

An old, mad, blind, despised, and dying king, –
Princes, the dregs of their dull race, who flow
Through public scorn, – mud from a muddy spring, –
Rulers who neither see, nor feel, nor know,
But leech-like to their fainting country cling,
Till they drop, blind in blood, without a blow, –
A people starved and stabbed in the unfilled field, –
An army, which liberticide and prey
Makes as a two-edged sword to all who wield, –

Golden and sanguine laws which tempt and slay;
Religion Christless, Godless – a book sealed;
A Senate, – Tune's worst statute unrepealed, –
Are graves, from which a glorious Phantom may
Burst, to illumine our tempestuous day.

PERCY BYSSHE SHELLEY

Ode to the West Wind

I

O wild West Wind, thou breath of Autumn's being,
Thou, from whose unseen presence the leaves dead
Are driven, like ghosts from an enchanter fleeing,

Yellow, and black, and pale, and hectic red,
Pestilence-stricken multitudes: O thou,
Who chariotest to their dark wintry bed

The wingéd seeds, where they lie cold and low,
Each like a corpse within its grave, until
Thine azure sister of the spring shall blow

Her clarion o'er the dreaming earth, and fill
(Driving sweet buds like flocks to feed in air)
With living hues and odours plain and hill:

Wild Spirit, which art moving everywhere;
Destroyer and preserver; hear, oh hear!

II

Thou on whose stream, 'mid the steep sky's commotion,
Loose clouds like earth's decaying leaves are shed,
Shook from the tangled boughs of Heaven and Ocean,

Angels of rain and lightning: there are spread
On the blue surface of thine airy surge.
Like the bright hair uplifted from the head

Of some fierce Maenad, even from the dim verge
Of the horizon to the zenith's height,
The locks of the approaching storm. Thou dirge

Of the dying year, to which this closing night
Will be the dome of a vast sepulchre,
Vaulted with all thy congregated might

Of vapours, from whose solid atmosphere
Black rain, and fire, and hail, will burst: oh, hear!

III

Thou who didst waken from his summer dreams
The blue Mediterranean, where he lay
Lulled by the coil of his crystalline streams,

Beside a pumice isle in Baiae's bay,
And saw in sleep old palaces and towers
Quivering within the wave's intenser day,

All overgrown with azure moss and flowers
So sweet, the sense faints picturing them! Thou
For whose path the Atlantic's level powers

Cleave themselves into chasms, while far below
The sea-blooms and the oozy woods which wear
The sapless foliage of the ocean, know

Thy voice, and suddenly grow grey with fear,
And tremble and despoil themselves: oh, hear!

IV

If I were a dead leaf thou mightest bear;
If I were a swift cloud to fly with thee;
A wave to pant beneath thy power, and share

The impulse of thy strength, only less free
Than thou, O uncontrollable! If even
I were as in my boyhood, and could be

The comrade of thy wanderings over Heaven,
As then, when to outstrip thy skiey speed
Scarce seemed a vision; I would ne'er have striven

As thus with thee in prayer in my sore need.
Oh, lift me as a wave, a leaf, a cloud!
I fall upon the thorns of life! I bleed!

A heavy weight of hours has chained and bowed
One too like thee: tameless, and swift, and proud.

Make me thy lyre, even as the forest is:
What if my leaves are falling like its own!
The tumult of thy mighty harmonies

Will take from both a deep, autumnal tone,
Sweet though in sadness. Be thou, Spirit fierce,
My spirit! Be thou me, impetuous one!

Drive my dead thoughts over the universe
Like withered leaves to quicken a new birth!
And, by the incantation of this verse,

Scatter, as from an unextinguished hearth
Ashes and sparks, my words among mankind!
Be through my lips to unawakened earth

The trumpet of a prophecy! O, wind,
If Winter comes, can Spring be far behind?

PERCY BYSSHE SHELLEY

Pleasant Sounds

The rustling of leaves under the feet in woods and under hedges. The crumping of cat-ice and snow down wood rides, narrow lanes and every street causeways. Rustling through a wood, or rather rushing while the wind halloos in the oak tops like thunder. The rustles of birds' wings startled from their nests, or flying unseen into the bushes.

The whizzing of larger birds overhead in a wood, such as crows, puddocks, buzzards etc.

The trample of robust wood larks on the brown leaves, and the patter of squirrels on the green moss. The fall of an acorn on the ground, the pattering of nuts on the hazel branches ere they fall from ripeness. The flirt of the ground-lark's wing from the stubbles, how sweet such pictures on dewy mornings when the dew flashes from its brown feathers.

JOHN CLARE

The Moors

Far spread the moory ground, a level scene
Bespread with rush and one eternal green
That never felt the rage of blundering plough
Though centuries wreathed spring's blossoms on its brow,
Still meeting plains that stretched them far away
In unchecked shadows of green, brown and grey.
Unbounded freedom ruled the wandering scene
Nor fence of ownership crept in between
To hide the prospect of the following eye –

Its only bondage was the circling sky.
One mighty flat undwarfed by bush and tree
Spread its faint shadow of immensity
And lost itself, which seemed to eke its bounds,
In the blue mist the horizon's edge surrounds.
Now this sweet vision of my boyish hours,
Free as spring clouds and wild as summer flowers,
Is faded all – a hope that blossomed free,
And hath been once, no more shall ever be.
Enclosure came and trampled on the grave
Of labour's rights and left the poor a slave,
And memory's pride, ere want to wealth did bow,
Is both the shadow and the substance now.
The sheep and cows were free to range as then
Where change might prompt, nor felt the bonds of men:
Cows went and came with evening, morn and night
To the wild pasture as their common right,
And sheep unfolded with the rising sun
Heard the swains shout and felt their freedom won,
Tracked the red fallow field and heath and plain,
Then met the brook and drank and roamed again –
The brook that dribbled on as clear as glass
Beneath the roots they hid among the grass –
While the glad shepherd traced their tracks along,
Free as the lark and happy as her song.
But now all's fled and flats of many a dye
That seemed to lengthen with the following eye,
Moors losing from the sight, far, smooth and blea,
Where swopt the plover in its pleasure free,
Are vanished now with commons wild and gay
As poets' visions of life's early day.
Mulberry bushes where the boy would run
To fill his hands with fruit are grubbed and done,

And hedgerow briars – flower-lovers overjoyed
Came and got flower pots – these are all destroyed,
And sky-bound moors in mangled garbs are left
Like mighty giants of their limbs bereft.
Fence now meets fence in owners' little bounds
Of field and meadow, large as garden grounds,
In little parcels little minds to please
With men and flocks imprisoned, ill at ease.
Each little path that led its pleasant way
As sweet as morning leading night astray,
Where little flowers bloomed round, a varied host,
That Travel felt delighted to be lost
Nor grudged the steps that he had ta'en as vain
When right roads traced his journey's end again;
Nay on a broken tree he'd sit awhile
To see the moors and fields and meadows smile,
Sometimes with cowslips smothered – then all white
With daisies – then the summer's splendid sight
Of corn fields crimson o'er, the 'headache' bloomed
Like splendid armies for the battle plumed;
He gazed upon them with wild fancy's eye
As fallen landscapes from an evening sky.
These paths are stopped – the rude philistine's thrall
Is laid upon them and destroyed them all.
Each little tyrant with his little sign
Shows where man claims, earth glows no more divine.
On paths to freedom and to childhood dear
A board sticks up to notice 'no road here'
And on the tree with ivy overhung
The hated sign by vulgar taste is hung
As though the very birds should learn to know
When they go there they must no further go.
Thus, with the poor, scared freedom bade good-bye

And much they feel it in the smothered sigh,
And birds and trees and flowers without a name
All sighed when lawless law's enclosure came,
And dreams of plunder in such rebel schemes
Have found too truly that they were but dreams.

JOHN CLARE

Summer Evening

The frog, half fearful, jumps across the path,
And little mouse that leaves its hole at eve
Nimbles with timid dread beneath the swath;
My rustling steps awhile their joys deceive,
Till past – and then the cricket sings more strong
And grasshoppers in merry moods still wear
The short night wean' with their fretting song.
Up from behind the mole-hill jumps die hare,
Cheat of his chosen bed, and from the bank
The yellow-hammer flutters in short fears
From off its nest hid in the grasses rank,
And drops again when no more noise it hears.
Thus nature's human link and endless thrall,
Proud man, still seems the enemy of all.

JOHN CLARE

Oor Location

A hunner funnels bleezin', reekin',
Coal an' ironstane, charrin', smeekin';
Navvies, miners, keepers, fillers,
Puddlers, rollers, iron millers;
Reestit, reekit, raggit laddies,
Firemen, enginemen, an' Paddies;
Boatmen, banksmen, rough an' rattlin',
Bout the wecht wi' colliers battlin',
Sweatin', swearin', fechtin', drinkin';
Change-house bells an' gill-stoups clinkin';
Police – ready men and willin' –
Aye at han' whan stoups are fillin';
Clerks an' counter-loupers plenty,
Wi' trim moustache and whiskers dainty –
Chaps that winna staun at trifles!
Min' ye, they can han'le rifles!
  'Bout the wives in oor location –
An' the lassies' botheration –
Some are decent, some are dandies,
An' a gey wheen drucken randies;
Aye to neebors' houses sailin',
Greetin' bairns ahint them trailin',
Gaun for nouther bread nor butter,
Juist to drink an' rin the cutter!
o the dreadfu' curse o' drinkin'!
Men are ill, but, tae my thinkin',
Leukin' through the drucken fock,
There's a Jenny for ilka Jock.
Oh the dool an' desolation,
An' the havock in the nation

Wrocht by dirty, drucken wives!
Oh hoo mony bairnies lives
Lost ilk year through their neglec'!
Like a millstane roun' the neck
O' the struggling toilin' masses
Hing drucken wives an' wanton lassies.
To see sae mony unwed mithers
Is sure a shame that taps a' ithers.
  An' noo I'm fairly set a-gaun;
On baith the whisky-shop and pawn
I'll speak my min' – and what for no?
Frae whence cums misery, want, an' wo
The ruin, crime, disgrace, an' shame
That quenches a' the lichts o' hame?
Ye needna speer, the feck ot's drawn
Oot o' the change-hoose an' the pawn.
  Sin an' Death, as poets tell,
On ilk side the doors o' hell
Wait to haurl mortals in;
Death gets a' that's catcht by sin:
There are doors where Death an' Sin
Draw their tens o' thoosan's in;
Thick an' thrang we see them gaun,
First the dram-shop, then the pawn;
Owre a' kin's o' ruination,
Drink's the King in oor location!

JANET HAMILTON

Auld Mither Scotlan'

Na, na, I wunna pairt wi' that,
   I downa gi'e it up;
O' Scotlan's hamely mither tongue
   I canna quat the grup.
It's bedded in my very he'rt,
   Ye needna rive an' rug;
It's in my e'e an' on my tongue,
   An' singin' in my lug.

O leeze me on the Scottish lass,
   Fresh frae her muirlan' hame,
Wi' gowden or wi' coal-black hair,
   Row'd up wi' bucklin'-kame;
Or wavin' roun' her snawy broo,
   Sae bonnie, braid, an' brent,
Gaun barefit wi' her kiltit coat,
   Blythe singin' ower the bent.

I heard her sing 'Auld Robin Gray',
   An' 'Yarrow's dowie den' –
O' Flodden, an' oor forest flouris
   Cut doon by Englishmen;
My saul was fir'd, my he'rt was fu',
   The tear was in my e'e:
Let ither lan's hae ither sangs –
   Auld Scotlan's sangs for me.

JANET HAMILTON

'This living hand, now warm and capable'

This living hand, now warm and capable
Of earnest grasping, would, if it were cold
And in the icy silence of the tomb,
So haunt thy days and chill thy dreaming nights
That thou would wish thine own heart dry of blood
So in my veins red life might stream again,
And thou be conscience-calm'd – see here it is –
I hold it towards you.

JOHN KEATS

A Song about Myself

I

There was a naughty boy
A naughty boy was he,
He would not stop at home,
He could not quiet be –
He took
In his Knapsack
A Book
Full of vowels
And a shirt
With some towels –
A slight cap
For a night cap –
A hair brush,

Comb ditto,
New Stockings
For old ones
Would split O!
This Knapsack
Tight at's back
He rivetted close
And followed his Nose
To the North,
To the North,
And followed his Nose
To the North.

II

There was a naughty boy
  And a naughty boy was he,
For nothing would he do
  But scribble poetry –
    He took
    An ink stand
    In his hand
    And a pen
    Big as ten
    In the other.
    And away
    In a Pother
    He ran
    To the mountains
    And fountains
    And ghostes
    And Postes
    And witches

And ditches
And wrote
In his coat
When the weather
Was cool,
Fear of gout
And without
When the weather
Was warm –
Och the charm
When we choose
To follow one's nose
To the north
To the north,
To follow one's nose
To the north!

III

There was a naughty boy
  And a naughty boy was he,
He kept little fishes
  In washing tubs three
      In spite
      Of the might
      Of the Maid
      Nor afraid
      Of his Granny-good –
      He often would
      Hurly burly
      Get up early
      And go
      By hook or crook

To the brook
And bring home
Miller's thumb,
Tittlebat
Not over fat,
Minnows small
As the stall
Of a glove,
Not above
The size
Of a nice
Little Baby's
Little fingers –
O he made
'Twas his trade
Of fish a pretty Kettle
A Kettle –
A Kettle
Of fish a pretty Kettle
A Kettle!

IV

There was a naughty Boy,
    And a naughty Boy was he,
He ran away to Scotland
    The people for to see –
        Then he found
        That the ground
        Was as hard,
        That a yard
        Was as long,
        That a song

[254]

Was as merry,
That a cherry
Was as red –
That lead
Was as weighty,
That fourscore
Was as eighty,
That a door
Was as wooden
As in England –
So he stood in his shoes
And he wondered,
He wondered,
He stood in his
Shoes and he wondered.

JOHN KEATS

On the Grasshopper and the Cricket

The poetry of earth is never dead:
    When all the birds are faint with the hot sun,
    And hide in cooling trees, a voice will run
From hedge to hedge about the new-mown mead;
That is the Grasshopper's – he takes the lead
    In summer luxury, – he has never done
    With his delights; for when tired out with fun
He rests at ease beneath some pleasant weed.

The poetry of earth is ceasing never:
   On a lone winter evening, when the frost
   Has wrought a silence, from the stove there shrills
The Cricket's song, in warmth increasing ever,
   And seems to one in drowsiness half lost,
   The Grasshopper's among some grassy hills.

JOHN KEATS

'Bright star, would I were steadfast as thou art'

Bright star, would I were steadfast as thou art –
   Not in lone splendour hung aloft the night
And watching, with eternal lids apart,
   Like nature's patient, sleepless Eremite,
The moving waters at their priestlike task
   Of pure ablution round earth's human shores.
Or gazing on the new soft-fallen mask
   Of snow upon the mountains and the moors –
No – yet still steadfast, still unchangeable,
   Pillow'd upon my fair love's ripening breast,
To feel for ever its soft fall and swell,
   Awake for ever in a sweet unrest,
Still, still to hear her tender-taken breath,
And so live ever – or else swoon to death.

JOHN KEATS

Grief

I tell you, hopeless grief is passionless;
That only men incredulous of despair
Half-taught in anguish, through the midnight air
Beat upward to God's throne in loud access
Of shrieking and reproach. Full desertness
In souls, as countries, lieth silent-bare
Under the blanching, vertical eye-glare
Of the absolute Heavens. Deep-hearted man, express
Grief for thy Dead in silence like to death:
Most like a monumental statue set
In everlasting watch and moveless woe,
Till itself crumble to the dust beneath.
Touch it: the marble eyelids are not wet;
If it could weep, it could arise and go.

ELIZABETH BARRETT BROWNING

When Our Two Souls

When our two souls stand up erect and strong,
Face to face, silent, drawing nigh and nigher,
Until the lengthening wings break into fire
At either curved point, – what bitter wrong
Can the earth do to us, that we should not long
Be here contented ? Think. In mounting higher,
The angels would press on us, and aspire
To drop some golden orb of perfect song
Into our deep dear silence. Let us stay

Rather on earth. Beloved, where the unfit
Contrarious moods of men recoil away
And isolate pure spirits, and permit
A place to stand and love in for a day,
With darkness and the death-hour rounding it.

ELIZABETH BARRETT BROWNING

'How do I love thee? Let me count the ways'

How do I love thee? Let me count the ways.
I love thee to the depth and breadth and height
My soul can reach, when feeling out of sight
For the ends of Being and ideal Grace.
I love thee to the level of every day's
Most quiet need, by sun and candlelight.
I love thee freely, as men strive for Right;
I love thee purely, as they turn from Praise.
I love thee with the passion put to use
In my old griefs, and with my childhood's faith.
I love thee with a love I seemed to lose
With my lost saints, – I love thee with the breath,
Smiles, tears, of all my life! – and, if God choose,
I shall but love thee better after death.

ELIZABETH BARRETT BROWNING

Lord Walter's Wife

'But why do you go?' said the lady, while both sate under the
yew,
And her eyes were alive in their depth, as the kraken beneath
the sea-blue.

'Because I fear you,' he answered; – 'because you are far too
fair,
And able to strangle my soul in a mesh of your
gold-coloured hair.'

'Oh, that,' she said, 'is no reason! Such knots are quickly
undone,
And too much beauty, I reckon, is nothing but too much sun.'

'Yet farewell so,' he answered; – 'the sunstroke 's fatal at
times.
I value your husband, Lord Walter, whose gallop rings still
from the limes.'

'O, that,' she said, 'is no reason. You smell a rose through a
fence:
If two should smell it, what matter? who grumbles, and
where's the pretence?'

'But I,' he replied, 'have promised another, when love was
free,
To love her alone, alone, who alone and afar loves me.'

'Why, that,' she said, 'is no reason. Love's always free, I am
    told.
Will you vow to be safe from the headache on Tuesday, and
    think it will hold?'

'But you,' he replied, 'have a daughter, a young little child,
    who was laid
In your lap to be pure; so I leave you: the angels would make
    me afraid.'

'O, that,' she said, 'is no reason. The angels keep out of the
    way;
And Dora, the child, observes nothing, although you should
    please me and stay.'

At which he rose up in his anger, – 'Why, now, you no longer
    are fair!
Why, now, you no longer are fatal, but ugly and hateful,
    I swear.'

At which she laughed out in her scorn, – 'These men! O, these
    men overnice,
Who are shocked if a colour not virtuous is frankly put on by
    a vice.'

Her eyes blazed upon him – 'And *you*! You bring us your
    vices so near
That we smell them! you think in our presence a thought 't
    would defame us to hear!

'What reason had you, and what right, – I appeal to your
    soul from my life, –
To find me too fair as a woman? Why, sir, I am pure, and a wife.

'Is the day-star too fair up above you? It burns you not. Dare
   you imply
I brushed you more close than the star does, when Walter had
   set me as high?

'If a man finds a woman too fair, he means simply adapted
   too much
To uses unlawful and fatal. The praise! – shall I thank you
   for such?

'Too fair? – not unless you misuse us! and surely if, once in
   a while,
You attain to it, straightway you call us no longer too fair,
   but too vile.

'A moment, – I pray your attention! – I have a poor word in
   my head
I must utter, though womanly custom would set it down
   better unsaid.

'You grew, sir, pale to impertinence, once when I showed you
   a ring.
You kissed my fan when I dropped it. No matter! I've broken
   the thing.

'You did me the honour, perhaps, to be moved at my side
   now and then
In the senses, – a vice, I have heard, which is common to
   beasts and some men

'Love's a virtue for heroes! – as white as the snow on high hills,
And immortal as every great soul is that struggles, endures,
   and fulfils.

'I love my Walter profoundly, – you, Maude, though you
  faltered a week,
For the sake of . . . what was it? an eyebrow? or, less still, a
  mole on a cheek?

'And since, when all's said, you're too noble to stoop to the
  frivolous cant
About crimes irresistible, virtues that swindle, betray, and
  supplant,

'I determined to prove to yourself that, whate'er you might
  dream or avow
By illusion, you wanted precisely no more of me than you
  have now.

'There! Look me full in the face! – in the face. Understand, if
  you can,
That the eyes of such women as I am are clean as the palm of
  a man.

'Drop his hand, you insult him. Avoid us for fear we should
  cost you a scar, –
You take us for harlots, I tell you, and not for the women we
  are.

'You wrong me: but then I consider . . . there's Walter! And so
  at the end,
I vowed that he should not be mulcted, by me, in the hand of
  a friend.

'Have I hurt you indeed? We are quits then. Nay, friend of my
   Walter, be mine!
Come, Dora, my darling, my angel, and help me to ask him
   to dine.'

ELIZABETH BARRETT BROWNING

'Come into the garden, Maud'

Come into the garden, Maud,
   For the black bat, night, has flown,
Come into the garden, Maud,
   I am here at the gate alone;
And the woodbine spices are wafted abroad,
   And the musk of the rose is blown.

For a breeze of morning moves,
   And the planet of Love is on high,
Beginning to faint in the light that she loves
   On a bed of daffodil sky,
To faint in the light of the sun she loves,
   To faint in his light, and to die.

All night have the roses heard
   The flute, violin, bassoon;
All night has the casement jessamine stirred
   To the dancers dancing in tune;
Till a silence fell with the waking bird,
   And a hush with the setting moon.

I said to the lily, 'There is but one
    With whom she has heart to be gay.
When will the dancers leave her alone?
    She is weary of dance and play.'
Now half to the setting moon are gone,
    And half to the rising day;
Low on the sand and loud on the stone
    The last wheel echoes away.

I said to the rose, 'The brief night goes
    In babble and revel and wine.
O young lord-lover, what sighs are those,
    For one that will never be thine?
But mine, but mine,' so I sware to the rose,
    'For ever and ever, mine.'

And the soul of the rose went into my blood,
    As the music clashed in the hall;
And long by the garden lake I stood,
    For I heard your rivulet fall
From the lake to the meadow and on to the wood,
    Our wood, that is dearer than all;

From the meadow your walks have left so sweet
    That whenever a March-wind sighs
He sets the jewel-print of your feet
    In violets blue as your eyes,
To the woody hollows in which we meet
    And the valleys of Paradise.

The slender acacia would not shake
    One long milk-bloom on the tree;
The white lake-blossom fell into the lake

As the pimpernel dozed on the lea;
But the rose was awake all night for your sake,
   Knowing your promise to me;
The lilies and roses were all awake,
   They sighed for the dawn and thee.

Queen rose of the rosebud garden of girls,
   Come hither, the dances are done,
In gloss of satin and glimmer of pearls,
   Queen lily and rose in one;
Shine out, little head, sunning over with curls,
   To the flowers, and be their sun.

There has fallen a splendid tear
   From the passion-flower at the gate.
She is coming, my dove, my dear;
   She is coming, my life, my fate;
The red rose cries, 'She is near, she is near;'
   And the white rose weeps, 'She is late;'
The larkspur listens, 'I hear, I hear;'
   And the lily whispers, 'I wait.'

She is coming, my own, my sweet;
   Were it ever so airy a tread,
My heart would hear her and beat,
   Were it earth in an earthy bed;
My dust would hear her and beat,
   Had I lain for a century dead;
Would start and tremble under her feet,
   And blossom in purple and red.

ALFRED, LORD TENNYSON

The Charge of the Light Brigade

Half a league, half a league,
  Half league onward,
All in the valley of Death
  Rode the six hundred.
'Forward, the Light Brigade!
Charge for the guns!' he said:
Into the valley of Death
  Rode the six hundred.

'Forward, the Light Brigade!'
Was there a man dismay'd?
  Not tho' the soldier knew
Some one had blunder'd:
Their's not to make reply,
Their's not to reason why,
Their's but to do and die:
Into the valley of Death
  Rode the six hundred.

Cannon to right of them,
Cannon to left of them,
Cannon in front of them
  Volley'd and thunder'd;
Storm'd at with shot and shell,
Boldly they rode and well,
Into the jaws of Death,
Into the mouth of Hell
  Rode the six hundred.

Flash'd all their sabres bare,
Flash'd as they turn'd in air
Sabring the gunners there,
Charging an army, while
   All the world wonder'd:
Plunged in the battery-smoke
Right thro' the line they broke;
Cossack and Russian
Reel'd from the sabre-stroke
   Shatter'd and sunder'd.
Then they rode back, but not
   Not the six hundred.

Cannon to right of them,
Cannon to left of them,
Cannon behind them
   Volley'd and thunder'd;
Storm'd at with shot and shell,
While horse and hero fell,
They that had fought so well
Came thro' the jaws of Death,
Back from the mouth of Hell,
All that was left of them,
   Left of six hundred.

When can their glory fade?
O the wild charge they made!
   All the world wonder'd.
Honour the charge they made!
Honour the Light Brigade,
   Noble six hundred!

ALFRED, LORD TENNYSON

Crossing the Bar

Sunset and evening star,
    And one clear call for me!
And may there be no moaning of the bar,
    When I put out to sea,

But such a tide as moving seems asleep,
    Too full for sound and foam,
When that which drew from out the boundless deep
    Turns again home.

Twilight and evening bell,
    And after that the dark!
And may there be no sadness of farewell,
    When I embark;

For tho' from out our bourne of Time and Place
    The flood may bear me far,
I hope to see my Pilot face to face
    When I have crost the bar.

ALFRED, LORD TENNYSON

The Visionary

Silent is the house: all are laid asleep:
One alone looks out o'er the snow-wreaths deep,
Watching every cloud, dreading every breeze
That whirls the wildering drift, and bends the groaning trees.

Cheerful is the hearth, soft the matted floor;
Not one shivering gust creeps through pane or door;
The little lamp burns straight, its rays shoot strong and far:
I trim it well, to be the wanderer's guiding-star.

Frown, my haughty sire! chide, my angry dame;
Set your slaves to spy; threaten me with shame:
But neither sire nor dame, nor prying serf shall know,
What angel nightly tracks that waste of frozen snow.

What I love shall come like visitant of air,
Safe in secret power from lurking human snare;
What loves me, no word of mine shall e'er betray,
Though for faith unstained my life must forfeit pay.

EMILY AND CHARLOTTE BRONTË

Home-Thoughts, from Abroad

Oh, to be in England
Now that April's there,
And whoever wakes in England
Sees, some morning, unaware,
That the lowest boughs and the brushwood sheaf
Round the elm-tree bole are in tiny leaf,
While the chaffinch sings on the orchard bough
In England – now!

And after April, when May follows,
And the whitethroat builds, and all the swallows!
Hark, where my blossomed pear-tree in the hedge
Leans to the field and scatters on the clover
Blossoms and dewdrops – at the bent spray's edge –
That's the wise thrush; he sings each song twice over,
Lest you should think he never could recapture
The first fine careless rapture!
And though the fields look rough with hoary dew,
All will be gay when noontide wakes anew
The buttercups, the little children's dower
– Far brighter than this gaudy melon-flower!

ROBERT BROWNING

Meeting at Night

The grey sea and the long black land;
And the yellow half-moon large and low;
And the startled little waves that leap
In fiery ringlets from their sleep,
As I gain the cove with pushing prow,
And quench its speed in the slushy sand.

Then a mile of warm sea-scented beach;
Three fields to cross till a farm appears;
A tap at the pane, the quick sharp scratch
And blue spurt of a lighted match,
And a voice less loud, thro' its joys and fears,
Than the two hearts beating each to each!

ROBERT BROWNING

Porphyria's Lover

The rain set early in to-night.
　The sullen wind was soon awake,
It tore the elm-tops down for spite,
　And did its worst to vex the lake:
　I listened with heart fit to break.
When glided in Porphyria; straight
　She shut the cold out and the storm,
And kneeled and made the cheerless grate
　Blaze up, and all the cottage warm;
　Which done, she rose, and from her form
Withdrew the dripping cloak and shawl,
　And laid her soiled gloves by, untied
Her hat and let the damp hair fall.
　And, last, she sat down by my side
　And called me. When no voice replied,
She put my arm about her waist.
　And made her smooth white shoulder bare
And all her yellow hair displaced.
　And stooping, made my cheek lie there
　And spread, o'er all, her yellow hair,
Murmuring how she loved me – she
　Too weak, for all her heart's endeavour,
To set its struggling passion free
　From pride, and vainer ties dissever,
　And give herself to me for ever.
But passion sometimes would prevail,
　Nor could to-night's gay feast restrain
A sudden thought of one so pale
　For love of her, and all in Vain :
　So, she was come through wind and rain.

Be sure I looked up at her eyes
   Happy and proud; at last I knew
Porphyria worshipped me; surprise
   Made my heart swell, and still it grew
   While I debated what to do.
That moment she was mine, mine, fair,
   Perfectly pure and good: I found
A thing to do, and all her hair
   In one long yellow string I wound
   Three times her little throat around,
And strangled her. No pain felt she;
   I am quite sure she felt no pain.
As a shut bud that holds the bee,
   I warily oped her lids: again
   Laughed the blue eyes without a stain.
And I untightened next the tress
   About her neck; her cheek once more
Blushed bright beneath my burning kiss.
   I propped her head up as before.
   Only, this time my shoulder bore
Her head, which droops upon it still;
   The smiling rosy little head,
So glad it has its utmost will.
   That all it scorned at once is fled,
   And I, its love, am gained instead!
Porphyria's love: she guessed not how
   Her darling one wish would be heard.
And thus we sit together now,
   And all night long we have not stirred,
   And yet God has not said a word!

ROBERT BROWNING

VII

OUR days WERE
A JOY,
AND OUR PATHS
THROUGH
FLOWERS...

Dover Beach

The sea is calm to-night.
The tide is full, the moon lies fair
Upon the straits; – on the French coast the light
Gleams and is gone; the cliffs of England stand,
Glimmering and vast, out in the tranquil bay.
Come to the window, sweet is the night-air!
Only, from the long line of spray
Where the sea meets the moon-blanch'd land,
Listen! you hear the grating roar
Of pebbles which the waves draw back, and fling,
At their return, up the high strand,
Begin, and cease, and then again begin,
With tremulous cadence slow, and bring
The eternal note of sadness in.

Sophocles long ago
Heard it on the Ægæan, and it brought
Into his mind the turbid ebb and flow
Of human misery; we
Find also in the sound a thought,
Hearing it by this distant northern sea.

The Sea of Faith
Was once, too, at the full, and round earth's shore
Lay like the folds of a bright girdle furl'd.
But now I only hear
Its melancholy, long, withdrawing roar,
Retreating, to the breath
Of the night-wind, down the vast edges drear
And naked shingles of the world.

Ah, love, let us be true
To one another! for the world, which seems
To lie before us like a land of dreams,
So various, so beautiful, so new,
Hath really neither joy, nor love, nor light,
Nor certitude, nor peace, nor help for pain;
And we are here as on a darkling plain
Swept with confused alarms of struggle and flight,
Where ignorant armies clash by night.

MATTHEW ARNOLD

A Christmas Carol

In the bleak mid-winter
   Frosty wind made moan,
Earth stood hard as iron,
   Water like a stone;
Snow had fallen, snow on snow,
   Snow on snow,
In the bleak mid-winter
   Long ago.

Our God, Heaven cannot hold Him
   Nor earth sustain;
Heaven and earth shall flee away
   When He comes to reign:
In the bleak mid-winter
   A stable-place sufficed
The Lord God Almighty
   Jesus Christ.

Enough for Him whom cherubim
  Worship night and day,
A breastful of milk
  And a mangerful of hay;
Enough for Him whom angels
  Fall down before,
The ox and ass and camel
  Which adore.

Angels and archangels
  May have gathered there,
Cherubim and seraphim
  Throng'd the air,
But only His mother
  In her maiden bliss
Worshipped the Beloved
  With a kiss.

What can I give Him,
  Poor as I am?
If I were a shepherd
  I would bring a lamb,
If I were a wise man
  I would do my part, –
Yet what I can I give Him,
  Give my heart.

CHRISTINA ROSSETTI

The Queen of Hearts

How comes it, Flora, that, whenever we
Play cards together, you invariably,
    However the pack parts,
    Still hold the Queen of Hearts?

I've scanned you with a scrutinising gaze,
Resolved to fathom these your secret ways:
    But, sift them as I will,
    Your ways are secret still.

I cut and shuffle; shuffle, cut, again;
But all my cutting, shuffling, proves in vain:
    Vain hope, vain forethought too;
    That Queen still falls to you.

I dropped her once, prepense; but, ere the deal
Was dealt, your instinct seemed her loss to feel:
    'There should be one card more,'
    You said, and searched the floor.

I cheated once; I made a private notch
In Heart-Queen's back, and kept a lynx-eyed watch;
    Yet such another back
    Deceived me in the pack:

The Queen of Clubs assumed by arts unknown
An imitative dint that seemed my own;
    This notch, not of my doing,
    Misled me to my ruin.

It baffles me to puzzle out the clue,
Which must be skill, or craft, or luck in you:
  Unless, indeed, it be
  Natural affinity.

CHRISTINA ROSSETTI

The Railway Bridge of the Silvery Tay

Beautiful Railway Bridge of the Silvery Tay!
With your numerous arches and pillars in so grand array,
And your central girders, which seem to the eye
To be almost towering to the sky.
The greatest wonder of the day,
And a great beautification to the River Tay,
Most beautiful to be seen,
Near by Dundee and the Magdalen Green.

Beautiful Railway Bridge of the Silvery Tay!
That has caused the Emperor of Brazil to leave
His home far away, *incognito* in his dress,
And view thee ere he passed along *en route* to Inverness.

Beautiful Railway Bridge of the Silvery Tay!
The longest of the present day
That has ever crossed o'er a tidal river stream,
Most gigantic to be seen,
Near by Dundee and the Magdalen Green.

Beautiful Railway Bridge of the Silvery Tay!
Which will cause great rejoicing on the opening day,
And hundreds of people will come from far away,
Also the Queen, most gorgeous to be seen,
Near by Dundee and the Magdalen Green.

Beautiful Railway Bridge of the Silvery Tay!
And prosperity to Provost Cox, who has given
Thirty thousand pounds and upwards away
In helping to erect the Bridge of the Tay,
Most handsome to be seen,
Near by Dundee and the Magdalen Green.

Beautiful Railway Bridge of the Silvery Tay!
I hope that God will protect all passengers
By night and by day,
And that no accident will befall them while crossing
The Bridge of the Silvery Tay,
For that would be most awful to be seen
Near by Dundee and the Magdalen Green.

Beautiful Railway Bridge of the Silvery Tay!
And prosperity to Messrs Bouche and Grothe,
The famous engineers of the present day,
Who have succeeded in erecting the Railway
Bridge of the Silvery Tay,
Which stands unequalled to be seen
Near by Dundee and the Magdalen Green.

WILLIAM MCGONAGALL

A Scherzo (a Shy Person's Wishes)

With the wasp at the innermost heart of a peach,
On a sunny wall out of tip-toe reach,
With the trout in the darkest summer pool,
With the fern-seed clinging behind its cool
Smooth frond, in the chink of an aged tree,
In the woodbine's horn with the drunken bee,
With the mouse in its nest in a furrow old,
With the chrysalis wrapt in its gauzy fold;
With things that are hidden, and safe, and bold,
With things that are timid, and shy, and free,
Wishing to be;
With the nut in its shell, with the seed in its pod,
With the corn as it sprouts in the kindly clod,
Far down where the secret of beauty shows
In the bulb of the tulip, before it blows;
With things that are rooted, and firm, and deep,
Quiet to lie, and dreamless to sleep;
With things that are chainless, and tameless, and proud,
With the fire in the jagged thunder-cloud,
With the wind in its sleep, with the wind in its waking,
With the drops that go to the rainbow's making,
Wishing to be with the light leaves shaking,
Or stones on some desolate highway breaking;
Far up on the lulls, where no foot surprises
The dew as it falls, or the dust as it rises;
To be couched with the beast in its torrid lair,

Or drifting on ice with the polar bear,
With the weaver at work at his quiet loom;
Anywhere, anywhere, out of this room!

DORA GREENWELL

Seven Times One: Exultation

There's no dew left on the daisies and clover,
There's no rain left in heaven:
I've said my 'seven times' over and over,
Seven times one are seven.

I am old, so old, I can write a letter;
My birthday lessons are done;
The lambs play always, they know no better;
They are only one times one.

O moon! in the night I have seen you sailing
And shining so round and low;
You were bright! ah bright! but your light is failing –
You are nothing now but a bow.

You moon, have you done something wrong in heaven
That God has hidden your face?
I hope if you have you will soon be forgiven,
And shine again in your place.

O velvet bee, you're a dusty fellow,
You've powdered your legs with gold!
O brave marsh marybuds, rich and yellow,
Give me your money to hold!

O columbine, open your folded wrapper,
Where two twin turtle-doves dwell!
O cuckoopint, toll me the purple clapper
That hangs in your clear green bell!

And show me your nest with the young ones in it;
I will not steal them away;
I am old! you may trust me, linnet, linnet –
I am seven times one today.

JEAN INGELOW

The Owl and the Pussy-Cat

The Owl and the Pussy-Cat went to sea
    In a beautiful pea-green boat.
They took some honey, and plenty of money,
    Wrapped up in a five-pound note.
The Owl looked up to the stars above,
    And sang to a small guitar,
'O lovely Pussy! O Pussy, my love,
    What a beautiful Pussy you are,
            You are,
            You are!
What a beautiful Pussy you are!'

Pussy said to the Owl, 'You elegant fowl!
   How charmingly sweet you sing!
O let us be married! too long we have tarried:
   But what shall we do for a ring?'
They sailed away, for a year and a day,
   To the land where the Bong-Tree grows,
And there in a wood a Piggy-wig stood,
   With a ring at the end of his nose,
         His nose,
         His nose,
   With a ring at the end of his nose.

'Dear Pig, are you willing to sell for one shilling
   Your ring?' Said the Piggy, 'I will.'
So they took it away, and were married next day
   By the Turkey who lives on the hill.
They dinèd on mince, and slices of quince,
   Which they ate with a runcible spoon;
And hand in hand, on the edge of the sand,
   They danced by the light of the moon,
         The moon,
         The moon,
   They danced by the light of the moon.

EDWARD LEAR

The Akond of Swat

Who or why, or which, or what,
                    Is the Akond of SWAT?

Is he tall or short, or dark or fair?
Does he sit on a stool or a sofa or chair,   or SQUAT,
                    The Akond of Swat?

Is he wise or foolish, young or old?
Does he drink his soup and his coffee cold,   or HOT,
                    The Akond of Swat?

Does he sing or whistle, jabber or talk,
And when riding abroad does he gallop or walk,   or TROT,
                    The Akond of Swat?

Does he wear a turban, a fez, or a hat?
Does he sleep on a mattress, a bed, or a mat,   or a COT,
                    The Akond of Swat?

When he writes a copy in round-hand size,
Does he cross his T's and finish his I's   with a DOT,
                    The Akond of Swat?

Can he write a letter concisely clear
Without a speck or a smudge or smear   or BLOT,
                    The Akond of Swat?

Do his people like him extremely well?
Or do they, whenever they can, rebel,   or PLOT,
                    At the Akond of Swat?

If he catches them then, either old or young,
Does he have them chopped in pieces or hung,   or SHOT,
                    The Akond of Swat?

Do his people prig in the lanes or park?
Or even at times, when days are dark,   GAROTTE?
                        O the Akond of Swat?

Does he study the wants of his own dominion?
Or doesn't he care for public opinion   a JOT,
                    The Akond of Swat?

To amuse his mind do his people show him
Pictures,   or any one's last new poem,   or WHAT,
                    For the Akond of Swat?

At night if he suddenly screams and wakes,
Do they bring him only a few small cakes,   or a LOT,
                    For the Akond of Swat?

Does he live on turnips, tea, or tripe?
Does he like his shawl to be marked with a stripe,   or a DOT,
                    The Akond of Swat?

Does he like to he on his back in a boat
Like the lady who lived in that isle remote,   SHALLOTT,
                    The Akond of Swat?

Is he quiet,   or always making a fuss?
Is his steward a Swiss or a Swede or a Russ,   or a SCOT,
                    The Akond of Swat?

Does he like to sit by the calm blue wave?
Or to sleep and snore in a dark green cave,   or a GROTT,
                    The Akond of Swat?

Does he drink small beer from a silver jug?
Or a bowl? or a glass? or a cup? or a mug?   or a POT,
                    The Akond of Swat?

Does he beat his wife with a gold-topped pipe,
When she lets the gooseberries grow too ripe,   or ROT,
                    The Akond of Swat?

Does he wear a white tie when he dines with friends,
And tie it neat in a bow with ends,   or a KNOT,
                    The Akond of Swat?

Does he like new cream, and hate mince-pies?
When he looks at the sun does he wink his eyes,   or NOT,
                    The Akond of Swat?

Does he teach his subjects to roast and bake?
Does he sail about on an inland lake, in   a YACHT,
                    The Akond of Swat?

Some one, or nobody, knows I wot
Who or which or why or what
                    Is the Akond of Swat!

EDWARD LEAR

The Walrus and the Carpenter

The sun was shining on the sea,
    Shining with all his might:
He did his very best to make
    The billows smooth and bright –
And this was odd, because it was
    The middle of the night.

The moon was shining sulkily,
    Because she thought the sun
Had got no business to be there
    After the day was done –
'It's very rude of him,' she said,
    'To come and spoil the fun.'

The sea was wet as wet could be,
    The sands were dry as dry.
You could not see a cloud, because
    No cloud was in the sky:
No birds were flying overhead –
    There were no birds to fly.

The Walrus and the Carpenter
    Were walking close at hand;
They wept like anything to see
    Such quantities of sand:
'If this were only cleared away,'
    They said, 'it *would* be grand.'

'If seven maids with seven mops
    Swept it for half a year,

Do you suppose,' the Walrus said,
　'That they could get it clear?'
'I doubt it,' said the Carpenter,
　And shed a bitter tear.

'O Oysters, come and walk with us!'
　The Walrus did beseech.
'A pleasant walk, a pleasant talk,
　Along the briny beach:
We cannot do with more than four,
　To give a hand to each.'

The eldest Oyster looked at him,
　But never a word he said:
The eldest Oyster winked his eye,
　And shook his heavy head –
Meaning to say he did not choose
　To leave the oyster-bed.

But four young Oysters hurried up,
　All eager for the treat;
Their coats were brushed, their faces washed,
　Their shoes were clean and neat –
And this was odd, because, you know,
　They hadn't any feet.

Four other Oysters followed them,
　And yet another four;
And thick and fast they came at last,
　And more, and more, and more –
All hopping through the frothy waves,
　And scrambling to the shore.

The Walrus and the Carpenter
  Walked on a mile or so,
And then they rested on a rock
  Conveniently low:
And all the little Oysters stood
  And waited in a row.

'The time has come,' the Walrus said,
  'To talk of many things:
Of shoes – and ships – and sealing-wax –
  Of cabbages – and kings –
And why the sea is boiling hot –
  And whether pigs have wings.'

'But wait a bit,' the Oysters cried,
  'Before we have our chat;
For some of us are out of breath,
  And all of us are fat!'
'No hurry!' said the Carpenter.
  They thanked him much for that.

'A loaf of bread,' the Walrus said,
  'Is what we chiefly need:
Pepper and vinegar besides
  Are very good indeed –
Now if you're ready, Oysters dear,
  We can begin to feed.'

'But not on us!' the Oysters cried,
  Turning a little blue.
'After such kindness, that would be

A dismal thing to do!'
'The night is fine,' the Walrus said.
   'Do you admire the view?

'It was so kind of you to come!
   And you are very nice!'
The Carpenter said nothing but
   'Cut us another slice:
I wish you were not quite so deaf –
   I've had to ask you twice!'

'It seems a shame,' the Walrus said,
   'To play them such a trick,
After we've brought them out so far,
   And made them trot so quick!'
The Carpenter said nothing but
   'The butter's spread too thick!'

'I weep for you,' the Walrus said:
   'I deeply sympathise.'
With sobs and tears he sorted out
   Those of the largest size,
Holding his pocket-handkerchief
   Before his streaming eyes.

'O Oysters,' said the Carpenter,
   'You've had a pleasant run!
Shall we be trotting home again?'
   But answer came there none –
And this was scarcely odd, because
   They'd eaten every one.

LEWIS CARROLL

Proud Songsters

The thrushes sing as the sun is going,
And the finches whistle in ones and pairs,
And as it gets dark loud nightingales
      In bushes
Pipe, as they can when April wears,
  As if all Time were theirs.

These are brand-new birds of twelve-months' growing,
Which a year ago, or less than twain,
No finches were, nor nightingales,
      Nor thrushes,
But only particles of grain,
  And earth, and air, and rain.

THOMAS HARDY

After a Journey

Hereto I come to view a voiceless ghost;
  Whither, O whither will its whim now draw me?
Up the cliff, down, till I'm lonely, lost,
  And the unseen waters' ejaculations awe me.
Where you will next be there's no knowing,
  Facing round about me everywhere,
    With your nut-coloured hair,
And grey eyes, and rose-flush coming and going.

Yes: I have re-entered your olden haunts at last;
   Through the years, through the dead scenes I have tracked
      you;
What have you now found to say of our past –
   Scanned across the dark space wherein I have lacked you?
Summer gave us sweets, but autumn wrought division?
   Things were not lastly as firstly well
     With us twain, you tell?
But all's closed now, despite Time's derision.

I see what you are doing: you are leading me on
   To spots we knew when we haunted here together,
The waterfall, above which the mist-bow shone
   At the then fair hour in the then fair weather,
And the cave just under, with a voice still so hollow
   That it seems to call out to me from forty years ago,
     When you were all aglow,
And not the thin ghost that I now frailly follow!

Ignorant of what there is flitting here to see,
   The waked birds preen and the seals flop lazily,
Soon you will have, Dear, to vanish from me,
   For the stars close their shutters and the dawn whitens
     hazily.
Trust me, I mind not, though Life lours,
   The bringing me here; nay, bring me here again!
     I am just the same as when
Our days were a joy, and our paths through flowers.

THOMAS HARDY

Neutral Tones

We stood by a pond that winter day,
And the sun was white, as though chidden of God,
And a few leaves lay on the starving sod;
   – They had fallen from an ash, and were grey.

Your eyes on me were as eyes that rove
Over tedious riddles of years ago;
And some words played between us to and fro
   On which lost the more by our love.

The smile on your mouth was the deadest thing
Alive enough to have strength to die;
And a grin of bitterness swept thereby
   Like an ominous bird a-wing . . .

Since then, keen lessons that love deceives,
And wrings with wrong, have shaped to me
Your face, and the God-curst sun, and a tree
   And a pond edged with greyish leaves.

THOMAS HARDY

The Convergence of the Twain

Lines on the loss of the Titanic

I

In a solitude of the sea
Deep from human vanity,
And the Pride of Life that planned her, stilly couches she.

II

Steel chambers, late the pyres
Of her salamandrine fires,
Cold currents thrid, and turn to rhythmic tidal lyres.

III

Over the mirrors meant
To glass the opulent
The sea-worm crawls – grotesque, slimed, dumb, indifferent.

IV

Jewels in joy designed
To ravish the sensuous mind
Lie lightless, all their sparkles bleared and black and blind.

V

Dim moon-eyed fishes near
Gaze at the gilded gear
And query: 'What does this vaingloriousness down here?' . . .

VI

Well: while was fashioning
This creature of cleaving wing,
The Immanent Will that stirs and urges everything

VII

Prepared a sinister mate
For her – so gaily great –
A Shape of Ice, for the time far and dissociate.

VIII

And as the smart ship grew
In stature, grace, and hue,
In shadowy silent distance grew the Iceberg too.

IX

Alien they seemed to be:
No morttal eye could see
The intimate welding of their later history,

X

Or sign that they were bent
By paths coincident
On being anon twin halves of one august event,

XI

Till the Spinner of the Years
Said 'Now!' And each one hears,
And consummation comes, and jars two hemispheres.

THOMAS HARDY

Felix Randal

Felix Randal the farrier, O is he dead then? my duty all
  ended,
Who have watched his mould of man, big-boned and hardy-
  handsome
Pining, pining, till time when reason rambled in it and some
Fatal four disorders, fleshed there, all contended?

Sickness broke him. Impatient, he cursed at first, but mended
Being anointed and all; though a heavenlier heart began some
Months earlier, since I had our sweet reprieve and ransom
Tendered to him. Ah well, God rest him all road ever he
  offended!

This seeing the sick endears them to us, us too it endears.
My tongue had taught thee comfort, touch had quenched thy
  tears,
Thy tears that touched my heart, child, Felix, poor Felix
  Randal;

How far from then forethought of, all thy more boisterous
  years,
When thou at the random grim forge, powerful amidst peers,
Didst fettle for the great grey drayhorse his bright and
  battering sandal!

GERARD MANLEY HOPKINS

God's Grandeur

The world is charged with the grandeur of God.
  It will flame out, like shining from shook foil;
  It gathers to a greatness, like the ooze of oil
Crushed. Why do men then now not reck his rod?
Generations have trod, have trod, have trod;
  And all is seared with trade; bleared, smeared with toil;
  And wears man's smudge and shares man's smell: the soil
Is bare now, nor can foot feel, being shod.

And for all this, nature is never spent;
  There lives the dearest freshness deep down things;
And though the last lights off the black West went
  Oh, morning, at the brown brink eastward, springs –
Because the Holy Ghost over the bent
  World broods with warm breast and with ah! bright wings.

GERARD MANLEY HOPKINS

Hurrahing in Harvest

Summer ends now; now, barbarous in beauty, the stooks arise
    Around; up above, what wind-walks! what lovely behaviour
    Of silk-sack clouds! has wilder, wilful-wavier
Meal-drift moulded ever and melted across skies?

I walk, I lift up, I lift up heart, eyes,
    Down all that glory in the heavens to glean our Saviour;
    And éyes, héart, what looks, what lips yet gave you a
Rapturous love's greeting of realer, of rounder replies?

And the azurous hung hills are his world-wielding shoulder
    Majestic – as a stallion stalwart, very-violet-sweet!
These things, these things were here and but the beholder
    Wanting: which two when they once meet,
The heart rears wings bold and bolder
    And hurls for him, O half hurls earth for him off under his
      feet.

GERARD MANLEY HOPKINS

The Sea and the Skylark

On ear and ear two noises too old to end
    Trench – right, the tide that ramps against the shore;
    With a flood or a fall, low lull-off or all roar,
Frequenting there while moon shall wear and wend.

Left hand, off land, I hear the lark ascend,
  His rash-fresh re-winded new-skeinèd score
  In crisps of curl off wild winch whirl, and pour
And pelt music, till none's to spill nor spend.

How these two shame this shallow and frail town!
  How ring right out our sordid turbid time,
Being pure! We, life's pride and cared-for crown,

  Have lost that cheer and charm of earth's past prime:
Our make and making break, are breaking, down
  To man's last dust, drain fast towards man's first slime.

GERARD MANLEY HOPKINS

'I wake and feel the fell of dark, not day'

I wake and feel the fell of dark, not day.
What hours, O what black hoürs we have spent
This night! what sights you, heart, saw; ways you went!
And more must, in yet longer light's delay.
  With witness I speak this. But where I say
Hours I mean years, mean life. And my lament
Is cries countless, cries like dead letters sent
To dearest him that lives alas! away.

I am gall, I am heartburn. God's most deep decree
Bitter would have me taste: my taste was me;
Bones built in me, flesh filled, blood brimmed the curse.
    Selfyeast of spirit a dull dough sours. I see
The lost are like this, and their scourge to be
As I am mine, their sweating selves; but worse.

GERARD MANLEY HOPKINS

London Snow

When men were all asleep the snow came flying,
In large white flakes falling on the city brown,
Stealthily and perpetually settling and loosely lying,
    Hushing the latest traffic of the drowsy town;
Deadening, muffling, stifling its murmurs failing;
Lazily and incessantly floating down and down:
    Silently sifting and veiling road, roof and railing;
Hiding difference, making unevenness even,
Into angles and crevices softly drifting and sailing.
    All night it fell, and when full inches seven
It lay in the depth of its uncompacted lightness,
The clouds blew off from a high and frosty heaven;
    And all woke earlier for the unaccustomed brightness
Of the winter dawning, the strange unheavenly glare:
The eye marvelled – marvelled at the dazzling whiteness;
    The ear hearkened to the stillness of the solemn air;
No sound of wheel rumbling nor of foot falling,
And the busy morning cries came thin and spare.
    Then boys I heard, as they went to school, calling,

They gathered up the crystal manna to freeze
Their tongues with tasting, their hands with snowballing;
    Or rioted in a drift, plunging up to the knees;
Or peering up from under the white-mossed wonder,
'O look at the trees!' they cried, 'O look at the trees!'

    With lessened load a few carts creak and blunder,
Following along the white deserted way,
A country company long dispersed asunder:
    When now already the sun, in pale display
Standing by Paul's high dome, spread forth below
His sparkling beams, and awoke the stir of the day.

    For now doors open, and war is waged with the snow;
And trains of sombre men, past tale of number,
Tread long brown paths, as toward their toil they go:
    But even for them awhile no cares encumber
Their minds diverted; the daily word is unspoken,
The daily thoughts of labour and sorrow slumber
At the sight of the beauty that greets them, for the charm
    they have broken.

ROBERT BRIDGES

On a Dead Child

Perfect little body, without fault or stain on thee,
With promise of strength and manhood full and fair!
    Though cold and stark and bare,
The bloom and the charm of life doth awhile remain on thee

Thy mother's treasure wert thou; – alas! no longer
To visit her heart with wondrous joy; to be

Thy father's pride; – ah, he
Must gather his faith together, and his strength make stronger,

To me, as I move thee now in the last duty,
Dost thou with a turn or gesture anon respond;
    Startling my fancy fond
With a chance attitude of the head, a freak of beauty.

Thy hand clasps, as 'twas wont, my finger, and holds it:
But the grasp is the clasp of Death, heartbreaking and stiff;
    Yet feels to my hand as if
'Twas still thy will, thy pleasure and trust that enfolds it.

So I lay thee there, thy sunken eyelids closing, –
Go lie thou there in thy coffin, thy last little bed! –
    Propping thy wise, sad head,
Thy firm, pale hands across thy chest disposing.

So quiet! doth the change content thee? – Death, whither hath
        he taken thee?
To a world, do I think, that rights the disaster of this?
    The vision of which I miss,
Who weep for the body, and wish but to warm thee
        and awaken thee?

Ah! little at best can all our hopes avail us
To lift this sorrow, or cheer us, when in the dark,
    Unwilling, alone we embark,
And the things we have seen and have known and have heard
        of, fail us.

ROBERT BRIDGES

Manly Sports

How brave is the hunter who nobly will dare
On horseback to follow the small timid hare;
Oh! ye soldiers who fall in defence of your flag,
What are you to the hero who brings down the stag?

Bright eyes glance admiring, soft hearts give their loves
To the knight who shoots best in 'the tourney of doves';
Nothing else with such slaughtering feats can compare,
To win manly applause, or the smiles of the fair.

A cheer for fox-hunting! Come all who can dare
Track this dangerous animal down to its lair;
'Tis first trapped, then set free for the huntsmen to follow
With horses and hounds, and with heartstirring halloo!

The brave knights on the moor when the grouse are a-drive,
Slay so many, you'd think, there'd be none left alive;
Oh! the desperate daring of slaughtering grouse,
Can only be matched in a real slaughterhouse.

The angler finds true Anglo-Saxon delight,
In trapping small fish, who so foolishly bite,
He enjoys the wild terror of creatures so weak,
And what manlier pleasures can any one seek?

MARION BERNSTEIN

The Lady Poverty

The Lady Poverty was fair:
But she has lost her looks of late,
With change of times and change of air.
Ah slattern ! she neglects her hair,
Her gown, her shoes; she keeps no state
As once when her pure feet were bare.

Or – almost worse, if worse can be –
She scolds in parlours, dusts and trims,
Watches and counts. Oh, is this she
Whom Francis met, whose step was free,
Who with Obedience carolled hymns,
In Umbria walked with Chastity?

Where is her ladyhood? Not here,
Not among modern kinds of men;
But in the stony fields, where clear
Through the thin trees the skies appear,
In delicate spate soil and fen,
And slender landscape and austere.

ALICE MEYNELL

'She was poor, but she was honest'

She was poor, but she was honest,
Victim of the squire's whim:
First he loved her, then he left her,
And she lost her honest name.

Then she ran away to London,
For to hide her grief and shame;
There she met another squire,
And she lost her name again.

See her riding in her carriage,
In the Park and all so gay:
All the nibs and nobby persons
Come to pass the time of day.

See the little old-world village
Where her aged parents live,
Drinking the champagne she sends them;
But they never can forgive.

In the rich man's arms she flutters,
Like a bird with broken wing:
First he loved her, then he left her,
And she hasn't got a ring.

See him in the splendid mansion,
Entertaining with the best,
While the girl that he has ruined,
Entertains a sordid guest.

See him in the House of Commons,
Making laws to put down crime,
While the victim of his passions
Trails her way through mud and slime.

Standing on the bridge at midnight,
She says; 'Farewell, blighted Love.'
There's a scream, a splash – Good Heavens!
What is she a-doing of?

Then they drag her from the river,
Water from her clothes they wrang,
For they thought that she was drownded;
But the corpse got up and sang:

'It's the same the whole world over;
It's the poor that gets the blame,
It's the rich that gets the pleasure.
Isn't it a blooming shame?'

ANON

The Woman of Llyn y Fan's Call to Her Cattle

Spotted cow that's light and freckled,
Dotted cow with white bespeckled,
Mottled cow so brightly deckled
　　Plod homewards now.

Kerry sheep long held in fold,
Merry sheep dong-belled with gold,
Fairy sheep song-spelled of old,
    Drift homewards now.

Goat on high that's dry of coat,
Goat with eye so sly to note,
Goat whose cry is wry in throat,
    Skip homewards now.

Horses tall and gay and bobtailed,
Horses small and bay and lobtailed,
Horses all, though grey and hobnailed,
    Clop homewards now.

ANON
translated from the Welsh by Gwyn Jones

Sonnet Found in a Deserted Mad-House

Oh that my soul a marrow-bone might seize!
For the old egg of my desire is broken,
Spilled is the pearly white and spilled the yolk, and
As the mild melancholy contents grease
My path the shorn lamb baas like bumblebees.
Time's trashy purse is as a taken token
Or like a thrilling recitation, spoken
By mournful mouths filled full of mirth and cheese.

And yet, why should I clasp the earthful urn?
Or find the frittered fig that felt the fast?
Or choose to chase the cheese around the churn?
Or swallow any pill from out the past?
Ah, no Love, not while your hot kisses burn
Like a potato riding on the blast.

ANON

Symphony in Yellow

An omnibus across the bridge
   Crawls like a yellow butterfly,
   And, here and there, a passer-by
Shows like a little restless midge.

Big barges full of yellow hay
   Are moored against the shadowy wharf,
   And, like a yellow silken scarf,
The thick fog hangs along the quay.

The yellow leaves begin to fade
   And flutter from the Temple elms,
   And at my feet the pale green Thames
Lies like a rod of rippled jade.

OSCAR WILDE

The Motor Bus

What is this that roareth thus?
Can it be a Motor Bus?
Yes, the swell and hideous hum
Indicat Motorem Bum!
Implet in the Corn and High
Terror me Motoris Bi:
Bo Motori clamitabo
Ne Motore caeder a Bo –
Dative be or Ablative
So thou only let us live:
Whither shall thy victims flee?
Spare us, spare us, Motor Be!
Thus I sang; and still anigh
Came in hordes Motores Bi,
Et complebat omne forum
Copia Motorum Borum.
How shall wretches live like us
Cincti Bis Motoribus?
Domine, defende nos
Contra nos Motores Bos!

A. D. GODLEY

Soliloquy of a Maiden Aunt

The ladies bow, and partners set,
And turn around and pirouette
        And trip the Lancers.

But no one seeks my ample chair,
Or asks me with persuasive air
        To join the dancers.

They greet me, as I sit alone
Upon my solitary throne,
        And pass politely.

Yet mine could keep the measured beat,
As surely as the youngest feet,
        And tread as lightly.

No other maiden had my skill,
In our old homestead on the hill –
        That merry May-time

When Allan closed the flagging ball,
And danced with me before them all,
        Until the day-time.

Again I laugh, and step alone,
And curtsey low as on my own
        His strong hand closes.

But Allan now seeks staid delight,
His son there, brought my niece to-night
       These early roses.

Time orders well, we have our Spring,
Our songs, and may-flower gathering,
       Our love and laughter.

And children chatter all the while,
And leap the brook and climb the stile
       And follow after.

And yet – the step of Allan's son,
Is not as light as was the one
       That went before it.

And that old lace, I think, falls down
Less softly on Priscilla's gown
       Than when I wore it.

DOLLIE RADFORD

'When first my way to fair I took'

When first my way to fair I took
  Few pence in purse had I,
And long I used to stand and look
  At things I could not buy.

Now times are altered: if I care
    To buy a thing, I can;
The pence are here and here's the fair,
    But where's the lost young man?

– To think that two and two are four
    And neither five nor three
The heart of man has long been sore
    And long 'tis like to be.

             A. E. HOUSMAN

'Here dead lie we because we did not choose'

Here dead lie we because we did not choose
    To live and shame the land from which we sprung.
Life, to be sure, is nothing much to lose;
    But young men think it is, and we were young.

             A. E. HOUSMAN

Tam i' the Kirk

O Jean, my Jean, when the bell ca's the congregation
Owre valley an' hill wi' the ding frae its iron mou',
When a'body's thochts is set on his ain salvation,
    Mine's set on you.

There's a reid rose lies on the Buik o' the Word 'afore ye
That was growin' braw on its bush at the keek o' day,
But the lad that pu'd yon flower i' the mornin's glory,
   He canna pray.

He canna pray; but there's nane i' the kirk will heed him
Whaur he sits sae still his lane at the side o' the wa',
For nane but the reid rose kens what my lassie gied him –
   It an' us twa!

He canna sing for the sang that his ain he'rt raises,
He canna see for the mist that's afore his e'en,
And a voice drouns the hale o' the psalms an' the paraphrases,
   Cryin' 'Jean! Jean! Jean!'

VIOLET JACOB

The Way Through the Woods

They shut the road through the woods
   Seventy years ago.
Weather and rain have undone it again,
   And now you would never know
There was once a road through the woods
   Before they planted the trees.
It is underneath the coppice and heath,
   And the thin anemones.
   Only the keeper sees
That, where the ring-dove broods,
   And the badgers roll at ease,
There was once a road through the woods.

Yet, if you enter the woods
    Of a summer evening late,
When the night-air cools on the trout-ringed pools
    Where the otter whistles his mate
(They fear not men in the woods,
    Because they see so few)
You will hear the beat of a horse's feet
    And the swish of a skirt in the dew,
    Steadily cantering through
The misty solitudes,
    As though they perfectly knew
The old lost road through the woods. . . .
But there is no road through the woods.

RUDYARD KIPLING

VIII

1900–1918

ALL THE BIRDS OF OXFORDSHIRE AND GLOUCESTERSHIRE...

The Wild Swans at Coole

The trees are in their autumn beauty,
The woodland paths are dry,
Under the October twilight the water
Mirrors a still sky;
Upon the brimming water among the stones
Are nine-and-fifty swans.

The nineteenth autumn has come upon me
Since I first made my count;
I saw, before I had well finished,
All suddenly mount
And scatter wheeling in great broken rings
Upon their clamorous wings.

I have looked upon those brilliant creatures,
And now my heart is sore.
All's changed since I, hearing at twilight,
The first time on this shore,
The bell-beat of their wings above my head,
Trod with a lighter tread.

Unwearied still, lover by lover,
They paddle in the cold
Companionable streams or climb the air;
Their hearts have not grown old;
Passion or conquest, wander where they will,
Attend upon them still.

But now they drift on the still water,
Mysterious, beautiful;
Among what rushes will they build,
By what lake's edge or pool
Delight men's eyes when I awake some day
To find they have flown away?

W. B. YEATS

The Song of Wandering Aengus

I went out to the hazel wood,
Because a fire was in my head,
And cut and peeled a hazel wand,
And hooked a berry to a thread;
And when white moths were on the wing,
And moth-like stars were flickering out,
I dropped the berry in a stream
And caught a little silver trout.

When I had laid it on the floor
I went to blow the fire aflame,
But something rustled on the floor,
And some one called me by my name:
It had become a glimmering girl
With apple blossom in her hair
Who called me by my name and ran
And faded through the brightening air.

Though I am old with wandering
Through hollow lands and hilly lands,
I will find out where she has gone,
And kiss her lips and take her hands;
And walk among long dappled grass,
And pluck till time and times are done
The silver apples of the moon,
The golden apples of the sun.

W. B. YEATS

No Second Troy

Why should I blame her that she filled my days
With misery, or that she would of late
Have taught to ignorant men most violent ways,
Or hurled the little streets upon the great,
Had they but courage equal to desire?
What could have made her peaceful with a mind
That nobleness made simple as a fire,
With beauty like a tightened bow, a kind
That is not natural in an age like this,
Being high and solitary and most stern?
Why, what could she have done, being what she is?
Was there another Troy for her to burn?

W. B. YEATS

Easter, 1916

I have met them at close of day
Coming with vivid faces
From counter or desk among grey
Eighteenth-century houses.
I have passed with a nod of the head
Or polite meaningless words,
Or have lingered awhile and said
Polite meaningless words,
And thought before I had done
Of a mocking tale or a gibe
To please a companion
Around the fire at the club,
Being certain that they and I
But lived where motley is worn:
All changed, changed utterly:
A terrible beauty is born.

That woman's days were spent
In ignorant good-will,
Her nights in argument
Until her voice grew shrill.
What voice more sweet than hers
When, young and beautiful,
She rode to harriers?
This man had kept a school
And rode our wingèd horse;
This other his helper and friend
Was coming into his force;
He might have won fame in the end,
So sensitive his nature seemed,

So daring and sweet his thought.
This other man I had dreamed
A drunken, vainglorious lout.
He had done most bitter wrong
To some who are near my heart,
Yet I number him in the song;
He, too, has resigned his part
In the casual comedy;
He, too, has been changed in his turn,
Transformed utterly:
A terrible beauty is born.

Hearts with one purpose alone
Through summer and winter seem
Enchanted to a stone
To trouble the living stream.
The horse that comes from the road,
The rider, the birds that range
From cloud to tumbling cloud,
Minute by minute they change;
A shadow of cloud on the stream
Changes minute by minute;
A horse-hoof slides on the brim,
And a horse plashes within it;
The long-legged moor-hens dive,
And hens to moor-cocks call;
Minute by minute they live:
The stone's in the midst of all.

Too long a sacrifice
Can make a stone of the heart.
O when may it suffice?
That is Heaven's part, our part

To murmur name upon name,
As a mother names her child
When sleep at last has come
On limbs that had run wild.
What is it but nightfall?
No, no, not night but death;
Was it needless death after all?
For England may keep faith
For all that is done and said.
We know their dream; enough
To know they dreamed and are dead;
And what if excess of love
Bewildered them till they died?
I write it out in a verse –
MacDonagh and MacBride
And Connolly and Pearse
Now and in time to be,
Wherever green is worn,
Are changed, changed utterly:
A terrible beauty is born.

W. B. YEATS

An Irish Airman Foresees his Death

I know that I shall meet my fate
Somewhere among the clouds above;
Those that I fight I do not hate,
Those that I guard I do not love;
My country is Kiltartan Cross,
My countrymen Kiltartan's poor,

No likely end could bring them loss
Or leave them happier than before.
Nor law, nor duty bade me fight,
Nor public men, nor cheering crowds,
A lonely impulse of delight
Drove to this tumult in the clouds;
I balanced all, brought all to mind,
The years to come seemed waste of breath,
A waste of breath the years behind
In balance with this life, this death.

W. B. YEATS

The Farmer's Bride

Three Summers since I chose a maid,
Too young maybe – but more's to do
At harvest-time than bide and woo.
   When us was wed she turned afraid
Of love and me and all things human;
Like the shut of a winter's day.
Her smile went out, and 'twasn't a woman –
   More like a little frightened fay.
      One night, in the Fall, she runned away.

'Out 'mong the sheep, her be,' they said,
'Should properly have been abed;
But sure enough she wasn't there
Lying awake with her wide brown stare.

So over seven-acre field and up-along across the down
    We chased her, flying like a hare
    Before our lanterns. To Church-Town
        All in a shiver and a scare
    We caught her, fetched her home at last
        And turned the key upon her, fast.

She does the work about the house
As well as most, but like a mouse:
    Happy enough to chat and play
    With birds and rabbits and such as they,
    So long as men-folk keep away.
'Not near, not near!' her eyes beseech
When one of us comes within reach.
    The women say that beasts in stall
    Look round like children at her call.
    I've hardly heard her speak at all.

Shy as a leveret, swift as he,
Straight and slight as a young larch tree,
Sweet as the first wild violets, she,
To her wild self. But what to me?

The short days shorten and the oaks are brown,
    The blue smoke rises to the low grey sky,
One leaf in the still air falls slowly down,
    A magpie's spotted feathers lie
On the black earth spread white with rime,
    The berries redden up to Christmas-time.
        What's Christmas-time without there be
        Some other in the house than we!

She sleeps up in the attic there
 Alone, poor maid. 'Tis but a stair
Betwixt us. Oh! my God! the down,
 The soft young down of her, the brown,
 The brown of her – her eyes, her hair, her hair!

CHARLOTTE MEW

On the Road to the Sea

We passed each other, turned and stopped for half an hour,
 then went our way,
 I who make other women smile did not make you –
But no man can move mountains in a day.
 So this hard thing is yet to do.

But first I want your life: – before I die I want to see
 The world that lies behind the strangeness of your eyes,
There is nothing gay or green there for my gathering, it may be,
 Yet on brown fields there lies
A haunting purple bloom: is there not something in grey skies
 And in grey sea?
 I want what world there is behind your eyes,
 I want your life and you will not give it me.

 Now, if I look, I see you walking down the years,
 Young, and through August fields – a face, a thought, a
 swinging dream perched on a stile – ;
 I would have liked (so vile we are!) to have taught you tears
 But most to have made you smile.

To-day is not enough or yesterday: God sees it all –
Your length on sunny lawns, the wakeful rainy nights – ;
   tell me – ; (how vain to ask),
        but it is not a question – just a call – ;
Show me then, only your notched inches climbing up the
   garden wall,
               I like you best when you are small.

        Is this a stupid thing to say
        Not having spent with you one day?
   No matter; I shall never touch your hair
   Or hear the little tick behind your breast,
        Still it is there,
        And as a flying bird
   Brushes the branches where it may not rest
        I have brushed your hand and heard
   The child in you: I like that best

So small, so dark, so sweet; and were you also then too grave
   and wise?
     Always I think. Then put your far off little hand in mine;
      – Oh! let it rest;
I will not stare into the early world beyond the opening eyes,
    Or vex or scare what I love best.
       But I want your life before mine bleeds away –
         Here – not in heavenly hereafters – soon, –
         I want your smile this very afternoon,
       (The last of all my vices, pleasant people used to say,
         I wanted and I sometimes got – the Moon!)

You know, at dusk, the last bird's cry,
And round the house the flap of the bat's low flight,
Trees that go black against the sky
And then – how soon the night!

No shadow of you on any bright road again,
And at the darkening end of this – what voice? whose
  kiss? As if you'd say!
It is not I who have walked with you, it will not be I
  who take away
Peace, peace, my little handful of the gleaner's grain
From your reaped fields at the shut of day.

Peace! Would you not rather die
Reeling, – with all the cannons at your ear?
So, at least, would I,
And I may not be here
To-night, to-morrow morning or next year.
Still I will let you keep your life a little while,
See dear?
I have made you smile.

CHARLOTTE MEW

The Trees are Down

They are cutting down the great plane-trees at the end of
     the gardens.
For days there has been the grate of the saw, the swish of
     the branches as they fall,
The crash of the trunks, the rustle of trodden leaves,
With the 'Whoops' and the 'Whoas,' the loud common talk,
    the loud common laughs of the men, above it all.

I remember one evening of a long past Spring
Turning in at a gate, getting out of a cart, and finding a large
    dead rat in the mud of the drive.
I remember thinking: alive or dead, a rat was a god-forsaken
    thing,
But at least, in May, that even a rat should be alive.

The week's work here is as good as done. There is just one bough
    On the roped bole, in the fine grey rain,
        Green and high
        And lonely against the sky.
          (Down now! –)
        And but for that,
        If an old dead rat
Did once, for a moment, unmake the Spring, I might never
    have thought of him again.

It is not for a moment the Spring is unmade to-day;
These were great trees, it was in them from root to stem:
When the men with the Whoops' and the 'Whoas' have
    carted the whole of the whispering loveliness away
Half the Spring, for me, will have gone with them.

It is going now, and my heart has been struck with the hearts
    of the planes;
Half my life it has beat with these, in the sun, in the rains,
            In the March wind, the May breeze,
In the great gales that came over to them across the roofs
    from the great seas.
            There was only a quiet rain when they were dying;
            They must have heard the sparrows flying,
And the small creeping creatures in the earth where they were
    lying –
            But I, all day, I heard an angel crying:
            'Hurt not the trees.'

CHARLOTTE MEW

Rooms

I remember rooms that have had their part
    In the steady slowing down of the heart.
The room in Paris, the room at Geneva,
The little damp room with the seaweed smell,
And that ceaseless maddening sound of the tide –
    Rooms where for good or for ill – things died.
But there is the room where we two lie dead,

Though every morning we seem to wake and might just as
    well seem to sleep again
As we shall somewhere in the other quieter, dustier bed
Out there in the sun – in the rain.

CHARLOTTE MEW

Ballade of Genuine Concern

A child at Brighton has been left to drown;
    A railway train has jumped the line at Crewe;
I haven't got the change for half a crown;
    I can't imagine what on earth to do . . .
    Three bisons have stampeded from the Zoo,
A German fleet has anchored in the Clyde;
    By God the wretched country's up the flue!
– The ice is breaking up on every side.

What! Further news? Rhodesian stocks are down?
    England, my England, can the news be true?
Cannot the Duke be got to come to town?
    Or will not Mr Hooper pull us through?
    And now the Bank is stopping payment, too,
The chief cashier has cut his throat and died,
    And Scotland Yard has failed to find a clue:
– The ice is breaking up on every side.

A raging mob inflamed by Charley Brown
    Is tearing up the rails at Waterloo;
They've hanged the Chancellor in wig and gown,
    The Speaker, and the Chief Inspector, too!

Police! Police! Is this the road to Kew?
I can't keep up: my garter's come untied:
  I shall be murdered by the savage crew.
  – The ice is breaking up on every side.

ENVOI

Prince of the Empire, Prince of Timbuctoo
Prince eight feet round and nearly four feet wide,
  Do try to run a little faster, do –
  – The ice is breaking up on every side.

HILAIRE BELLOC

Hannaker Mill

Sally is gone that was so kindly,
  Sally is gone from Hannaker Hill.
And the briar grows ever since then so blindly
  And ever since then the clapper is still,
  And the sweeps have fallen from Hannaker Mill.

Hannaker Hill is in desolation:
  Ruin a-top and a field unploughed.
And Spirits that call on a falling nation,
  Spirits that loved her calling aloud:
  Spirits abroad in a windy cloud.

Spirits that call and no one answers;
  Hannaker's down and England's done.
Wind and thistle for pipe and dancers,
  And never a ploughman under the sun:
  Never a ploughman. Never a one.

HILAIRE BELLOC

The Villain

While joy gave clouds the light of stars,
  That beamed where'er they looked;
And calves and lambs had tottering knees,
  Excited, while they sucked;
While every bird enjoyed his song,
  Without one thought of harm or wrong –
  I turned my head and saw the wind,
    Not far from where I stood,
  Dragging the corn by her golden hair,
    Into a dark and lonely wood.

W. H. DAVIES

No

A drear, wind-weary afternoon,
Drenched with rain was the autumn air;
As weary, too, though not of the wind,
  I fell asleep in my chair.

Lost in that slumber I dreamed a dream
And out of its strangeness in stealth awoke;
No longer alone. Though who was near
   I opened not eyes to look;

But stayed for a while in half-heavenly joy,
Half-earthly grief; nor moved:
More conscious, perhaps, than – had she been there –
   Of whom, – and how much, – I loved.

WALTER DE LA MARE

The Birthnight

Dearest, it was a night
That in its darkness rocked Orion's stars;
A sighing wind ran faintly white
Along the willows, and the cedar boughs
Laid their wide hands in stealthy peace across
The starry silence of their antique moss:
No sound save rushing air
Cold, yet all sweet with Spring,
And in thy mother's arms, couched weeping there,
   Thou, lovely thing.

WALTER DE LA MARE

The Rolling English Road

Before the Roman came to Rye or out to Severn strode,
The rolling English drunkard made the rolling English road.
A reeling road, a rolling road, that rambles round the shire,
And after him the parson ran, the sexton and the squire;
A merry road, a mazy road, and such as we did tread
The night we went to Birmingham by way of Beachy Head.

I knew no harm of Bonaparte and plenty of the Squire,
And for to fight the Frenchman I did not much desire;
But I did bash their baggonets because they came arrayed
To straighten out the crooked road an English drunkard
  made,
Where you and I went down the lane with ale-mugs in our
  hands,
The night we went to Glastonbury by way of Goodwin
  Sands.

His sins they were forgiven him; or why do flowers run
Behind him; and the hedges all strengthening in the sun?
The wild thing went from left to right and knew not which
  was which,
But the wild rose was above him when they found him in the
  ditch.
God pardon us, nor harden us; we did not see so clear
The night we went to Bannockburn by way of Brighton Pier.

My friends we will not go again or ape an ancient rage,
Or stretch the folly of our youth to be the shame of age,
But walk with clearer eyes and ears this path that wandereth,
And see undrugged in evening light the decent inn of death;
For there is good news yet to hear and fine things to be seen,
Before we go to Paradise by way of Kensal Green.

G. K. CHESTERTON

Ballade of Liquid Refreshment

Last night we started with some dry vermouth;
    Some ancient sherry with a golden glow;
Then many flagons of the soul of fruit
    Such as Burgundian vineyards only grow;
    A bottle each of port was not *de trop;*
And then old brandy till the east was pink
    – But talking makes me hoarse as any crow.
Excuse me while I go and have a drink.

Some talk of Alexander: some impute
    Absorbency to Mirabeau-Tonneau;
Some say that General Grant and King Canute,
    Falstaff and Pitt and Edgar Allan Poe,
    Prince Charlie, Carteret, Hans Breitmann – so
The list goes on – they say that these could clink
    The can, and take their liquor – *A propos!*
Excuse me while I go and have a drink.

Spirit of all that lives, from God to brute,
　　Spirit of love and life, of sun and snow,
Spirit of leaf and limb, of race and root,
　　How wonderfully art thou prison'd! Lo!
　　I quaff the cup, I feel the magic flow,
And Superman succeeds to Missing Link,
　　(I say, 'I quaff'; but am I quaffing? No!
Excuse me while I go and have a drink.)

ENVOI

Hullo there, Prince! Is that you down below
Kicking and frying by the brimstone brink?
　　Well, well! It had to come some time, you know.
Excuse me while I go and have a drink.

E. C. BENTLEY

Adlestrop

Yes. I remember Adlestrop –
The name, because one afternoon
Of heat the express-train drew up there
Unwontedly. It was late June.

The steam hissed. Someone cleared his throat.
No one left and no one came
On the bare platform. What I saw
Was Adlestrop – only the name

And willows, willow-herb, and grass,
And meadowsweet, and haycocks dry,
No whit less still and lonely fair
Than the high cloudlets in the sky.

And for that minute a blackbird sang
Close by, and round him, mistier,
Farther and farther, all the birds
Of Oxfordshire and Gloucestershire.

EDWARD THOMAS

Words

Out of us all
That make rhymes,
Will you choose
Sometimes –
As the winds use
A crack in a wall
Or a drain,
Their joy or their pain
To whistle through –
Choose me,
You English words?

I know you:
You are light as dreams,
Tough as oak,
Precious as gold,
As poppies and corn,
Or an old cloak:

Sweet as our birds
To the ear,
As the burnet rose
In the heat
Of Midsummer:
Strange as the races
Of dead and unborn:
Strange and sweet
Equally,
And familiar,
To the eye,

As the dearest faces
That a man knows,
And as lost homes are:
But though older far
Than oldest yew, –
As our hills are, old. –
Worn new
Again and again:
Young as our streams
After rain:
And as dear
As the earth which you prove
That we love.

Make me content
With some sweetness
From Wales
Whose nightingales
Have no wings, –
From Wiltshire and Kent
And Herefordshire,

And the villages there, –
From the names, and the things
No less.

Let me sometimes dance
With you,
Or climb
Or stand perchance
In ecstasy,
Fixed and free
In a rhyme,
As poets do.

EDWARD THOMAS

What shall I give?

What shall I give my daughter the younger
More than will keep her from cold and hunger?
I shall not give her anything.
If she shared South Weald and Havering,
Their acres, the two brooks running between,
Paine's Brook and Weald Brook,
With pewit, woodpecker, swan, and rook,
She would be no richer than the queen
Who once on a time sat in Havering Bower
Alone, with the shadows, pleasure and power.
She could do no more with Samarcand,
Or the mountains of a mountain land
And its far white house above cottages
Like Venus above the Pleiades.

Her small hands I would not cumber
With so many acres and their lumber,
But leave her Steep and her own world
And her spectacled self with hair uncurled,
Wanting a thousand little things
That time without contentment brings.

EDWARD THOMAS

Tall Nettles

Tall nettles cover up, as they have done
These many springs, the rusty harrow, the plough
Long worn out, and the roller made of stone:
Only the elm butt tops the nettles now.

This corner of the farmyard I like most:
As well as any bloom upon a flower
I like the dust on the nettles, never lost
Except to prove the sweetness of a shower.

EDWARD THOMAS

The Nightingale Near the House

Here is the soundless cypress on the lawn:
It listens, listens. Taller trees beyond
Listen. The moon at the unruffled pond
    Stares. And you sing, you sing.

That star-enchanted song falls through the air
From lawn to lawn down terraces of sound,
Darts in white arrows on the shadowed ground;
  While all the night you sing.

My dreams are flowers to which you are a bee,
As all night long I listen, and my brain
Receives your song, then loses it again
  In moonlight on the lawn.

Now is your voice a marble high and white,
Then like a mist on fields of paradise;
Now is a raging fire, then is like ice,
  Then breaks, and it is dawn.

HAROLD MONRO

Overheard on a Saltmarsh

Nymph, nymph, what are your beads?

Green glass, goblin. Why do you stare at them?

Give them me.

        No.

Give them me. Give them me.

            No.

Then I will howl all night in the reeds,
Lie in the mud and howl for them.

Goblin, why do you love them so?

They are better than stars or water,
Better than voices of winds that sing,
Better than any man's fair daughter,
Your green glass beads on a silver ring.

Hush, I stole them out of the moon.

Give me your beads, I want them.

      No.

I will howl in a deep lagoon
For your green glass beads, I love them so.
Give them me. Give them.

     No.

HAROLD MONRO

The Lion and Albert

There's a famous seaside place called Blackpool,
That's noted for fresh air and fun,
And Mr and Mrs Ramsbottom
Went there with young Albert, their son.

A grand little lad was young Albert,
All dressed in his best; quite a swell
With a stick with an 'orse's 'ead 'andle,
The finest that Woolworth's could sell.

They didn't think much to the Ocean:
The waves, they was fiddlin' and small,
There was no wrecks and nobody drownded,
Fact, nothing to laugh at at all.

So, seeking for further amusement,
They paid and went into the Zoo,
Where they'd Lions and Tigers and Camels,
And old ale and sandwiches too.

There were one great big Lion called Wallace;
His nose were all covered with scars –
He lay in a somnolent posture,
With the side of his face on the bars.

Now Albert had heard about Lions,
How they was ferocious and wild –
To see Wallace lying so peaceful,
Well, it didn't seem right to the child.

So straightway the brave little feller,
Not showing a morsel of fear,
Took his stick with it's 'orse's 'ead 'andle
. . . And pushed it in Wallace's ear.

You could see that the Lion didn't like it,
For giving a kind of a roll,
He pulled Albert inside the cage with 'im,
And swallowed the little lad 'ole.

Then Pa, who had seen the occurence,
And didn't know what to do next,
Said 'Mother! Yon Lion's 'et Albert',
And Mother said, 'Well I am vexed!'

Then Mr and Mrs Ramsbottom –
Quite rightly, when all's said and done –
Complained to the Animal Keeper,
That the Lion had eaten their son.

The keeper was quite nice about it;
He said 'What a nasty mishap.
Are you sure that it's your boy he's eaten?'
Pa said 'Am I sure? There's his cap!'

The manager had to be sent for.
He came and he said 'What's to do?'
Pa said 'Yon Lion's 'et Albert,
And 'im in his Sunday clothes, too.'

The Mother said, 'Right's right, young feller;
I think it's a shame and a sin,
For a lion to go and eat Albert,
And after we've paid to come in.'

The manager wanted no trouble,
He took out his purse right away,
Saying 'How much to settle the matter?'
And Pa said 'What do you usually pay?'

But Mother had turned a bit awkward
When she thought where her Albert had gone.
She said 'No! someone's got to be summonsed' –
So that was decided upon.

Then off they went to the P'lice Station,
In front of the Magistrate chap;
They told 'im what happened to Albert,
And proved it by showing his cap.

The Magistrate gave his opinion
That no one was really to blame
And he said that he hoped the Ramsbottoms
Would have further sons to their name.

At that Mother got proper blazing,
'And thank you, sir, kindly,' said she.
'What waste all our lives raising children
To feed ruddy Lions? Not me!'

MARRIOTT EDGAR

Mrs Reece Laughs

Laughter, with us, is no great undertaking,
A sudden wave that breaks and dies in breaking.
Laughter with Mrs Reece is much less simple:
It germinates, it spreads, dimple by dimple,
From small beginnings, things of easy girth,
To formidable redundancies of mirth.
Clusters of subterranean chuckles rise
And presently the circles of her eyes
Close into slits and all the woman heaves
As a great elm with all its mounds of leaves
Wallows before the storm. From hidden sources
A mustering of blind volcanic forces
Takes her and shakes her till she sobs and gapes.
Then all that load of bottled mirth escapes
In one wild crow, a lifting of huge hands,
And creaking stays, and visage that expands
In scarlet ridge and furrow. Thence collapse,
A hanging head, a feeble hand that flaps
An apron-end to stir an air and waft
A steaming face. And Mrs Reece has laughed.

MARTIN ARMSTRONG

The Fired Pot

In our town, people live in rows.
The only irregular thing in a street is the steeple,
And where that points to, God only knows,
And not the poor disciplined people!

And I have watched the women growing old,
Passionate about pins, and pence, and soap,
Till the heart within my wedded breast grew cold,
And I lost hope.

But a young soldier came to our town,
He spoke his mind most candidly.
He asked me quickly to lie down,
And that was very good for me.

For though I gave him no embrace –
Remembering my duty –
He altered the expression of my face,
And gave me back my beauty.

ANNA WICKHAM

Meditation at Kew

Alas! for all the pretty women who marry dull men,
Go into the suburbs and never come out again,
Who lose their pretty faces, and dim their pretty eyes,
Because no one has skill or courage to organise.

What do these pretty women suffer when they marry?
They bear a boy who is like Uncle Harry,
A girl, who is like Aunt Eliza, and not new.
These old dull races must breed true.

I would enclose a common in the sun,
And let the young wives out to laugh and run;
I would steal their dull clothes and go away,
And leave the pretty naked things to play.

Then I would make a contract with hard Fate
That they see all the men in the world and choose a mate,
And I would summon all the pipers in the town
That they dance with Love at a feast, and dance him down.

From the gay unions of choice
We'd have a race of splendid beauty, and of thrilling voice.
The World whips frank gay love with rods,
But frankly gaily shall be got the gods.

ANNA WICKHAM

Survivors

No doubt they'll soon get well; the shock and strain
    Have caused their stammering, disconnected talk.
Of course they're 'longing to go out again,' –
    These boys with old, scared faces, learning to walk.
They'll soon forget their haunted nights; their cowed
    Subjection to the ghosts of friends who died, –
Their dreams that drip with murder; and they'll be proud

Of glorious war that shatter'd all their pride . . .
Men who went out to battle, grim and glad;
   Children, with eyes that hate you, broken and mad.

SIEGFRIED SASSOON

The General

'Good-morning; good-morning!' the General said
When we met him last week on our way to the line.
Now the soldiers he smiled at are most of 'em dead,
And we're cursing his staff for incompetent swine.
'He's a cheery old card,' grunted Harry to jack
As they slogged up to Arras with rifle and pack.

      . . .

But he did for them both by his plan of attack.

SIEGFRIED SASSOON

Everyone Sang

Everyone suddenly burst out singing;
And I was filled with such delight
As prisoned birds must find in freedom,
Winging wildly across the white
Orchards and dark-green fields; on – on –
   and out of sight.

Everyone's voice was suddenly lifted;
And beauty came like the setting sun:
My heart was shaken with tears; and horror
Drifted away ... O, but Everyone
Was a bird; and the song was wordless;
    the singing will never be done.

Falling Asleep

Voices moving about in the quiet house:
Thud of feet and a muffled shutting of doors:
Everyone yawning. Only the clocks are alert.

    Out in the night there's autumn-smelling gloom
Crowded with whispering trees; across the park
A hollow cry of hounds like lonely bells:
And I know that the clouds are moving across the moon;
The low, red, rising moon. Now herons call
And wrangle by their pool; and hooting owls
Sail from the wood above pale stooks of oats.

    Waiting for sleep, I drift from thoughts like these;
And where to-day was dream-like, build my dreams.
Music ... there was a bright white room below,
And someone singing a song about a soldier,
One hour, two hours ago: and soon the song
Will be '*last night*'; but now the beauty swings
Across my brain, ghost of remembered chords

Which still can make such radiance in my dream
That I can watch the marching of my soldiers,
And count their faces; faces; sunlit faces.

   Falling asleep . . . the herons, and the hounds . . .
September in the darkness; and the world
I've known; all fading past me into peace.

SIEGFRIED SASSOON

August 1914

What in our lives is burnt
In the fire of this?
The heart's dear granary?
The much we shall miss?

Three lives hath one life –
Iron, honey, gold.
The gold, the honey gone –
Left is the hard and cold.

Iron are our lives
Molten right through our youth.
A burnt space through ripe fields,
A fair mouth's broken tooth.

ISAAC ROSENBERG

Break of Day in the Trenches

The darkness crumbles away –
It is the same old druid Time as ever.
Only a live thing leaps my hand –
A queer sardonic rat –
As I pull the parapet's poppy
To stick behind my ear.
Droll rat, they would shoot you if they knew
Your cosmopolitan sympathies
(And God knows what antipathies).
Now you have touched this English hand
You will do the same to a German –
Soon, no doubt, if it be your pleasure
To cross the sleeping green between.
It seems you inwardly grin as you pass
Strong eyes, fine limbs, haughty athletes
Less chanced than you for life,
Bonds to the whims of murder,
Sprawled in the bowels of the earth,
The torn fields of France.
What do you see in our eyes
At the shrieking iron and flame
Hurled through still heavens?
What quaver – what heart aghast?
Poppies whose roots are in man's veins
Drop, and are ever dropping;
But mine in my ear is safe,
Just a little white with the dust.

ISAAC ROSENBERG

Lunch Hour

Withdrawn for a little space from the confusion
  Of pulled potatoes littered on broken earth,
We lay in the shadowed ditch, a peaceful circle
  Of food, drink, smoke, and mirth.

The smell of the ditch was hot and sweet, and heavy
  With poppy flowers, and tangled with nettle-weed.
In the grass a cricket chirped his eternal question,
    Like a thin tune on a reed.

Blue tobacco-smoke drifted and curled about us;
  Its eddying wove for us a mystic screen.
The field and its littered trenches dropped, and shimmered
    In the clear gulf between

Real and dream; the gulf where shadowless silence
  Dwells and beauty is strange, and thin, and far,
And the world is quiet and flat, as pictures woven
    On old tapestries are.

So we lay and laughed in the breathless noon-tide.
  Your laughter, and your faces, burnt with the sun,
Were as far and as near as heaven, and as mystic. . . .
    And the lunch hour was done.

Stiffly we stooped again in the sun-baked trenches,
    And flung the lifted potatoes into pails.
And the earth stood out once more in relief and shadow,
    Wholesome, like fairy-tales.

ROSE MACAULAY

The Silent One

Who died on the wires, and hung there, one of two –
Who for his hours of life had chattered through
Infinite lovely chatter of Bucks accent:
Yet faced unbroken wires; stepped over, and went
A noble fool, faithful to his stripes – and ended.
But I weak, hungry, and willing only for the chance
Of line – to fight in the line, lay down under unbroken
Wires, and saw the flashes and kept unshaken,
Till the politest voice – a finicking accent, said:
'Do you think you might crawl through there: there's a hole.'
Darkness, shot at: I smiled, as politely replied –
'I'm afraid not. Sir.' There was no hole no way to be seen
Nothing but chance of death, after tearing of clothes.
Kept flat, and watched the darkness, hearing bullets whizzing –
And thought of music – and swore deep heart's deep oaths
(Polite to God) and retreated and came on again,
Again retreated – and a second time faced the screen.

IVOR GURNEY

First Time In

After the dread tales and red yarns of the Line
Anything might have come to us; but the divine
Afterglow brought us up to a Welsh colony
Hiding in sandbag ditches, whispering consolatory
Soft foreign things. Then we were taken in
To low huts candle-lit, shaded close by slitten
Oilsheets, and there but boys gave us kind welcome,
So that we looked out as from the edge of home,
Sang us Welsh things, and changed all former notions
To human hopeful things. And the next day's guns
Nor any Line-pangs ever quite could blot out
That strangely beautiful entry to war's rout;
Candles they gave us, precious and shared over-rations –
Ulysses found little more in his wanderings without doubt.
'David of the White Rock', the 'Slumber Song' so soft, and that
Beautiful tune to which roguish words by Welsh pit boys
Are sung – but never more beautiful than here under the
   guns' noise.

IVOR GURNEY

The Soaking

The rain has come, and the earth must be very glad
Of its moisture, and the made roads, all dust clad;
It lets a veil down on the lucent dark,
And not of any bright ground thing shows its spark.

Tomorrow's grey morning will show cowparsley,
Hung all with shining drops, and the river will be
Duller because of the all soddenness of things,
Till the skylark breaks his reluctance, hangs shaking, and sings.

IVOR GURNEY

Anthem for Doomed Youth

What passing bells for those who die as cattle?
    Only the monstrous anger of the guns.
    Only the stuttering rifles' rapid rattle
Can patter out their hasty orisons.
No mockeries for them from prayers or bells,
    Nor any voice of mourning save the choirs, –
The shrill, demented choirs of wailing shells;
    And bugles calling for them from sad shires.
What candles may be held to speed them all?
    Not in the hands of boys, but in their eyes
Shall shine the holy glimmers of good-byes.
    The pallor of girls' brows shall be their pall;
Their flowers the tenderness of patient minds,
And each slow dusk a drawing-down of blinds.

WILFRED OWEN

Disabled

He sat in a wheeled chair, waiting for dark,
And shivered in his ghastly suit of grey,
Legless, sewn short at elbow. Through the park
Voices of boys rang saddening like a hymn,
Voices of play and pleasure after day,
Till gathering sleep had mothered them from him.

*

About this time Town used to swing so gay
When glow-lamps budded in the light blue trees,
And girls glanced lovelier as the air grew dim,
– In the old times, before he threw away his knees.
Now he will never feel again how slim
Girls' waists are, or how warm their subtle hands.
All of them touch him like some queer disease.

*

There was an artist silly for his face,
For it was younger than his youth, last year,
Now, he is old; his back will never brace;
He's lost his colour very far from here,
Poured it down shell-holes till the veins ran dry,
And half his lifetime lapsed in the hot race
And leap of purple spurted from his thigh.
One time he liked a bloodsmear down his leg,
After the matches, carried shoulder-high.
It was after football, when he'd drunk a peg,
He thought he'd better join. – He wonders why.

Someone had said he'd look a god in kilts,
That's why; and maybe, too, to please his Meg,
Aye, that was it, to please the giddy jilts
He asked to join. He didn't have to beg;
Smiling they wrote his lie: aged nineteen years.
Germans he scarcely thought of; all their guilt
And Austria's, did not move him. And no fears
Of Fear came yet. He thought of jewelled hilts
For daggers in plaid socks; of smart salutes;
And care of arms; and leave; and pay arrears;
Esprit de corps; and hints for young recruits.
And soon, he was drafted out with drums and cheers.

*

Some cheered him home, but not as crowds cheer Goal.
Only a solemn man who brought him fruits
Thanked him; and then inquired about his soul.

*

Now, he will spend a few sick years in institutes,
And do what things the rules consider wise,
And take whatever pity they may dole.
Tonight he noticed how the women's eyes
Passed from him to the strong men that were whole.
How cold and late it is! Why don't they come
And put him into bed? Why don't they come?

WILFRED OWEN

Dulce et Decorum Est

Bent double, like old beggars under sacks,
Knock-kneed, coughing like hags, we cursed through sludge,
Till on the haunting flares we turned our backs
And towards our distant rest began to trudge.
Men marched asleep. Many had lost their boots
But limped on, blood-shod. All went lame; all blind;
Drunk with fatigue; deaf even to the hoots
Of tired, outstripped Five-Nines that dropped behind.

Gas! Gas! Quick, boys! – An ecstasy of fumbling,
Fitting the clumsy helmets just in time;
But someone still was yelling out and stumbling
And flound'ring like a man in fire or lime ...
Dim, through the misty panes and thick green light,
As under a green sea, I saw him drowning.

In all my dreams, before my helpless sight,
He plunges at me, guttering, choking, drowning.

If in some smothering dreams you too could pace
Behind the wagon that we flung him in,
And watch the white eyes writhing in his face,
His hanging face, like a devil's sick of sin;
If you could hear, at every jolt, the blood
Come gargling from the froth-corrupted lungs,
Obscene as cancer, bitter as the cud
Of vile, incurable sores on innocent tongues, –

My friend, you would not tell with such high zest
To children ardent for some desperate glory,
The old Lie: Dulce et decorum est
Pro patria more.

WILFRED OWEN

Insensibility

I

Happy are men who yet before they are killed
Can let their veins run cold.
Whom no compassion fleers
Or makes their feet
Sore on the alleys cobbled with their brothers.
The front line withers,
But they are troops who fade, not flowers
For poets' tearful fooling:
Men, gaps for filling:
Losses who might have fought
Longer; but no one bothers.

II

And some cease feeling
Even themselves or for themselves.
Dullness best solves
The tease and doubt of shelling,
And Chance's strange arithmetic
Comes simpler than the reckoning of their shilling.
They keep no check on armies' decimation.

Happy are these who lose imagination:
They have enough to carry with ammunition.
Their spirit drags no pack,
Their old wounds save with cold can not more ache.
Having seen all things red,
Their eyes are rid
Of the hurt of the colour of blood for ever.
And terror's first constriction over,
Their hearts remain small-drawn.
Their senses in some scorching cautery of battle
Now long since ironed,
Can laugh among the dying, unconcerned.

Happy the soldier home, with not a notion
How somewhere, every dawn, some men attack,
And many sighs are drained.
Happy the lad whose mind was never trained:
His days are worth forgetting more than not.
He sings along the march
Which we march taciturn, because of dusk,
The long, forlorn, relentless trend
From larger day to huger night.

We wise, who with a thought besmirch
Blood over all our soul,
How should we see our task
But through his blunt and lashless eyes?
Alive, he is not vital overmuch;

Dying, not mortal overmuch;
Nor sad, nor proud,
Nor curious at all.
He cannot tell
Old men's placidity from his.

VI

But cursed are dullards whom no cannon stuns,
That they should be as stones;
Wretched are they, and mean
With paucity that never was simplicity.
By choice they made themselves immune
To pity and whatever moans in man
Before the last sea and the hapless stars;
Whatever mourns when many leave these shores;
Whatever shares
The eternal reciprocity of tears.

WILFRED OWEN

IX

I think we are in RATS' ALLEY WHERE THE DEAD MEN LOST THEIR bones ...

The Love Song of J. Alfred Prufrock

S'io credessi che mia risposta fosse
a persona che mai tornasse al mondo,
questa fiamma staria senza più scosse.
Ma per ciò che giammai di questo fondo
non tornò vivo alcun, s'i' odo il vero,
senza tema d'infamia ti rispondo.

Let us go then, you and I,
When the evening is spread out against the sky
Like a patient etherised upon a table;
Let us go, through certain half-deserted streets,
The muttering retreats
Of restless nights in one-night cheap hotels
And sawdust restaurants with oyster-shells:
Streets that follow like a tedious argument
Of insidious intent
To lead you to an overwhelming question . . .

Oh, do not ask, 'What is it?'
Let us go and make our visit.

In the room the women come and go
Talking of Michelangelo.

The yellow fog that rubs its back upon the window-panes,
The yellow smoke that rubs its muzzle on the window-panes,
Licked its tongue into the corners of the evening,
Lingered upon the pools that stand in drains,
Let fall upon its back the soot that falls from chimneys,

Slipped by the terrace, made a sudden leap,
And seeing that it was a soft October night,
Curled once about the house, and fell asleep.

And indeed there will be time
For the yellow smoke that slides along the street
Rubbing its back upon the window-panes;
There will be time, there will be time
To prepare a face to meet the faces that you meet;
There will be time to murder and create,
And time for all the works and days of hands
That lift and drop a question on your plate;
Time for you and time for me,
And time yet for a hundred indecisions,
And for a hundred visions and revisions,
Before the taking of a toast and tea.

In the room the women come and go
Talking of Michelangelo.

And indeed there will be time
To wonder, 'Do I dare?' and, 'Do I dare?'
Time to turn back and descend the stair,
With a bald spot in the middle of my hair –
(They will say: 'How his hair is growing thin!')
My morning coat, my collar mounting firmly to the chin,
My necktie rich and modest, but asserted by a simple pin –
(They will say: But how his arms and legs are thin!')
Do I dare
Disturb the universe?
In a minute there is time
For decisions and revisions which a minute will reverse.
For I have known them all already, known them all –

Have known the evenings, mornings, afternoons,
I have measured out my life with coffee spoons;
I know the voices dying with a dying fall
Beneath the music from a farther room.
    So how should I presume?

And I have known the eyes already, known them all –
The eyes that fix you in a formulated phrase,
And when I am formulated, sprawling on a pin,
When I am pinned and wriggling on the wall,
Then how should I begin
To spit out all the butt-ends of my days and ways?
    And how should I presume?

And I have known the arms already, known them all –
Arms that are braceleted and white and bare
(But in the lamplight, downed with light brown hair!)
Is it perfume from a dress
That makes me so digress?
Arms that lie along a table, or wrap about a shawl.
    And should I then presume?
    And how should I begin?

                .   .   .   .   .   .

Shall I say, I have gone at dusk through narrow streets
And watched the smoke that rises from the pipes
Of lonely men in shirt-sleeves, leaning out of windows? . . .

I should have been a pair of ragged claws
Scuttling across the floors of silent seas.

                .   .   .   .   .   .

And the afternoon, the evening, sleeps so peacefully!
Smoothed by long fingers,
Asleep . . . tired . . . or it malingers,
Stretched on the floor, here beside you and me.
Should I, after tea and cakes and ices,
Have the strength to force the moment to its crisis?
But though I have wept and fasted, wept and prayed,
Though I have seen my head (grown slightly bald) brought in
  upon a platter,
I am no prophet – and here's no great matter;
I have seen the moment of my greatness flicker,
And I have seen the eternal Footman hold my coat, and
  snicker,
And in short, I was afraid.

And would it have been worth it, after all,
After the cups, the marmalade, the tea,
Among the porcelain, among some talk of you and me,
Would it have been worth while,
To have bitten off the matter with a smile,
To have squeezed the universe into a ball
To roll it towards some overwhelming question,
To say: 'I am Lazarus, come from the dead,
Come back to tell you all, I shall tell you all' –
If one, settling a pillow by her head,
    Should say: 'That is not what I meant at all.
    That is not it, at all.'

And would it have been worth it, after all,
Would it have been worth while,
After the sunsets and the dooryards and the sprinkled streets,
After the novels, after the teacups, after the skirts that trail
  along the floor –

And this, and so much more? –
It is impossible to say just what I mean!
But as if a magic lantern threw the nerves in patterns on a
    screen:
Would it have been worth while
If one, settling a pillow or throwing off a shawl,
And turning toward the window, should say:
    'That is not it at all,
    That is not what I meant, at all.'

.   .   .   .   .

No! I am not Prince Hamlet, nor was meant to be;
Am an attendant lord, one that will do
To swell a progress, start a scene or two,
Advise the prince; no doubt, an easy tool,
Deferential, glad to be of use,
Politic, cautious, and meticulous;
Full of high sentence, but a bit obtuse;
At times, indeed, almost ridiculous –
Almost, at times, the Fool.

I grow old . . . I grow old . . .
I shall wear the bottoms of my trousers rolled.

Shall I part my hair behind? Do I dare to eat a peach?
I shall wear white flannel trousers, and walk upon the beach.
I have heard the mermaids singing, each to each.

I do not think that they will sing to me.

I have seen them riding seaward on the waves
Combing the white hair of the waves blown back
When the wind blows the water white and black.

We have lingered in the chambers of the sea
By sea-girls wreathed with seaweed red and brown
Till human voices wake us, and we drown.

T. S. ELIOT

from The Waste Land

A GAME OF CHESS

The Chair she sat in, like a burnished throne,
Glowed on the marble, where the glass
Held up by standards wrought with fruited vines
From which a golden Cupidon peeped out
(Another hid his eyes behind his wing)
Doubled the flames of sevenbranched candelabra
Reflecting light upon the table as
The glitter of her jewels rose to meet it,
From satin cases poured in rich profusion.
In vials of ivory and coloured glass
Unstoppered, lurked her strange synthetic perfumes,
Unguent, powdered, or liquid – troubled, confused
And drowned the sense in odours; stirred by the air
That freshened from the window, these ascended
In fattening the prolonged candle-flames,
Flung their smoke into the laquearia,
Stirring the pattern on the coffered ceiling.

Huge sea-wood fed with copper
Burned green and orange, framed by the coloured stone,
In which sad light a carvèd dolphin swam.
Above the antique mantel was displayed
As though a window gave upon the sylvan scene
The change of Philomel, by the barbarous king
So rudely forced; yet there the nightingale
Filled all the desert with inviolable voice
And still she cried, and still the world pursues,
'Jug Jug' to dirty ears.
And other withered stumps of time
Were told upon the walls; staring forms
Leaned out, leaning, hushing the room enclosed.
Footsteps shuffled on the stair.
Under the firelight, under the brush, her hair
Spread out in fiery points
Glowed into words, then would be savagely still.

'My nerves are bad to-night. Yes, bad. Stay with me.
'Speak to me. Why do you never speak. Speak.
'What are you thinking of? What thinking? What?
'I never know what you are thinking. Think.'

I think we are in rats' alley
Where the dead men lost their bones.

'What is that noise?'
                      The wind under the door.
'What is that noise now? What is the wind doing?'
                      Nothing again nothing.
                                             'Do
'You know nothing? Do you see nothing? Do you remember
'Nothing?'

                    I remember
Those are pearls that were his eyes.
'Are you alive, or not? Is there nothing in your head?'
                                                    But

O O O O that Shakespeherian Rag –
It's so elegant
So intelligent

'What shall I do now? What shall I do?
'I shall rush out as I am, and walk the street
'With my hair down, so. What shall we do tomorrow?
'What shall we ever do?'
                            The hot water at ten.
And if it rains, a closed car at four.
And we shall play a game of chess,
(The ivory men make company between us)
Pressing lidless eyes and waiting for a knock upon the door.

When Lil's husband got demobbed, I said –
I didn't mince my words, I said to her myself,
HURRY UP PLEASE ITS TIME
Now Albert's coming back, make yourself a bit smart.
He'll want to know what you done with that money he
      gave you
To get yourself some teeth. He did, I was there.
You have them all out, Lil, and get a nice set,
He said, I swear, I can't bear to look at you.
And no more can't I, I said, and think of poor Albert,
He's been in the army four years, he wants a good time,
And if you don't give it him, there's others will, I said.
Oh is there, she said. Something o' that, I said.

Then I'll know who to thank, she said, and give me a straight
    look.
H<small>URRY UP PLEASE ITS TIME</small>
If you don't like it you can get on with it, I said.
Others can pick and choose if you can't.
But if Albert makes off, it won't be for lack of telling.
You ought to be ashamed, I said, to look so antique.
(And her only thirty-one.)
I can't help it, she said, pulling a long face,
It's them pills I took, to bring it off, she said.
(She's had five already, and nearly died of young George.)
The chemist said it would be all right, but I've never been
    the same.
You *are* a proper fool, I said.
Well, if Albert won't leave you alone, there it is, I said,
What you get married for if you don't want children?
H<small>URRY UP PLEASE ITS TIME</small>
Well, that Sunday Albert was home, they had a hot gammon,
And they asked me in to dinner, to get the beauty of it hot –
H<small>URRY UP PLEASE ITS TIME</small>
H<small>URRY UP PLEASE ITS TIME</small>
Goonight Bill. Goonight Lou. Goonight May. Goonight.
Ta ta. Goonight. Goonight.
Good night, ladies, good night, sweet ladies, good night, good
    night.

                                            T. S. ELIOT

Full Moon

She was wearing coral taffeta trousers
Someone had bought her from Isfahan,
And the little gold coat with pomegranate blossoms,
And the coral-hafted feather fan,
But she ran down a Kentish lane in the moonlight,
And skipped in the pool of moon as she ran.

She cared not a rap for all the big planets,
For Betelgeuse or Aldebaran,
And all the big planets cared nothing for her,
That small impertinent charlatan,
As she climbed on a Kentish stile in the moonlight,
And laughed at the sky through the sticks of her fan.

VITA SACKVILLE-WEST

The Ballad of Persse O'Reilly

Have you heard of one Humpty Dumpty
How he fell with a roll and a rumble
And curled up like Lord Olofa Crumple
By the butt of the Magazine Wall,
    (Chorus) Of the Magazine Wall,
          Hump, helmet and all?

He was one time our King of the Castle
Now he's kicked about like a rotten old parsnip.
And from Green street he'll be sent by order of His Worship

To the penal jail of Mountjoy
    (Chorus) To the jail of Mountjoy!
        Jail him and joy.

He was fafafather of all schemes for to bother us
Slow coaches and immaculate contraceptives for the populace,
Mare's milk for the sick, seven dry Sundays a week,
Openair love and religion's reform,
    (Chorus) And religious reform,
        Hideous in form.

Arrah, why, says you, couldn't he manage it?
I'll go bail, my fine dairyman darling,
Like the bumping bull of the Cassidys
All your butter is in your horns.
    (Chorus) His butter is in his horns.
        Butter his horns!

(Repeat) Hurrah there, Hosty, frosty Hosty, change that shirt
    on ye,
Rhyme the rann, the king of all ranns!

        Balbaccio, balbuccio!

We had chaw chaw chops, chairs, chewing gum, the chicken-
    pox and china chambers
Universally provided by this soffsoaping salesman.
Small wonder He'll Cheat E'erawan our local lads nicknamed
    him
When Chimpden first took the floor
    (Chorus) With his bucketshop store
        Down Bargainweg, Lower.

[379]

So snug he was in his hotel premises sumptuous
But soon we'll bonfire all his trash, tricks and trumpery
And 'tis short till sheriff Clancy'll be winding up his
   unlimited company
With the bailiff's bom at the door,
     (Chorus) Bimbam at the door.
           Then he'll bum no more.

Sweet bad luck on the waves washed to our island
The hooker of that hammerfast viking
And Gall's curse on the day when Eblana bay
Saw his black and tan man-o'-war.
     (Chorus) Saw his man-o'-war
           On the harbour bar.

Where from? roars Poolbeg. Cookingha'pence, he bawls
Donnez-moi scampitle, wick an wipin'fampiny
Fingal Mac Oscar Onesine Bargearse Boniface
Thok's min gammelhole Norveegickers moniker
Og as ay are at gammelhore Norveegickers cod.
     (Chorus) A Norwegian camel old cod.
           He is, begod.

Lift it, Hosty, lift it, ye devil ye! up with the rann, the
   rhyming rann!

It was during some fresh water garden pumping
Or, according to the *Nursing Mirror*, while admiring the
   monkeys
That our heavyweight heathen Humpharey
Made bold a maid to woo
     (Chorus) Woohoo, what'll she doo!
           The general lost her maidenloo!

He ought to blush for himself, the old hayheaded philosopher,
For to go and shove himself that way on top of her.
Begob, he's the crux of the catalogue
Of our antediluvial zoo,
    (Chorus) Messrs. Billing and Coo.
               Noah's larks, good as noo.

He was joulting by Wellinton's monument
Our rotorious hippopopotamuns
When some bugger let down the backtrap of the omnibus
And he caught his death of fusiliers
    (Chorus) With his rent in his rears.
               Give him six years.

'Tis sore pity for his innocent poor children
But look out for his missus legitimate!
When that frew gets a grip of old Earwicker
Won't there be earwigs on the green?
    (Chorus) Big earwigs on the green,
               The largest ever you seen.

    Suffoclose! Shikespower! Seudodanto! Anonymoses!

Then we'll have a free trade Gaels' band and mass meeting
For to sod the brave son of Scandiknavery.
And we'll bury him down in Oxmanstown
Along with the devil and Danes,
    (Chorus) With the deaf and dumb Danes,
               And all their remains.

And not all the king's men nor his horses
Will resurrect his corpus
For there's no true spell in Connacht or hell
    (bis) That's able to raise a Cain.

JAMES JOYCE

Ducks

I

From troubles of the world
I turn to ducks,
Beautiful comical things
Sleeping or curled
Their heads beneath white wings
By water cool,
Or finding curious things
To eat in various mucks
Beneath the pool,
Tails uppermost, or waddling
Sailor-like on the shores
Of ponds, or paddling
– Left! right! – with fanlike feet
Which are for steady oars
When they (white galleys) float
Each bird a boat
Rippling at will the sweet
Wide waterway . . .
When night is fallen *you* creep
Upstairs, but drakes and dillies

Nest with pale water-stars,
Moonbeams and shadow bars,
And water-lilies:
Fearful too much to sleep
Since they've no locks
To click against the teeth
Of weasel and fox.
And warm beneath
Are eggs of cloudy green
Whence hungry rats and lean
Would stealthily suck
New life, but for the mien,
The bold ferocious mien
Of the mother-duck.

II

Yes, ducks are valiant things
On nests of twigs and straws,
And ducks are soothy things
And lovely on the lake
When that the sunlight draws
Thereon their pictures dim
In colours cool.
And when beneath the pool
They dabble, and when they swim
And make their rippling rings,
O ducks are beautiful things!

But ducks are comical things: –
As comical as you.
Quack!
They waddle round, they do.

They eat all sorts of things,
And then they quack.
By barn and stable and stack
They wander at their will,
But if you go too near
They look at you through black
Small topaz-tinted eyes
And wish you ill.
Triangular and clear
They leave their curious track
In mud at the water's edge,
And there amid the sedge
And slime they gobble and peer
Saying 'Quack! quack!'

III

When God had finished the stars and whirl of coloured suns
He turned His mind from big things to fashion little ones,
Beautiful tiny things (like daisies) He made, and then
He made the comical ones in case the minds of men
    Should stiffen and become
    Dull, humourless and glum:
And so forgetful of their Maker be
As to take even themselves – *quite seriously*.
Caterpillars and cats are lively and excellent puns:
All God's jokes are good – even the practical ones!
And as for the duck, I think God must have smiled a bit
Seeing those bright eyes blink on the day He fashioned it.
And He's probably laughing still at the sound that came out
    of its bill!

F. W. HARVEY

A Saturday in the '20s

The child came to the dark library,
Afraid. Feeling the darkness of the men
Sitting so silently – not reading –
On the tilted chairs.

The steps to go in were loaded with darkness.
Men stood hinged on their heavy arms
A smell of cloth-pudding boiling on a winter day –
The child knew this smell
Damp caps over embittered minds, they smell the same.
Men's gear stricken, like the ancient smoke
Above the table. No one was smoking.
Yet there it hung.

Then the lame man stumped with his keys.
Opening cases,
Muttering. What was a child doing here,
Among darkened men? Wanting locked books?
The child snatched and fled

While the books bloomed in a fire between the covers,
Waiting to burst for her – Saturday's great new rose.
The men lolled silent, holding their empty hands
On their dark knees. She was afraid.
Yet above fear, she wanted their books
That they did not read.

What the dark men wanted
She was too young and well cared for to understand.

JEAN EARLE

The Bonnie Broukit Bairn

For Peggy

Mars is braw in crammasy,
Venus in a green silk goun,
The auld mune shak's her gowden feathers,
Their starry talk's a wheen o' blethers,
Nane for thee a thochtie sparin',
Earth, thou bonnie broukit bairn!
– *But greet, an' in your tears ye'll droun*
The haill clanjamfrie!

HUGH MACDIARMID

Back Bedroom

The dirty licht that through the winnock seeps
Into this unkempt room has glozed strange sichts;
Heaven like a Peepin' Tam 'twixt chimley-pots
Keeks i' the drab fore-nichts.

The folk that hed it last – the selfsame bed –
Were a great hulkin' cairter an' his bride.
She deed i' child-birth – on this verra spot
Whaur we'll lie side by side.

An' everything's deid-grey except oor een.
Wi' wee waugh jokes we strip an' intae bed . . .
An' suddenly oor een sing oot like stars
An' a' oor misery's shed.

What tho' the auld dour licht is undeceived?
What tho' a callous morn oure shairly comes?
For a wee while we ken but een like stars,
An' oor herts gaen' like drums.

Mony's the dreich back bedroom whaur the same
Sad little miracle tak's place ilk' nicht,
An' orra shapes o' sickly-hued mankind
Cheenge into forms o' licht.

HUGH MACDIARMID

Mary's Song

I wad ha'e gi'en him my lips tae kiss,
Had I been his, had I been his;
Barley breid and elder wine,
Had I been his as he is mine.

The wanderin' bee it seeks the rose;
Tae the lochan's bosom the burnie goes;
The grey bird cries at evenin's fa',
'My luve, my fair one, come awa',

My beloved sall ha'e this he'rt tae break,
Reid, reid wine and the barley cake,
A he'rt tae break, and a mou' tae kiss,
Tho' he be nae mine, as I am his.

MARION ANGUS

The Blue Jacket

When there comes a flower to the stingless nettle,
    To the hazel bushes, bees,
I think I can see my little sister
    Rocking herself by the hazel trees.

Rocking her arms for very pleasure
    That every leaf so sweet can smell,
And that she has on her the warm blue jacket
    Of mine, she liked so well.

Oh to win near you, little sister!
   To hear your soft lips say –
'I'll never tak' up wi' lads or lovers,
   But a baby I maun hae.

'A baby in a cradle rocking,
   Like a nut, in a hazel shell,
And a new blue jacket, like this o' Annie's,
   It sets me aye sae well.'

MARION ANGUS

Alas! Poor Queen

She was skilled in music and the dance
And the old arts of love
At the court of the poisoned rose
And the perfumed glove,
And gave her beautiful hand
To the pale Dauphin
A triple crown to win –
And she loved little dogs
   And parrots
   And red-legged partridges
And the golden fishes of the Duc de Guise
And a pigeon with a blue ruff
She had from Monsieur d'Elbœuf.

Master John Knox was no friend to her;
She spoke him soft and kind,
Her honeyed words were Satan's lure
The unwary soul to bind
'Good sir, doth a lissome shape
And a comely face
Offend your God His Grace
Whose Wisdom maketh these
Golden fishes of the Duc de Guise?'

She rode through Liddesdale with a song;
'Ye streams sae wondrous strang,
Oh, mak' me a wrack as I come back
But spare me as I gang,'
While a hill-bird cried and cried
Like a spirit lost
By the grey storm-wind tost.

Consider the way she had to go.
Think of the hungry snare,
The net she herself had woven,
Aware or unaware,
Of the dancing feet grown still,
The blinded eyes –
Queens should be cold and wise,
And she loved little things,
    Parrots
  And red-legged partridges
And the golden fishes of the Duc de Guise
And the pigeon with the blue ruff
She had from Monsieur d'Elbœuf.

MARION ANGUS

The Bells of Rhymney

O what can you give me?
Say the sad bells of Rhymney.
Is there hope for the future?
Cry the brown bells of Merthyr.
Who made the mineowner?
Say the black bells of Rhondda.
And who robbed the miner?
Cry the grim bells of Blaina.
They will plunder willy-nilly,
Say the bells of Caerphilly.
They have fangs, they have teeth
Shout the loud bells of Neath.
To the south, things are sullen,
Say the pink bells of Brecon.
Even God is uneasy,
Say the moist bells of Swansea.
Put the vandals in court
Cry the bells of Newport.
All would be well if – if – if –
Say the green bells of Cardiff.
Why so worried, sisters, why
Sing the silver bells of Wye.

IDRIS DAVIES

The Angry Summer

Mrs Evans fach, you want butter again.
How will you pay for it now, little woman
With your husband out on strike, and full
Of the fiery language? Ay, I know him,
His head is full of fire and brimstone
And a lot of palaver about communism,
And me, little Dan the grocer
Depending so much on private enterprise.

What, depending on the miners and their
Money too? O yes, in a way, Mrs Evans,
Yes, in a way I do, mind you.
Come tomorrow, little woman, and I'll tell you then
What I have decided overnight,
Go home now and tell that rash red husband of yours
That your grocer cannot afford to go on strike
Or what would happen to the butter from Carmarthen?
Good day for now, Mrs Evans fach.

IDRIS DAVIES

Cascando

I

why not merely the despaired of
occasion of
wordshed

is it not better abort than be barren

the hours after you are gone are so leaden
they will always start dragging too soon
the grapples clawing blindly the bed of want
bringing up the bones the old loves
sockets filled once with eyes like yours
all always is it better too soon than never
the black want splashing their faces
saying again nine days never floated the loved
nor nine months
nor nine lives

II

saying again
if you do not teach me I shall not learn
saying again there is a last
even of last times
last times of begging
last times of loving
of knowing not knowing pretending
a last even of last times of saying
if you do not love me I shall not be loved
if I do not love you I shall not love

the churn of stale words in the heart again
love love love thud of the old plunger
pestling the unalterable
whey of words
terrified again
of not loving
of loving and not you
of being loved and not by you
of knowing not knowing pretending
pretending

I and all the others that will love you
if they love you

III

unless they love you

SAMUEL BECKETT

Piano

Softly, in the dusk, a woman is singing to me;
Taking me back down the vista of years, till I see
A child sitting under the piano, in the boom of the tingling
    strings
And pressing the small, poised feet of a mother who smiles as
    she sings.

In spite of myself, the insidious mastery of song
Betrays me back, till the heart of me weeps to belong
To the old Sunday evenings at home, with winter outside
And hymns in the cosy parlour, the tinkling piano our guide.

So now it is vain for the singer to burst into clamour
With the great black piano appassionato. The glamour
Of childish days is upon me, my manhood is cast
Down in the flood of remembrance, I weep like a child for
   the past.

D. H. LAWRENCE

Innocent England

    Oh what a pity, Oh! don't you agree
    that figs aren't found in the land of the free!

    Fig-trees don't grow in my native land;
    there's never a fig-leaf near at hand

    when you want one; so I did without;
    and that is what the row's about.

    Virginal, pure policemen came
    and hid their faces for very shame,

    while they carried the shameless things away
    to gaol, to be hid from the light of day.

And Mr Mead, that old, old lily
said: 'Gross! coarse! hideous!' – and I, like a silly

thought he meant the faces of the police-court officials,
and how right he was, and I signed my initials

to confirm what he said: but alas, he meant
my pictures, and on the proceedings went.

The upshot was, my pictures must burn
that English artists might finally learn

when they painted a nude, to put a *cache sexe* on,
a cache sexe, a cache sexe, or else begone!

A fig-leaf; or, if you cannot find it
a wreath of mist, with nothing behind it.

A wreath of mist is the usual thing
in the north, to hide where the turtles sing.

Though they never sing, they never sing,
don't you dare to suggest such a thing

or Mr Mead will be after you.
– But what a pity I never knew

A wreath of English mist would do
as a cache sexe! I'd have put a whole fog.

But once and forever barks the old dog,
so my pictures are in prison, instead of in the Zoo.

D. H. LAWRENCE

Week-night Service

The five old bells
Are hurrying and eagerly calling.
Imploring, protesting
They know, but clamorously falling
Into gabbling incoherence, never resting,
Like spattering showers from a bursten sky-rocket dropping
In splashes of sound, endlessly, never stopping.

The silver moon
That somebody has spun so high
To settle the question, yes or no, has caught
In the net of the night's balloon,
And sits with a smooth bland smile up there in the sky
Smiling at naught,
Unless the winking star that keeps her company
Makes little jests at the bells' insanity,
As if *he* knew aught!

The patient Night
Sits indifferent, hugged in her rags,
She neither knows nor cares
Why the old church sobs and brags;
The light distresses her eyes, and tears
Her old blue cloak, as she crouches and covers her face,
Smiling, perhaps, if we knew it, at the bells' loud clattering
    disgrace.

The wise old trees
Drop their leaves with a faint, sharp hiss of contempt,
While a car at the end of the street goes by with a laugh;
As by degrees
The poor bells cease, and the Night is exempt,
And the stars can chaff
The ironic moon at their ease, while the dim old church
Is peopled with shadows and sounds and ghosts that lurch
In its cenotaph.

D. H. LAWRENCE

The Fox

A hundred yards from the peak, while the bells
Of the churches on the slopes called to prayer
And the unspent sun of marvellous July
Called to the mountain, – it was then,
On unfelt feet and with silent stride,
He paced his rare wonders before us.
We did not move, we did not breathe,
A moment paralysed; like a trinity in stone
We stood, while in untroubled midstep
He paused in surprise, and above
His single hesitant step the two steady flames
Of his eyes held us.

Then, without haste or fear,
He slipped his russet coat over the ridge;
It happened, it ended, like a shooting star.

ROBERT WILLIAMS PARRY
translated from the Welsh by Barry Tobin

Childhood

I used to think that grown-up people chose
To have stiff backs and wrinkles round their nose,
And veins like small fat snakes on either hand,
On purpose to be grand.
Till through the banisters I watched one day
My great-aunt Etty's friend who was going away,
And how her onyx beads had come unstrung.
I saw her grope to find them as they rolled;
And then I knew that she was helplessly old,
As I was helplessly young.

FRANCES CORNFORD

To a Fat Lady Seen from a Train

O why do you walk through the fields in gloves,
    Missing so much and so much?
O fat white woman whom nobody loves,
    Why do you walk through the fields in gloves,

When the grass is soft as the breast of doves
  And shivering-sweet to the touch?
O why do you walk through the fields in gloves,
  Missing so much and so much?

FRANCES CORNFORD

The Ponnage Pool

. . . Sing
Some simple silly sang
O' willows or o' mimulus
A river's banks alang
  – HUGH MACDIARMID

I mind o' the Ponnage Pule,
The reid brae risin',
Morphie Lade.
An' the saumon that louped the dam,
A tree i' Martin's Den
Wi' names carved on it;
But I ken na wha I am.

Ane o' the names was mine,
An' still I own it.
Naething it kens
O' a' that mak's up me.
Less I ken o' mysel'
Than the saumon wherefore
It rins up Esk frae the sea.

[400]

I am the deep o' the pule,
The fish, the fisher,
The river in spate,
The brune of the far peat-moss,
The shingle bricht wi' the flooer
O' the yellow mim'lus,
The martin fleein' across.

I mind o' the Ponnage Pule
On a shinin' mornin',
The saumon fishers
Nettin' the bonny brutes –
I' the slithery dark o' the boddom
O' Charon's Coble
Ae day I'll faddom my doobts.

HELEN B. CRUICKSHANK

The Interrogation

We could have crossed the road but hesitated,
And then came the patrol;
The leader conscientious and intent,
The men surly, indifferent.
While we stood by and waited
The interrogation began. He says the whole
Must come out now, who, what we are,
Where we have come from, with what purpose, whose
Country or camp we plot for or betray.
Question on question.

We have stood and answered through the standing day
And watched across the road beyond the hedge
The careless lovers in pairs go by,
Hand linked in hand, wandering another star,
So near we could shout to them. We cannot choose
Answer or action here,
Though still the careless lovers saunter by
And the thoughtless field is near.
We are on the very edge,
Endurance almost done,
And still the interrogation is going on.

EDWIN MUIR

The Late Wasp

You that through all the dying summer
Came every morning to our breakfast table,
A lonely bachelor mummer,
And fed on the marmalade
So deeply, all your strength was scarcely able
To prise you from the sweet pit you had made, –
You and the earth have now grown older,
And your blue thoroughfares have felt a change;
They have grown colder;
And it is strange
How the familiar avenues of the air

Crumble now, crumble; the good air will not hold,
All cracked and perished with the cold;
And down you dive through nothing and through despair.

EDWIN MUIR

from In Parenthesis

It's difficult with the weight of the rifle.
Leave it – under the oak.
Leave it for a salvage-bloke
let it lie bruised for a monument
dispense the authenticated fragments to the faithful.
It's the thunder-besom for us
it's the bright bough borne
it's the tensioned yew for a Genoese jammed arbalest and a
scarlet square for a mounted *mareschal*, it's that county-mob
back to back. Majuba mountain and Mons Cherubim and
spreaded mats for Sydney Street East, and come to Bisley for a
Silver Dish. It's R.S.M. O'Grady says, it's the soldier's best
friend if you care for the working parts and let us be 'aving
those springs released smartly in Company billets on wet
forenoons and clickerty-click and one up the spout and you
men must really cultivate the habit of treating this weapon with
the very greatest care and there should be a healthy rivalry
among you – it should be a matter of very proper pride and
  Marry it man! Marry it!
Cherish her, she's your very own.
  Coax it man coax it – it's delicately and ingeniously made
– it's an instrument of precision – it costs us tax-payers, money
– I want you men to remember that.

Fondle it like a granny – talk to it – consider it as you would a friend – and when you ground these arms she's not a rooky's gas-pipe for greenhorns to tarnish.

    You've known her hot and cold.
You would choose her from among many.
You know her by her bias, and by her exact error at 300, and by the deep scar at the small, by the fair flaw in the grain, above the lower sling-swivel – but leave it under the oak.

DAVID JONES

Aubade

    Jane, Jane,
    Tall as a crane,
    The morning light creaks down again;

    Comb your cockscomb-ragged hair,
    Jane, Jane, come down the stair.

    Each dull blunt wooden stalactite
    Of rain creaks, hardened by the light,

    Sounding like an overtone
    From some lonely world unknown.

    But the creaking empty light
    Will never harden into sight,

    Will never penetrate your brain
    With overtones like the blunt rain.

The light would show (if it could harder.)
Eternities of kitchen garden,

Cockscomb flowers that none will pluck
And wooden flowers that 'gin to cluck.

In the kitchen you must light
Flames as staring, red and white,

As carrots or as turnips, shining
Where the cold dawn light lies whining.

Cockscomb hair on the cold wind
Hang limp, turns the milk's weak mind. . .

    Jane, Jane,
    Tall as a crane,
    The morning light creaks down again!

EDITH SITWELL

Still Falls the Rain

The Raids, 1940. Night and Dawn

Still falls the Rain –
Dark as the world of man, black as our loss –
Blind as the nineteen hundred and forty nails
Upon the Cross.

Still falls the Rain
With a sound like the pulse of the heart that is changed to the
    hammer-beat
In the Potter's Field, and the sound of the impious feet

On the Tomb:
                Still falls the Rain
In the Field of Blood where the small hopes breed and the
    human brain
Nurtures its greed, that worm with the brow of Cain.

Still falls the Rain –
At the feet of the Starved Man hung upon the Cross.
Christ that each day, each night, nails there, have mercy on us –
On Dives and on Lazarus:
Under the Rain the sore and the gold are as one.

Still falls the Rain –
Still falls the Blood from the Starved Man's wounded Side:
He bears in His Heart all wounds, – those of the light that
    died,
The last faint spark
In the self-murdered heart, the wounds of the sad
    uncomprehending dark,
The wounds of the baited bear, –
The blind and weeping bear whom the keepers beat
On his helpless flesh . . . the tears of the hunted hare.

Still falls the Rain –
Then – O Ile leape up to my God: who pulles me doune –
See, see where Christ's blood streames in the firmament:

It flows from the Brow we nailed upon the tree
Deep to the dying, to the thirsting heart
That holds the fires of the world, – dark-smirched with pain
As Caesar's laurel crown.

Then sounds the voice of One who like the heart of man
Was once a child who among beasts has lain –
'Still do I love, still shed my innocent light, my Blood, for thee.'

EDITH SITWELL

Desire in Spring

I love the cradle songs the mothers sing
In lonely places when the twilight drops,
The slow endearing melodies that bring
Sleep to the weeping lids; and, when she stops,
I love the roadside birds upon the tops
Of dusty hedges in a world of Spring.

And when the sunny rain drips from the edge
Of midday wind, and meadows lean one way,
And a long whisper passes thro' the sedge,
Beside the broken water let me stay,
While these old airs upon my memory play,
And silent changes colour up the hedge.

FRANCIS LEDWIDGE

To a Conscript of 1940

Qui n'a pas une fois désespéré del'honneur, ne sera jamais un héros.
– GEORGES BERNANOS

A soldier passed me in the freshly fallen snow,
His footsteps muffled, his face unearthly grey;
And my heart gave a sudden leap
As I gazed on a ghost of five-and-twenty years ago.

I shouted 'Halt!' and my voice had the old accustom'd ring
And he obeyed it as it was obeyed
In the shrouded days when I too was one
Of an army of young men marching

Into the unknown. He turned towards me and I said:
'I am one of those who went before you
Five-and-twenty years ago: one of the many who never returned,
Of the many who returned and yet were dead.

We went where you are going, into the rain and the mud;
We fought as you will fight
With death and darkness and despair;
We gave what you will give – our brains and our blood.

We think we gave in vain. The world was not renewed.
There was hope in the homestead and anger in die sheets,
But the old world was restored and we returned
To the dreary field and workshop, and the immemorial feud

Of rich and poor. Our victory was our defeat.
Power was retained where power had been misused
And youth was left to sweep away
The ashes that the fires had strewn beneath our feet.

But one thing we learned: there is no glory in the dead
Until the soldier wears a badge of tarnish'd braid;
There are heroes who have heard the valley and have seen
The glitter of a garland round their head.

Theirs is the hollow victory. They are deceived.
But you, my brother and my ghost, if you can go
Knowing that there is no reward, no certain use
In all your sacrifice, then honour is reprieved.

To fight without hope is to fight with grace,
The self reconstructed, the false heart is repaired.'
Then I turned with a smile, and he answered my salute
As he stood against the fretted hedge which was like white lace.

HERBERT READ

Refugee Blues

Say this city has ten million souls,
Some are living in mansions, some are living in holes:
Yet there's no place for us, my dear, yet there's no place for us.

Once we had a country and we thought it fair,
Look in the atlas and you'll find it there:
We cannot go there now, my dear, we cannot go there now.

In the village churchyard there grows an old yew,
Every spring it blossoms anew:
Old passports can't do that, my dear, old passports can't do that.

The consul banged the table and said,
'If you've got no passport you're officially dead':
But we are still alive, my dear, but we are still alive.

Went to a committee; they offered me a chair;
Asked me politely to return next year:
But where shall we go to-day, my dear, but where shall we go
    to-day?

Came to a public meeting; the speaker got up and said;
'If we let them in, they will steal our daily bread':
He was talking of you and me, my dear, he was talking of
    you and me,

Thought I heard the thunder rumbling in the sky;
It was Hitler over Europe, saying, 'They must die':
O we were in his mind, my dear, O we were in his mind.

Saw a poodle in a jacket fastened with a pin,
Saw a door opened and a cat let in:
But they weren't German Jews, my dear, but they weren't
    German Jews.

Went down the harbour and stood upon the quay.
Saw the fish swimming as if they were free:
Only ten feet away, my dear, only ten feet away.

Walked through a wood, saw the birds in the trees;
They had no politicians and sang at their ease:
They weren't the human race, my dear, they weren't the
    human race.

Dreamed I saw a building with a thousand floors,
A thousand windows and a thousand doors:
Not one of them was ours, my dear, not one of them was ours.

Stood on a great plain in the falling snow;
Ten thousand soldiers marched to and fro:
Looking for you and me, my dear, looking for you and me.

W. H. AUDEN

Night Mail

Commentary for a G.P.O. Film

I

This is the Night Mail crossing the Border,
Bringing the cheque and the postal order,

Letters for the rich, letters for the poor,
The shop at the corner, the girl next door.

Pulling up Beattock, a steady climb:
The gradient's against her, but she's on time.

Past cotton-grass and moorland boulder,
Shovelling white steam over her shoulder,

Snorting noisily, she passes
Silent miles of wind-bent grasses.

Birds turn their heads as she approaches,
Stare from bushes at her blank-faced coaches.

Sheep-dogs cannot turn her course;
They slumber on with paws across.

In the farm she passes no one wakes,
But a jug in a bedroom gently shakes.

II

Dawn freshens. Her climb is done.
Down towards Glasgow she descends,
Towards the steam tugs yelping down a glade of cranes,
Towards the fields of apparatus, the furnaces
Set on the dark plain like gigantic chessmen.
All Scotland waits for her:
In dark glens, beside pale-green lochs,
Men long for news.

Letters of thanks, letters from banks,
Letters of joy from girl and boy,
Receipted bills and invitations
To inspect new stock or to visit relations,
And applications for situations,
And timid lovers' declarations,
And gossip, gossip from all the nations,
News circumstantial, news financial,
Letters with holiday snaps to enlarge in,
Letters with faces scrawled on the margin,
Letters from uncles, cousins and aunts,
Letters to Scotland from the South of France,
Letters of condolence to Highlands and Lowlands,
Written on paper of every hue,
The pink, the violet, the white and the blue,
The chatty, the catty, the boring, the adoring,
The cold and official and the heart's outpouring,
Clever, stupid, short and long,
The typed and the printed and the spelt all wrong.

IV

Thousands are still asleep,
Dreaming of terrifying monsters
Or a friendly tea beside the band in Cranston's or
    Crawford's:
Asleep in working Glasgow, asleep in well-set Edinburgh,
Asleep in granite Aberdeen,
They continue their dreams,
But shall wake soon and hope for letters,

And none will hear the postman's knock
Without a quickening of the heart.
For who can bear to feel himself forgotten?

W. H. AUDEN

In Memory of W. B. Yeats

I

He disappeared in the dead of winter:
The brooks were frozen, the airports almost deserted,
And snow disfigured the public statues;
The mercury sank in the mouth of the dying day.
What instruments we have agree
The day of his death was a dark cold day.

Far from his illness
The wolves ran on through the evergreen forests,
The peasant river was untempted by the fashionable quays;
By mourning tongues
The death of the poet was kept from his poems.

But for him it was his last afternoon as himself,
An afternoon of nurses and rumours;
The provinces of his body revolted,
The squares of his mind were empty,
Silence invaded the suburbs,
The current of his feeling failed; he became his admirers.

Now he is scattered among a hundred cities
And wholly given over to unfamiliar affections,
To find his happiness in another kind of wood
And be punished under a foreign code of conscience.
The words of a dead man
Are modified in the guts of the living.

But in the importance and noise of to-morrow
When the brokers are roaring like beasts on the floor of
     the Bourse,
And the poor have the sufferings to which they are fairly
     accustomed,
And each in the cell of himself is almost convinced of his
     freedom,
A few thousand will think of this day
As one thinks of a day when one did something slightly unusual.

What instruments we have agree
The day of his death was a dark cold day.

II

You were silly like us; your gift survived it all:
The parish of rich women, physical decay,
Yourself. Mad Ireland hurt you into poetry.
Now Ireland has her madness and her weather still,
For poetry makes nothing happen: it survives
In the valley of its making where executives
Would never want to tamper, flows on south
From ranches of isolation and the busy griefs,
Raw towns that we believe and die in; it survives,
A way of happening, a mouth.

Earth, receive an honoured guest:
William Yeats is laid to rest.
Let the Irish vessel lie
Emptied of its poetry.

In the nightmare of the dark
All the dogs of Europe bark,
And the living nations wait,
Each sequestered in its hate;

Intellectual disgrace
Stares from every human face,
And the seas of pity lie
Locked and frozen in each eye.

Follow, poet, follow right
To the bottom of the night,
With your unconstraining voice
Still persuade us to rejoice;

With the farming of a verse
Make a vineyard of the curse,
Sing of human unsuccess
In a rapture of distress;

In the deserts of the heart
Let the healing fountain start,
In the prison of his days
Teach the free man how to praise.

W. H. AUDEN

Carrickfergus

I was born in Belfast between the mountain and the gantries
   To the hooting of lost sirens and the clang of trams:
Thence to Smoky Carrick in County Antrim
   Where the bottle-neck harbour collects the mud which jams

The little boats beneath the Norman castle,
   The pier shining with lumps of crystal salt;
The Scotch Quarter was a line of residential houses
   But the Irish Quarter was a slum for the blind and halt.

The brook ran yellow from the factory stinking of chlorine,
   The yarn-mill called its funeral cry at noon;
Our lights looked over the lough to the lights of Bangor
   Under the peacock aura of a drowning moon.

The Norman walled this town against the country
   To stop his ears to the yelping of his slave
And built a church in the form of a cross but denoting
   The list of Christ on the cross in the angle of the nave.

I was the rector's son, born to the anglican order,
   Banned for ever from the candles of the Irish poor;
The Chichesters knelt in marble at the end of a transept
   With ruffs about their necks, their portion sure.

The war came and a huge camp of soldiers
   Grew from the ground in sight of our house with long
Dummies hanging from gibbets for bayonet practice
   And the sentry's challenge echoing all day long;

A Yorkshire terrier ran in and out by the gate-lodge
    Barred to civilians, yapping as if taking affront:
Marching at ease and singing 'Who Killed Cock Robin?'
    The troops went out by the lodge and off to the Front.

The steamer was camouflaged that took me to England –
    Sweat and khaki in the Carlisle train;
I thought that the war would last for ever and sugar
    Be always rationed and that never again

Would the weekly papers not have photos of sandbags
    And my governess not make bandages from moss
And people not have maps above the fireplace
    With flags on pins moving across and across –

Across the hawthorn hedge the noise of bugles,
    Flares across the night,
Somewhere on the lough was a prison ship for Germans,
    A cage across their sight.

I went to school in Dorset, the world of parents
    Contracted into a puppet world of sons
Far from the mill girls, the smell of porter, the salt-mines
    And the soldiers with their guns.

                                        LOUIS MACNEICE

Soap Suds

This brand of soap has the same smell as once in the big
House he visited when he was eight: the walls of the
   bathroom open
To reveal a lawn where a great yellow ball rolls back through
   a hoop
To rest at the head of a mallet held in the hands of a child.

And these were the joys of that house: a tower with a telescope;
Two great faded globes, one of the earth, one of the stars;
A stuffed black dog in the hall; a walled garden with bees;
A rabbit warren; a rockery; a vine under glass; the sea.

To which he has now returned. The day of course is fine
And a grown-up voice cries Play! The mallet slowly swings,
Then crack, a great gong booms from the dog-dark hall and
   the ball
Skims forward through the hoop and then through the next
   and then

Through hoops where no hoops were and each dissolves in turn
And the grass has grown head-high and an angry voice
   cries Play!
But the ball is lost and the mallet slipped long since from
   the hands
Under the running tap that are not the hands of a child.

LOUIS MACNEICE

Snow

The room was suddenly rich and the great bay-window was
Spawning snow and pink roses against it
Soundlessly collateral and incompatible:
World is suddener than we fancy it.

World is crazier and more of it than we think,
Incorrigibly plural. I peel and portion
A tangerine and spit the pips and feel
The drunkenness of things being various.

And the fire flames with a bubbling sound for world
Is more spiteful and gay than one supposes –
On the tongue on the eyes on the ears in the palms of
   one's hands –
There is more than glass between the snow and the huge roses.

LOUIS MACNEICE

Ghosts in New Houses

There's something dreadful about ghosts in new houses:
Ghosts in old houses are bad enough:
But ghosts in new houses are terrible.
The very newness of these new desolate houses
Would be terrible enough without the ghosts.
But the ghosts are new too.
Blue girls in blue blouses

And people at their Sunday roasts
In broad daylight, within these new houses
On streets where men are sweeping broken glass.

MALCOLM LOWRY

What the Gardener Said to Mrs Traill

– And now they turn poor poetry outdoors.
But in the olden time it was not so,
For it was once the language of man's woe,
And, through the tongues of prophets, of God's laws,
And, through the tongues of angels, of that cause
For which great souls have burned, and dwarf oaks grow.
I, who am friend to love-lies-bleeding, know
A healing in that name, and for these shores.
But now they use hard words for simple things,
For the wild flowers, and the flowers of the lake.
Gayfeather, blazing star, are words that move
Few today, yet have more than a seed's wings.
If ever sinful man like me can speak
With God who humbly calls such names with love.

MALCOLM LOWRY

He Liked the Dead

As the poor end of each dead day drew near
he tried to count the things which he held dear.
No Rupert Brooke and no great lover, he
remembered little of simplicity:
his soul had never been empty of fear
and he would sell it thrice now for a tarot of beer.
He seemed to have known no love, to have valued dread
above all human feelings. He liked the dead.
The grass was not green not even grass to him;
nor was sun, sun; rose, rose; smoke, smoke; limb, limb.

MALCOLM LOWRY

Lessons of the War

To Alan Michell

Vixi duellis nuper idoneus
Et militavi non sine gloria

I. NAMING OF PARTS

To-day we have naming of parts. Yesterday,
We had daily cleaning. And to-morrow morning,
We shall have what to do after firing. But to-day,
To-day we have naming of parts. Japonica
Glistens like coral in all of the neighbouring gardens,
 And to-day we have naming of parts.

This is the lower sling swivel. And this
Is the upper sling swivel, whose use you will see,
When you are given your slings. And this is the piling swivel,
Which in your case you have not got. The branches
Hold in the gardens their silent, eloquent gestures,
     Which in our case we have not got.

This is the safety-catch, which is always released
With an easy flick of the thumb. And please do not let me
See anyone using his finger. You can do it quite easy
If you have any strength in your thumb. The blossoms
Are fragile and motionless, never letting anyone see
     Any of them using their finger.

And this you can see is the bolt. The purpose of this
Is to open the breech, as you see. We can slide it
Rapidly backwards and forwards: we call this
Easing the spring. And rapidly backwards and forwards
The early bees are assaulting and fumbling the flowers:
     They call it easing the Spring.

They call it easing the Spring: it is perfectly easy
If you have any strength in your thumb: like the bolt,
And the breech, and the cocking-piece, and the point of
     balance,
Which in our case we have not got; and the almond-blossom
Silent in all of the gardens and the bees going backwards and
     forwards,
     For to-day we have naming of parts.

Not only how far away, but the way that you say it
Is very important. Perhaps you may never get
The knack of judging a distance, but at least you know
How to report on a landscape: the central sector,
The right of arc and that, which we had last Tuesday,
    And at least you know

That maps are of time, not place, so far as the army
Happens to be concerned – the reason being,
Is one which need not delay us. Again, you know
There are three kinds of tree, three only, the fir and the poplar,
And those which have bushy tops to; and lastly
       That things only seem to be things.

A barn is not called a bam, to put it more plainly,
Or a field in the distance, where sheep may be safely grazing.
You must never be over-sure. You must say, when reporting:
At five o'clock in the central sector is a dozen
Of what appear to be animals; whatever you do,
      Don't call the bleeders *sheep*.

I am sure that's quite clear; and suppose, for the sake of example,
The one at the end, asleep, endeavours to tell us
What he sees over there to the west, and how far away,
After first having come to attention. There to the west,
On the fields of summer the sun and the shadows bestow
       Vestments of purple and gold.

The still white dwellings are like a mirage in the heat,
And under the swaying elms a man and a woman
Lie gently together. Which is, perhaps, only to say

That there is a row of houses to the left of arc,
And that under some poplars a pair of what appear to be humans
Appear to be loving.

Well that, for an answer, is what we might rightly call
Moderately satisfactory only, the reason being,
Is that two things have been omitted, and those are important.
The human beings, now: in what direction are they,
And how far away, would you say? And do not forget
There may be dead ground in between.

There may be dead ground in between; and I may not have got
The knack of judging a distance; I will only venture
A guess that perhaps between me and the apparent lovers,
(Who, incidentally, appear by now to have finished,)
At seven o'clock from the houses, is roughly a distance
Of about one year and a half.

HENRY REED

In Hospital: Poona (1)

Last night I did not fight for sleep
But lay awake from midnight while the world
Turned its slow features to the moving deep
Of darkness, till I knew that you were furled,

Beloved, in the same dark watch as I
And sixty degrees of longitude beside
Vanished as though a swan in ecstasy
Had spanned the distance from your sleeping side.

And like to swan or moon the whole of Wales
Glided within the parish of my care:
I saw the green tide leap on Cardigan,
Your red yacht riding like a legend there.

And the great mountains Dafydd and Llewelyn,
Plynlimmon, Cader Idris and Eryri
Threshing the darkness back from head and fin,
And also the small nameless mining valley

Whose slopes are scratched with streets and sprawling graves
Dark in the lap of firwoods and great boulders
Where you lay waiting, listening to the waves
My hot hands touched your white despondent shoulders

And then ten thousand miles of daylight grew
Between us, and I heard the wild daws crake
In India's starving throat; whereat I knew
That Time upon the heart can break
But love survives the venom of the snake.

ALUN LEWIS

All Day it has Rained . . .

All day it has rained, and we on the edge of the moors
Have sprawled in our bell-tents, moody and dull as boors,
Groundsheets and blankets spread on the muddy ground
And from the first grey wakening we have found
No refuge from the skirmishing fine rain
And the wind that made the canvas heave and flap

And the taut wet guy-ropes ravel out and snap.
All day the rain has glided, wave and mist and dream,
Drenching the gorse and heather, a gossamer stream
Too light to stir the acorns that suddenly
Snatched from their cups by the wild south-westerly
Pattered against the tent and our upturned dreaming faces.
And we stretched out, unbuttoning our braces,
Smoking a Woodbine, darning dirty socks,
Reading the Sunday papers – I saw a fox
And mentioned it in the note I scribbled home; –
And we talked of girls, and dropping bombs on Rome,
And thought of the quiet dead and the loud celebrities
Exhorting us to slaughter, and the herded refugees;
– Yet thought softly, morosely of them, and as indifferently
As of ourselves or those whom we
For years have loved, and will again
Tomorrow maybe love; but now it is the rain
Possesses us entirely, the twilight and the rain.

And I can remember nothing dearer or more to my heart
Than the children I watched in the woods on Saturday
Shaking down burning chestnuts for the schoolyard's merry
    play,
Or the shaggy patient dog who followed me
By Sheet and Steep and up the wooded scree
To the Shoulder O' Mutton where Edward Thomas
    brooded long
On death and beauty – till a bullet stopped his song.

ALUN LEWIS

The Mountain over Aberdare

From this high quarried ledge I see
The place for which the Quakers once
Collected clothes, my father's home,
Our stubborn bankrupt village sprawled
In jaded dusk beneath its nameless hills;
The drab streets strung across the cwm,
Derelict workings, tips of slag
The gospellers and gamblers use
And children scrutting for the coal
That winter dole cannot purvey;
Allotments where the collier digs
While engines hack the coal within his brain;
Grey Hebron in a rigid cramp,
White cheap-jack cinema, the church
Stretched like a sow beside the stream;
And mourners in their Sunday best
Holding a tiny funeral, singing hymns
That drift insidious as the rain
Which rises from the steaming fields
And swathes about the skyline crags
Till all the upland gorse is drenched
And all the creaking mountain gates
Drip brittle tears of crystal peace;
And in a curtained parlour women hug
Huge grief, and anger against God.

But now the dusk, more charitable than Quakers,
Veils the cracked cottages with drifting may
And rubs the hard day off the slate.
The colliers squatting on the ashtip
Listen to one who holds them still with tales,
While that white frock that floats down the dark alley
Looks just like Christ; and in the lane
The clink of coins among the gamblers
Suggests the thirty pieces of silver.

I watch the clouded years
Rune the rough foreheads of these moody hills,
This wet evening, in a lost age.

ALUN LEWIS

A Wartime Dawn

Dulled by the slow glare of the yellow bulb,
As far from sleep still as at any hour
Since distant midnight; with a hollow skull
In which white vapours seem to reel
Among limp muddles of old thought; till eyes
Collapse into themselves like clams in mud . . .
Hand paws the wall to reach the chilly switch;
Then nerve-shot darkness gradually shakes
Throughout the room. *Lie still* . . . Limbs twitch;
Relapse to immobility's faint ache. And time
A while relaxes; space turns wholly black.

But deep in the velvet crater of the ear
A chip of sound abruptly irritates.
A second, a third chirp; and then another far
Emphatic trill and chirrup shrills in answer; notes
From all directions round pluck at the strings
Of hearing with frail finely-sharpened claws.
And in an instant, every wakened bird
Across surrounding miles of air
Outside, is sowing like a scintillating sand
Its throat's incessantly replenished store
Of tuneless singsong, timeless, aimless, blind.

Draw now with prickling hand the curtains back;
Unpin the blackout-cloth; let in
Grim crack-of-dawn's first glimmer through the glass.
All's yet half sunk in Yesterday's stale death,
Obscurely still beneath a moist-tinged blank
Sky like the inside of a deaf mute's mouth . . .
Nearest within the window's sight, ash-pale
Against a cinder coloured wall, the white
Pearblossom hovers like a stare; rain-wet
The further housetops weakly shine; and there,
Beyond, hangs flaccidly a lone barrage-balloon.

An incommunicable desolation weighs
Like depths of stagnant water on this break of day. –
Long meditation without thought. – Until a breeze
From some pure Nowhere straying, stirs
A pang of poignant odour from the earth, an unheard sigh
Pregnant with sap's sweet tang and raw soil's fine
Aroma, smell of stone, and acrid breath
Of gravel puddles. While the brooding green
Of nearby gardens' grass and trees, and quiet flat
Blue leaves, the distant lilac mirages, are made
Clear by increasing daylight, and intensified.

Now head sinks into pillows in retreat
Before this morning's hovering advance;
(Behind loose lids, in sleep's warm porch, half hears
White hollow clink of bottles, – dragging crunch
Of milk-cart wheels, – and presently a snatch
Of windy whistling as the newsboy's bike winds near.
Distributing to neighbour's peaceful steps
Reports of last-night's battles); at last sleeps.
While early guns on Norway's bitter coast
Where faceless troops are landing, renew fire:
And one more day of War starts everywhere.

DAVID GASCOYNE

Canoe

Well, I am thinking this may be my last
summer, but cannot lose even a part of
pleasure in the old-fashioned art of
idleness. I cannot stand aghast

at whatever doom hovers in the background;
while grass and buildings and the somnolent river,
who know they are allowed to last for ever,
exchange between them the whole subdued sound

of this hot time. What sudden fearful fate
can deter my shade wandering next year
from a return? Whistle and I will hear
and come another evening, when this boat

travels with you alone towards Iffley:
as you lie looking up for thunder again,
this cool touch does not betoken rain;
it is my spirit that kisses your mouth lightly.

KEITH DOUGLAS

X

1945–1970

Fern Hill

Now as I was young and easy under the apple boughs
About the lilting house and happy as the grass was green,
    The night above the dingle starry,
        Time let me hail and climb
      Golden in the heydays of his eyes,
And honoured among wagons I was prince of the apple towns
And once below a time I lordly had the trees and leaves
        Trail with daisies and barley
    Down the rivers of the windfall light.

And as I was green and carefree, famous among the barns
About the happy yard and singing as the farm was home,
    In the sun that is young once only,
        Time let me play and be
      Golden in the mercy of his means,
And green and golden I was huntsman and herdsman, the calves
Sang to my horn, the foxes on the hills barked clear and cold,
        And the sabbath rang slowly
    In the pebbles of the holy streams.

All the sun long it was running, it was lovely, the hay
Fields high as the house, the tunes from the chimneys, it was air
    And playing, lovely and watery
        And fire green as grass.
      And nightly under the simple stars
As I rode to sleep the owls were bearing the farm away,
All the moon long I heard, blessed among stables, the night-jars
        Flying with the ricks, and the horses
        Flashing into the dark.

And then to awake, and the farm, like a wanderer white
With the dew, come back, the cock on his shoulder: it was all
    Shining, it was Adam and maiden,
        The sky gathered again
    And the sun grew round that very day.
So it must have been after the birth of the simple light
In the first, spinning place, the spellbound horses walking warm
    Out of the whinnying green stable
      On to the fields of praise.

And honoured among foxes and pheasants by the gay house
Under the new made clouds and happy as the heart was long,
    In the sun born over and over,
        I ran my heedless ways,
    My wishes raced through the house high hay
And nothing I cared, at my sky blue trades, that time allows
In all his tuneful turning so few and such morning songs
    Before the children green and golden
      Follow him out of grace,

Nothing I cared, in the lamb white days, that time would
    take me
Up to the swallow thronged loft by the shadow of my hand,
    In the moon that is always rising,
        Nor that riding to sleep
    I should hear him fly with the high fields
And wake to the farm forever fled from the childless land.
Oh as I was young and easy in the mercy of his means,
      Time held me green and dying
    Though I sang in my chains like the sea.

DYLAN THOMAS

Poem on His Birthday

In the mustardseed sun,
By full tilt river and switchback sea
   Where the cormorants scud,
In his house on stilts high among beaks
   And palavers of birds
This sandgrain day in the bent bay's grave
   He celebrates and spurns
His driftwood thirty-fifth wind turned age;
   Herons spire and spear.

Under and round him go
Flounders, gulls, on their cold, dying trails,
   Doing what they are told,
Curlews aloud in the congered waves
   Work at their ways to death,
And the rhymer in the long tongued room,
   Who tolls his birthday bell,
Toils towards the ambush of his wounds;
   Herons, steeple stemmed, bless.

In the thistledown fall,
He sings towards anguish; finches fly
   In the claw tracks of hawks
On a seizing sky; small fishes glide
   Through wynds and shells of drowned
Ship towns to pastures of otters. He
   In his slant, racking house
And the hewn coils of his trade perceives
   Herons walk in their shroud,

The livelong river's robe
Of minnows wreathing around their prayer;
    And far at sea he knows,
Who slaves to his crouched, eternal end
    Under a serpent cloud,
Dolphins dive in their turnturtle dust,
    The rippled seals streak down
To kill and their own tide daubing blood
    Slides good in the sleek mouth.

    In a cavernous, swung
Wave's silence, wept white angelus knells.
    Thirty-five bells sing struck
On skull and scar where his loves lie wrecked.
    Steered by the falling stars.
And to-morrow weeps in a blind cage
    Terror will rage apart
Before chains break to a hammer flame
    And love unbolts the dark

    And freely he goes lost
In the unknown, famous light of great
    And fabulous, dear God.
Dark is a way and light is a place,
    Heaven that never was
Nor will be ever is always true,
    And, in that brambled void,
Plenty as blackberries in the woods
    The dead grow for His joy.

There he might wander bare
With the spirits of the horseshoe bay
    Or the stars' seashore dead,
Marrow of eagles, the roots of whales
    And wishbones of wild geese,
With blessed, unborn God and His Ghost,
    And every soul His priest,
Gulled and chanter in young Heaven's fold
    Be at cloud quaking peace,

But dark is a long way.
He, on the earth of the night, alone
    With all the living, prays,
Who knows the rocketing wind will blow
    The bones out of the hills,
And the scythed boulders bleed, and the last
    Rage shattered waters kick
Masts and fishes to the still quick stars,
    Faithlessly unto Him

Who is the light of old
And air shaped Heaven where souls grow wild
    As horses in the foam:
Oh, let me midlife mourn by the shrined
    And druid herons' vows
The voyage to ruin I must run,
    Dawn ships clouted aground,
Yet, though I cry with tumbledown tongue,
    Count my blessings aloud;

Four elements and five
Senses, and man a spirit in love
    Tangling through this spun slime
To his nimbus bell cool kingdom come
    And the lost, moonshine domes,
And the sea that hides his secret selves
    Deep in its black, base bones,
Lulling of spheres in the seashell flesh,
    And this last blessing most,

    That the closer I move
To death, one man through his sundered hulks,
    The louder the sun blooms
And the tusked, ramshackling sea exults;
    And every wave of the way
And gale I tackle, the whole world then,
    With more triumphant faith
Than ever was since the world was said,
    Spins its morning of praise,

    I hear the bouncing hills
Grow larked and greener at berry brown
    Fall and the dew larks sing
Taller this thunderclap spring, and how
    More spanned with angels ride
The mansouled fiery islands! Oh,
    Holier then their eyes,
And my shining men no more alone
    As I sail out to die.

DYLAN THOMAS

In my Craft or Sullen Art

In my craft or sullen art
Exercised in the still night
When only the moon rages
And the lovers lie abed
With all their griefs in their arms,
I labour by singing light
Not for ambition or bread
Or the strut and trade of charms
On the ivory stages
But for the common wages
Of their most secret heart.

Not for the proud man apart
From the raging moon I write
On these spindrift pages
Nor for the towering dead
With their nightingales and psalms
But for the lovers, their arms
Round the griefs of the ages,
Who pay no praise or wages
Nor heed my craft or art.

DYLAN THOMAS

Anne Donne

I lay in in London;
And round my bed my live children were crying,
And round my bed my dead children were singing.
As my blood left me it set the clappers swinging:
Tolling, jarring, jowling, all the bells of London
Were ringing as I lay dying –
John Donne, Anne Donne, Undone!

Ill-done, well-done, all done.
All fearing done, all striving and all hoping,
All weanings, watchings, done; all reckonings whether
Of debts, of moons, summed; all hither and thither
Sucked in the one ebb. Then, on my bed in London,
I heard him call me, reproaching:
Undone, Anne Donne, Undone!

Not done, not yet done!
Wearily I rose up at his bidding.
The sweat still on my face, my hair dishevelled,
Over the bells and the tolling seas I travelled,
Carrying my dead child, so lost, so light a burden,
To Paris, where he sat reading
And showed him my ill news. That done,
Went back, lived on in London.

SYLVIA TOWNSEND WARNER

Tilth

*Robert Graves, the British veteran, is no longer in the
poetic swim. He still resorts to traditional metres and
rhyme, and to such out-dated words as* tilth; *with-
holding his 100% approbation also from contem-
porary poems that favour sexual freedom.*

— From a New York critical weekly

Gone are the drab monosyllabic days
When 'agricultural labour' still was *tilth;*
And '100% approbation', *praise;*
And 'pornographic modernism', *filth* –
Yet still I stand by *tilth* and *filth* and *praise.*

ROBERT GRAVES

The Christmas Robin

The snows of February had buried Christmas
Deep in the woods, where grew self-seeded
The fir-trees of a Christmas yet unknown,
Without a candle or a strand of tinsel.

Nevertheless when, hand in hand, plodding
Between the frozen ruts, we lovers paused
And 'Christmas trees!' cried suddenly together,
Christmas was there again, as in December.

We velveted our love with fantasy
Down a long vista-row of Christmas trees,
Whose coloured candles slowly guttered down
As grandchildren came trooping round our knees.

But he knew better, did the Christmas robin –
The murderous robin with his breast aglow
And legs apart, in a spade-handle perched:
He prophesied more snow, and worse than snow.

ROBERT GRAVES

An Old Woman Speaks of the Moon

She was urgent to speak of the moon: she offered delight
And wondering praise to be shared by the girl in the shop,
Lauding the goddess who blessed her each sleepless night
Greater and brighter till full: but the girl could not stop.

She turned and looked up in my face, and hastened to cry
How beautiful was the orb, how the constant glow
Comforted in the cold night the old waking eye:
How fortunate she, whose lodging was placed that so

She in the lonely night, in her lonely age,
She from her poor lean bed might behold the undying
Letter of loveliness written on heaven's page,
The sharp silver arrows leap down to where she was lying.

The dying spoke love to the immortal, the foul to the fair,
The withered to the still-flowering, the bound to the free:
The nipped worm to the silver swan that sails through the air:
And I took it as good, and a happy omen to me.

RUTH PITTER

Wild Honey

You, the man going along the road alone,
Careless or wretched, rarely thoughtful, never serene,
Possessing nothing worth having; man of the sickly pleasures,
Man of the mawkish, wrong-headed sorrows, typical man:

The wealth is there, man of the empty pocket,
The gold is there, man of the greying hair,
And the sweetness, man whose life is bitter as ashes,
The good work, the accomplished work, the wonderful artifice,
The wonderful artefact, man of the useless hands.

There in the riddled tree, hanging in darkness,
There in the roof of the house and the wall-hollow,
The new like pearl, the old like magical amber,
Hidden with cunning, guarded by fiery thousands
(See where they stream like smoke from the hole in the gable),
There in the bank of the brook the immortal secret,
In the ground under your feet the treasure of nations,
Under the weary foot of the fool, the wild honey.

RUTH PITTER

Sin

Take off the business suit, the old-school tie,
The gown, the cap, drop the reviews, awards,
Certificates, stand naked in your sty,
A little carnivore, clothed in dried turds.
The snot that slowly fills our passages
Seeps up from hollows where the dead beasts lie;
Dumb stamping dances spell our messages,
We only know what makes our arrows fly.
Lost in the wood, we sometimes glimpse the sky
Between the branches, and the words drop down
We cannot hear, the alien voices high

And hard, singing salvation, grace, life, dawn.
Like wolves, we lift our snouts: Blood, blood, we cry,
The blood that bought us so we need not die.

D. GWENALLT JONES
translated from the Welsh by Rowan Williams

Lovers are Separate

'Do you hear the bells?'

'What bells?'

'The swinging bells the singing bells
Downed bells drowned bells
Hear the flying sound the dying sound
Tossed sound lost sound
Of the old bells sea-cold singing bells
Under the sea.'

'Bells? I hear nothing
But the even breath of the sea.
And look, oh come closer and look with me –
From this rock we stare down into depths so clear
We should see any bells that might be there.
No, there is nothing.
Only the chrysoprase water, deep,
Making a large, bare, twilit room
Such as I've wandered through in sleep,
A dream home . . .'

'Yes; but I tell you I hear the bells ringing!
Almost, I see the wild swinging
And then the swung sound the up-flung sound
Balanced high aloft – high aloft – listen now, right overhead!
Hear it top-
            -pling stumbling sliding and tumbling
All down the silver air into the green sea
To be lost.
Again lost
As the dead
In that hollow sea.

'And still you heard nothing?'

'Alas, we could not have drawn closer and yet I heard nothing
But the even breath of the sea.'

FRANCES BELLERBY

Ends Meet

My grandmother came down the steps into the garden.
She shone in the gauzy air.
She said: 'There's an old woman at the gate –
See what she wants, my dear.'

My grandmother's eyes were blue like the damsels
Darting and swerving above the stream,
Or like the kingfisher arrow shot into darkness
Through the archway's dripping gleam.

My grandmother's hair was silver as sunlight.
The sun had been poured right over her, I saw,
And ran down her dress and spread a pool for her shadow
To float in. And she would live for evermore.

There was nobody at the gate when I got there.
Not even a shadow hauling along the road,
Nor my yellow snail delicate under the ivy,
Nor my sheltering cold-stone toad.

But the sunflowers aloft were calm. They'd seen no one.
They were sucking light, for ever and a day.
So I busied myself with going away unheeded
And with having nothing to say.

No comment, nothing to tell, or to think,
Whilst the day followed the homing sun.
There was no old woman at my grandmother's gate.

And there isn't at mine.

FRANCES BELLERBY

from The Sound of the Wind that is Blowing

The land of Y Llain was on the high marsh
on the border between Caron-is-Clawdd and Padarn Odwyn
slanting from Cae Top down to Y Waun,
and beyond Cae Top was a glade of dark trees –
pines and tall larches – to break the cold wind,
the wind from the north.
And there were the small four-sided fields
like checkerboard, or a patchwork quilt,
and around each of the fields, a hedge.

      My father planted the hedges farthest from the house, –
The hedges of Cae Top and Cae Brwyn, –
myself a youngster at his heels
putting the plants in his hand;
three hawthorns and a beech-tree,
three hawthorns and a beech-tree in turn;
his feet measuring the distance between them along the top of
    the ditch,
squeezing them solidly into the loose earth-and-chalk.
Then the patterned wiring outside them –
the square posts of peeled oak-wood
sunk deep in the living earth –
and I getting to turn the wiring-engine on the post
while he did the stapling,
the hammer ringing in my ears with the pounding.
And I daring on the sly
to send a telegram back over the taut wires
to the other children at the far end of the ditch,
the note of music raising its pitch
with each turn I gave the old wiring-engine's handle.

My grandfather, said my father, had planted the Middle
    Fields
– Cae Cwteri, Cae Polion, Cae Troi –
but generations we knew nothing at all about,
except for the mark of their handiwork on Cae Lloi and Cae
    Moch
had planted the tall strong stout-trunked trees round the house,
and set sweet-plums here and there in the hedges.
    And there we children would be
safe in a fold in the ditch under the hedges,
the dried leaves a coverlet to keep us warm
(like the babes in the story hidden with leaves by the birds).
The breeze that trickled through the trunks of the hedges
was not enough to ruffle the wren's and the robin's feathers:
but above the hedges and the trees, above the house,
aloft in the firmament, the wind was
tumbling the clouds, tickling them till their white laughter
was unruly hysteria like children on a kitchen floor,
till the excess of play turns suddenly strange
and the laughter's whiteness scowls, and darkens,
and the tears burst forth, and the clouds escape
in a race from the wind, from the tickling and the tumbling,
escaping headlong from the wind's provocation –
the pursuing wind outside me,
and I fast in the fold in the ditch beneath the leaves
listening to its sound, outside,
with nothing at all occuring within what I am
because of the care and craft of generations of my fathers
planting their hedges prudnetly to shelter me in my day, –
nothing – despite my wishing and wishing . . .

J. KITCHENER DAVIES
translated from the Welsh by Joseph P. Clancy

The River God of the River Mimram
in Hertfordshire

I may be smelly and I may be old,
Rough in my pebbles, reedy in my pools,
But where my fish float by I bless their swimming
And I like the people to bathe in me, especially women.
But I can drown the fools
Who bathe too close to the weir, contrary to rules,
And they take a long time drowning
As I throw them up now and then in a spirit of clowning.
Hi yih, yippity-yap, merrily I flow,
Oh I may be an old foul river but I have plenty of go.
Once there was a lady who was too bold,
She bathed in me by the tall black cliff where the water
    runs cold,
So I brought her down here
To be my beautiful dear.

STEVIE SMITH

Correspondence between Mr Harrison in
Newcastle and Mr Sholto Peach Harrison in Hull

Sholto Peach Harrison you are no son of mine
And do you think I bred you up to cross the River Tyne
And do you think I bred you up (and mother says the same)
And do you think I bred you up to live a life of shame
To live a life of shame my boy as you are thinking to

Down south in Kingston-upon-Hull a traveller in glue?
Come back my bonny boy nor break your father's heart
Come back and marry Lady Susan Smart
She has a mint in Anglo-Persian oil
And Sholto never more need think of toil.

You are an old and evil man my father
I tell you frankly Sholto had much rather
Travel in glue unrecompensed unwed
Than go to church with oily Sue and afterwards to bed.

STEVIE SMITH

Infelice

Walking swiftly with a dreadful duchess,
He smiled too briefly, his face was as pale as sand,
He jumped into a taxi when he saw me coming,
Leaving me alone with a private meaning,
He loves me so much, my heart is singing.
Later at the Club when I rang him in the evening
They said: Sir Rat is dining, is dining, is dining,
No Madam, he left no message, ah how his silence speaks,
He loves me too much for words, my heart is singing.
The Pullman seats are here, the tickets for Paris, I am waiting,
Presently the telephone rings, it is his valet speaking,
Sir Rat is called away, to Scotland, his constituents,
(Ah the dreadful duchess, but he loves me best)
Best pleasure to the last, my heart is singing.
One night he came, it was four in the morning,
Walking slowly upstairs, he stands beside my bed,

Dear darling, lie beside me, it is too cold to stand speaking,
He lies down beside me, his face is like the sand,
He is in a sleep of love, my heart is singing.
Sleeping softly softly, in the morning I must wake him,
And waking he murmurs, I only came to sleep.
The words are so sweetly cruel, how deeply he loves me,
I say them to myself alone, my heart is singing.
Now the sunshine strengthens, it is ten in the morning,
He is so timid in love, he only needs to know,
He is my little child, how can he come if I do not call him,
I will write and tell him everything, I take the pen and write:
I love you so much, my heart is singing.

STEVIE SMITH

The Long Garden

It was the garden of the golden apples,
A long garden between a railway and a road,
In the sow's rooting where the hen scratches
We dipped our fingers in the pockets of God.

In the thistly hedge old boots were flying sandals
By which we travelled through the childhood skies,
Old buckets rusty-holed with half-hung handles
Were drums to play when old men married wives.

The pole that lifted the clothes-line in the middle
Was the flag-pole on a prince's palace when
We looked at it through fingers crossed to riddle
In evening sunlight miracles for men.

It was the garden of the golden apples,
And when the Carrick train went by we knew
That we could never die till something happened
Like wishing for a fruit that never grew,

Or wanting to be up on Candle-Fort
Above the village with its shops and mill.
The racing cyclists' gasp-gapped reports
Hinted of pubs where life can drink his fill.

And when the sun went down into Drumcatton
And the New Moon by its little finger swung
From the telegraph wires, we knew how God had happened
And what the blackbird in the whitehorn sang.

It was the garden of the golden apples,
The half-way house where we had stopped a day
Before we took the west road to Drumcatton
Where the sun was always setting on the play.

PATRICK KAVANAGH

Epic

I have lived in important places, times
When great events were decided: who owned
That half a rood of rock, a no-man's land
Surrounded by our pitchfork-armed claims.
I heard the Duffys shouting 'Damn your soul'
And old McCabe, stripped to the waist, seen
Step the plot defying blue cast-steel –
'Here is the march along these iron stones'.
That was the year of the Munich bother. Which
Was most important? I inclined
To lose my faith in Ballyrush and Gortin
Till Homer's ghost came whispering to my mind.
He said: I made the *Iliad* from such
A local row. Gods make their own importance.

PATRICK KAVANAGH

What Is a Man?

What is living? Finding a great hall
Inside a cell.
What is knowing? One root
To all the branches.

What is believing? Holding out
Until relief comes.
And forgiving? Crawling through thorns
To the side of an old foe.

What is singing? Winning back
The first breath of creation:
And work should be a song
Made of wheat or wood.

What is statecraft? Something
Still on all fours.
And defence of the realm?
A sword thrust in a baby's hand.

What is being a nation? A talent
Springing in the heart.
And love of country? Keeping house
Among a cloud of witness.

What is this world to the great powers?
A circle turning.
And to the lowly of the earth?
A cradle rocking.

WALDO WILLIAMS
translated from the Welsh by Emyr Humphreys

Listening to Collared Doves

I am homesick now for middle age, as then
For youth. For youth is our home-land: we were born
And lived there long, though afterwards moved on
From state to state, too slowly acclimatising
Perhaps and never fluent, through the surprising
Countries, in any languages but one.

This mourning now for middle age, no more
For youth, confirms me old as not before
Age rounds the world, they say, to childhood's far
Archaic shores; it may be so at last,
But what now (strength apart) I miss the most
Is time unseen like air, since everywhere.

And yet, when in the months and in the skies
That were the cuckoos', and in the nearer trees
That were the deep-voiced wood-pigeons', it is
Instead now the collared doves that call and call
(Their three flat notes growing traditional),
I think we live long enough, listening to these.

I draw my line out from their simple curve
And say, our natural span may be enough;
And think of one I knew and her long life;
And how the climate changed and how the sign-
Posts changed, defaced, from her Victorian
Childhood and youth, through our century of grief,

And how she adapted as she could, not one
By nature adaptable, bred puritan
(Though quick to be pleased and having still her own
Lightness of heart). She died twenty years ago,
Aged, of life – it seems, all she could do
Having done, all the change that she could know having known.

E. J. SCOVELL

Northumbrian Sequence: IV

Let in the wind
Let in the rain
Let in the moors tonight.

The storm beats on my window-pane,
Night stands at my bed-foot,
Let in the fear,
Let in the pain,
Let in the trees that toss and groan,
Let in the north tonight.

Let in the nameless formless power
That beats upon my door,
Let in the ice, let in the snow,
The banshee howling on the moor,
The bracken-bush on the bleak hillside,
Let in the dead tonight.

The whistling ghost behind the dyke,
The dead that rot in the mire,
Let in the thronging ancestors
The unfulfilled desire,
Let in the wraith of the dead earl,
Let in the unborn tonight.

Let in the cold,
Let in the wet,
Let in the loneliness,
Let in the quick,
Let in the dead,
Let in the unpeopled skies.

Oh how can virgin fingers weave
A covering for the void,
How can my fearful heart conceive
Gigantic solitude?
How can a house so small contain
A company so great?
Let in the dark,
Let in the dead,
Let in your love tonight.

Let in the snow that numbs the grave,
Let in the acorn-tree,
The mountain stream and mountain stone,
Let in the bitter sea.

Fearful is my virgin heart
And frail my virgin form,
And must I then take pity on
The raging of the storm
That rose up from the great abyss
Before the earth was made,
That pours the stars in cataracts
And shakes this violent world?

Let in the fire,
Let in the power,
Let in the invading might.

Gentle must my fingers be
And pitiful my heart
Since I must bind in human form
A living power so great,

A living impulse great and wild
That cries about my house
With all the violence of desire
Desiring this my peace.

Pitiful my heart must hold
The lonely stars at rest,
Have pity on the raven's cry
The torrent and the eagle's wing,
The icy water of the tarn
And on the biting blast.

Let in the wound,
Let in the pain,
Let in your child tonight.

KATHLEEN RAINE

To my sister Sian

Do you remember Sian? How dearly do you remember?
(Autobiography)

Nature and Time are against us now:
no more we leap up the river like salmon,
nor dive through its fishy holes
sliding along its summer corridor
with all the water from Wales, nor tear it to silver
shreds with our childish arms when it bolted our path for
   the day,

nor wade wearing our bindings
of string weed, white-flowering from our nakedness;
nor lie in the hot yellow fields with the cows.

We go home separately Sian.
Strangest of all changes, that you have one door,
I another! Dreamily I write to our childhood,
sisters with a brotherly friendship, one loyal to both.
There hang the black woods still with candles of daffodils
lighting the draught of the wind, and our parted language
speaks to each of us of the keepers' cot in the bracken corner
and the stream bed where the water had faded to rock.
Easily we keep our secrets now, for no-one cares
if we dare the red floods together, two little fools in the
    darkness
whose souls flew high above danger, whose bodies
death had a hundred times in its reach.

Forever we
did not end, but passed over our paths,
I following you, dabbling our hands in the birds' nests,
darting through ghost walk and haunted graveyard
when the year was dead in the church tower.
We had one home together. That put us beyond all danger:
that set us forever, that and our unfathomable friendship with
    trees,
fields and horizons. Two children
soilitary, pilgrimy, silent, inscrutably wishing
forever dallying with lostness, whether our choice
was through the jay woods, or over the mushroom
    mountains,
or the old cider orchards.

Our secrets
were eternal and will always be. Forever dallying
with lostness, at last we were lost and all paths
were the path of our unforgettable double childhood.
All our secrets were one – secrecy.
The memory of what we kept secret is gone, but the secret is
   true.
All the places were us, we were all the places,
and the inscrutable innocent altars of nature.
I see two children slipping into a wood
speechlessly happy. Two lives lived have not changed it.
For our ways, our fields, our river, our lostness
were children. So we were our country.

MARGIAD EVANS

Brither Worm

I saw a lang worm snoove throu the space atween twa stanes,
pokan its heid, if it had ane, up throu a hole in the New Toun,
up throu a crack ye wad hardly hae seen in an area of stane,
unkenn'd upliftit tons of mason-wark piled on the soil
wi causey-streets, biggit of granite setts, like blank waas flat
  on the grund,
plainstane pavements of Thurso slabs laid owre the stane-
  aircht cellars.
the area fifteen feet doun, wi weill-fittan flagstanes, Regency
  wark.
Nou, in my deedit stane-and-lime property awntert a nesh
  and perfect worm,

and I was abasit wi thochts of what was gaun-on ablow my
    feet,
that the feu'd and rentit grand was the soil of the
    Drumsheuch Forest,
and that life gaed on inunder the grund-waa-stane and had
    sent out a spy,
jalousan some Frien of the Worms had brocht a maist
    welcome shoure,
whan I on my side of the crust had teemit a pail of water,
meaning to gie the place a guid scrub-doun wi a stable-besom.
Sae a lang, saft, sappy and delicate pink and naukit cratur
neatly wan out frae atween thae weil-fittan chiselled,
    unnaitural stanes.
I watched and thocht lang of the wonders of Nature, and
    didna muve,
and thocht of the deeps of the soil, deeper nor the sea, and I
    made nae sound.
A rat raxt frae a crack atween twa stanes.
My hale body sheuk wi the grue.
It keekit at me, and was gane.

ROBERT GARIOCH

I'm Neutral

Last night in Scotland Street I met a man
that gruppit my lapel – a kinna foreign
cratur he seemed; he tellt me, There's a war on
atween the Lang-nebs and the Big-heid Clan.

I wasna fasht, I took him for a moron,
naething byordnar, but he said, Ye're wan
of thae lang-nebbit folk, and if I can,
I'm gaunnae pash ye doun and rype your sporran.

Says he, I'll get a medal for this job:
we're watchan ye, we ken fine what ye're at,
ye're with us or agin us, shut your gob.

He gied a clout that knockit aff my hat,
bawlan, A fecht! Come on, the Big-heid Mob!
Aweill, I caa'd him owre, and that was that.

ROBERT GARIOCH

Ghaisties

Cauld are the ghaisties in yon kirkyaird,
    and cauld the airms
that they mell wi the mists of the timm breists of their loves;
at the heid of their bed cauld angels staund on guaird,
    and marble doves.
They ken-na the fear of Gode, as they sleep ayont sin,
    nor the terror of man,
and there's nane but the angels to glunch at their trueloves'
  chairms,
yet they lang for the reek of the creeshie swat frae the skin
    and the grup of a haun.

But we in the warld are alowe
wi the glawmer of bluid-reid flame
that loups to the bluid in yer tongue's tip as it tingles on
   mine,
      and the howe
of the back we love wi our finger-nebbs, and the wame,
brent-white, wi a flush aneath like cramosie wine,
hou it curves to meet my ain!
      O, ma sonsie frow,
whit tho the flesh be bruckle, and fiends be slee,
the joys of the solid earth we'll pree or they dwine,
we'll lauch at daith, and man, and the fiend, aa three, afore
   we dee.

ROBERT GARIOCH

Poem From Llanybri

If you come my way that is. . .
Between now and then, I will offer you
A fist full of rock cress fresh from the bank
The valley tips of garlic red with dew
Cooler than shallots, a breath you can swank

In the village when you come. At noon-day
I will offer you a choice bowl of cawl
Served with a 'lover's' spoon and a chopped spray
Of leeks or savori fach, not used now,

In the old way you'll understand. The din
Of children singing through the eyelet sheds
Ringing 'smith hoops, chasing the butt of hens;
Or I can offer you Cwmcelyn spread

With quartz stones from the wild scratchings of men:
You will have to go carefully with clogs
Or thick shoes for it's treacherous the fen,
The East and West Marshes also have bogs.

Then I'll do the lights, fill the lamp with oil,
Get coal from the shed, water from the well;
Pluck and draw pigeon with crop of green foil
This your good supper from the lime-tree fell.

A sit by the hearth with blue flames rising,
No talk. Just a stare at 'Time' gathering
Healed thoughts, pool insight, like swan sailing
Peace and sound around the home, offering

You a night's rest and my day's energy.
You must come – start this pilgrimage
Can you come? – send an ode or elegy
In the old way and raise our heritage.

LYNETTE ROBERTS

Poem

We must uprise O my people. Though
Secretly trenched in sorrel, we must
Upshine outshine the day's sun: and day
Intensified by the falling prism
Of rain shall curve our smile with straw.

Bring plimsole plover to the tensile sand
And with cuprite crest and petulant feet
Distil our notes into febrile reeds
Crisply starched at the water-rail of tides.
On gault and greensand a gramophone stands:

In zebrine stripes strike out the pilotless
Age: from saxophone towns brass out the dead:
Disinter futility, that we entombing men
Might bridle our runaway hearts.
On tamarisk, on seafield pools shivering

With water-cats, ring out the square slate notes.
Shape the birdbox trees with neumes. Wind sound
Singular into cool and simple corners,
Round pale bittern grass, and all unseen
Unknown places of sheltered rubble

Where whimbrels, redshanks, sandpipers ripple
For the wing of living. Under tin of earth
And wooden boles where owls break music:
From this killing world against humanity,
Uprise against, outshine the day's sun.

LYNETTE ROBERTS

For a Child Expected

Lovers whose lifted hands are candles in winter,
Whose gentle ways like streams in the easy summer,
Lying together
For secret setting of a child, love what they do,
Thinking they make that candle immortal, those streams
    forever flow,
And yet do better than they know.

So the first flutter of a baby felt in the womb,
Its little signal and promise of riches to come,
Is taken in its father's name;
Its life is the body of his love, like his caress,
First delicate and strange, that daily use
Makes dearer and priceless.

Our baby was to be the living sign of our joy,
Restore to each the other's lost infancy;
To a painter's pillaging eye
Poet's coiled hearing, add the heart we might earn
By the help of love; all that our passion would yield
We put to planning our child.

The world flowed in; whatever we liked we took:
For its hair, the gold curls of the November oak
We saw on our walk;
Snowberries that make a Milky Way in the wood
For its tender hands; calm screen of the frozen flood
For our care of its childhood.

But the birth of a child is an uncontrollable glory;
Cat's cradle of hopes will hold no living baby,
Long though it lay quietly.
And when our baby stirs and struggles to be born
It compels humility: what we began
Is now its own.

For *as the sun that shines through glass*
So Jesus in His Mother was.
Therefore every human creature,
Since it shares in His nature,
In candle-gold passion or white
Sharp star should show its own way of light.
May no parental dread or dream
Darken our darling's early beam:
May she grow to her right powers
Unperturbed by passion of ours.

ANNE RIDLER

Black Friday

Oot behind a lorry,
Peyin nae heed,
Ablow a doubledecker,
A poor wean deid.

Perra worn sannies,
Wee durrty knees,
Heh, erra polis,
Stand back please!

Lookit the conductriss.
Face as white as chalk,
Heh, see the driver but
Cannae even talk.

Anyone a witness?
Na, we niver saw.
Glad ah'm no the polis
Goin tae tell its maw.

Weemen windae-hingin
Herts in their mooth,
It's no oor close, Lizzie
Oh Gawdstrewth!

Screams on the landin,
Twa closes doon,
It's no wee Hughie!
Poor Nellie Broon.

Phone up the shipyard.
Oh, what a shame!
Yes, we'll inform him,
Please repeat the name.

See Big Hughie,
Jokin wi the squad,
Better knock off, Heug,
Oh dear God.

Whit – no his laddie?
Aw, bloody hell!
D'ye see Hughie's face but,
He's just a boy himsel.

JAMES COPELAND

Dead ponies

There is death enough in Europe without these
Dead ponies on the mountain.
They are the underlining, the emphasis of death.
It is not wonderful that when they live
Their eyes are shadowed under mats of hair.
Despair and famine do not gripe so hard
When the bound earth and sky are kept remote
Behind clogged hairs.

The snows engulfed them, pressed their withered haunches flat,
Filled up their nostrils, burdened the cage of their ribs,
The snow retreated. Their bodies stink to heaven,
Potently crying out to raven and hawk and dog;
Come! Pick us clean; cleanse our fine bones of blood.

They were never lovely save as foals,
Before their necks grew long, uncrested;
Hut the wildness of the mountain was in their stepping,
The pride of Spring burnt in their haunches,
They were tawny as the rushes of the marsh.

The prey-birds have had their fill, and preen their feathers:
Soft entrails have gone to make the hawk arrogant.

BRENDA CHAMBERLAIN

The Bee Meeting

Who are these people at the bridge to meet me? They are the
    villagers –
The rector, the midwife, the sexton, the agent for bees.
In my sleeveless summery dress I have no protection,
And they are all gloved and covered, why did nobody tell me?
They are smiling and taking out veils tacked to ancient hats.

I am nude as a chicken neck, does nobody love me?
Yes, here is the secretary of bees with her white shop smock,
Buttoning the cuffs at my wrists and the slit from my neck to
    my knees.

Now I am milkweed silk, the bees will not notice.
They will not smell my fear, my fear, my fear.

Which is the rector now, is it that man in black?
Which is the midwife, is that her blue coat?
Everybody is nodding a square black head, they are knights
   in visors,
Breastplates of cheesecloth knotted under the armpits.
Their smiles and their voices are changing. I am led through a
   beanfield.

Strips of tinfoil winking like people,
Feather dusters fanning their hands in a sea of bean flowers,
Creamy bean flowers with black eyes and leaves like bored
   hearts,
Is it blood clots the tendrils are dragging up that string?
No, no, it is scarlet flowers that will one day be edible.

Now they are giving me a fashionable white straw Italian hat
And a black veil that molds to my face, they are making me
   one of them.
They are leading me to the shorn grove, the circle of hives.
Is it the hawthorn that smells so sick?
The barren body of hawthorn, etherising its children.

Is it some operation that is taking place?
It is the surgeon my neighbors are waiting for,
This apparition in a green helmet,
Shining gloves and white suit.
Is it the butcher, the grocer, the postman, someone I know?

I cannot run, I am rooted, and the gorse hurts me
With its yellow purses, its spiky armory.
I could not run without having to run forever.
The white hive is snug as a virgin,
Sealing off her brood cells, her honey, and quietly humming.

Smoke rolls and scarves in the grove.
The mind of the hive thinks this is the end of everything.
Here they come, the outriders, on their hysterical elastics.
If I stand very still, they will think I am cow-parsley,
A gullible head untouched by their animosity,

Not even nodding, a personage in a hedgerow.
The villagers open the chambers, they are hunting the queen.
Is she hiding, is she eating honey? She is very clever.
She is old, old, old, she must live another year, and she knows it.
While in their fingerjoint cells the new virgins

Dream of a duel they will win inevitably,
A curtain of wax dividing them from the bride flight,
The upflight of the murderess into a heaven that loves her.
The villagers are moving the virgins, there will be no killing.
The old queen does not show herself, is she so ungrateful?

I am exhausted, I am exhausted –
Pillar of white in a blackout of knives.
I am the magician's girl who does not flinch.
The villagers are untying their disguises, they are shaking
    hands.
Whose is that long white box in the grove, what have they
    accomplished, why am I cold.

SYLVIA PLATH

Blackberrying

Nobody in the lane, and nothing, nothing but blackberries,
Blackberries on either side, though on the right mainly,
A blackberry alley, going down in hooks, and a sea
Somewhere at the end of it, heaving. Blackberries
Big as the ball of my thumb, and dumb as eyes
Ebon in the hedges, fat
With blue-red juices. These they squander on my fingers.
I had not asked for such a blood sisterhood; they must love me.
They accommodate themselves to my milkbottle, flattening
    their sides.

Overhead go the choughs in black, cacophonous flocks –
Bits of burnt paper wheeling in a blown sky.
Theirs is the only voice, protesting, protesting.
I do not think the sea will appear at all.
The high, green meadows are glowing, as if lit from within.
I come to one bush of berries so ripe it is a bush of flies,
Hanging their bluegreen bellies and their wing panes in a
    Chinese screen.
The honey-feast of the berries has stunned them; they believe
    in heaven.
One more hook, and the berries and bushes end.

The only thing to come now is the sea.
From between two hills a sudden wind funnels at me,
Slapping its phantom laundry in my face.
These hills are too green and sweet to have tasted salt.
I follow the sheep path between them. A last hook brings me
To the hills' northern face, and the face is orange rock

That looks out on nothing, nothing but a great space
Of white and pewter lights, and a din like silversmiths
Beating and beating at an intractable metal.

SYLVIA PLATH

Addiction to an Old Mattress

No, this is not my life, thank God . . .
. . . worn out like this, and crippled by brain-fag;
Obsessed first by one person, and then
(Almost at once) most horribly besotted by another;
These Februaries, full of draughts and cracks,
They belong to the people in the streets, the others
Out there – haberdashers, writers of menus.

Salt breezes! Bolsters from Istanbul!
Barometers, full of contempt, controlling moody isobars.
Sumptuous tittle-tattle from a summer crowd
That's fed on lemonades and matinees. And seas
That float themselves about from place to place, and then
Spend *hours* – just moving some clear sleets across glass stones.
Yalta: deck-chairs in Asia's gold cake; thrones.

Meanwhile . . . I live on . . . powerful, disobedient,
Inside their draughty haberdasher's climate,
With these people . . . who are going to obsess me,
Potatoes, dentists, people I hardly know, it's unforgivable

For this is not my life
But theirs, that I am living.
And I wolf, bolt, gulp it down, day after day.

ROSEMARY TONKS

The Sofas, Fogs and Cinemas

I have lived it, and lived it,
My nervous, luxury civilisation,
My sugar-loving nerves have battered me to pieces.

. . . Their idea of literature is hopeless.
Make them drink their own poetry!
Let them eat their gross novel, full of mud.

It's quiet; just the fresh, chilly weather . . . and he
Gets up from his dead bedroom, and comes in here
And digs himself into the sofa.
He stays there up to two hours in the hole – and talks
– Straight into the large subjects, he faces up to *everything*
It's . . . . . . damnably depressing.
(That great lavatory coat . . . the cigarillo burning
In the little dish . . . And when he calls out: 'Ha!'
Madness! – you no longer possess your own furniture.)

On my bad days (and I'm being broken
At this very moment) I speak of my ambitions . . . and he
Becomes intensely gloomy, with the look of something jugged,
Morose, sour, mouldering away, with lockjaw . . .

I grow coarse; and more modern (*I*, who am driven mad
By my ideas; who go nowhere;
Who dare not leave my frontdoor, lest an idea . . .)
All right. I admit everything, everything!

Oh yes, the opera (Ah, but the cinema)
He particularly enjoys it, enjoys it *horribly,* when someone's ill
At the last minute; and they specially fly in
A new, gigantic, Dutch soprano. He wants to help her
With her arias. Old goat! Blasphemer!
He wants to help her with her arias!

No, I . . . go to the cinema,
I particularly like it when the fog is thick, the street
Is like a hole in an old coat, and the light is brown as
    laudanum,
. . . the fogs! the fogs! The cinemas
Where the criminal shadow-literature flickers over our faces,
The screen is spread out like a thundercloud – that bangs
And splashes you with acid . . . or lies derelict, with lighted
    waters in it,
And in the silence, drips and crackles – taciturn, luxurious.
. . . The drugged and battered Philistines
Are all around you in the auditorium . . .

And he . . . is somewhere else, in his dead bedroom clothes,
He wants to make me think his thoughts
And they will be *enormous,* dull – (just the sort
To keep away from).
. . . when I see that cigarillo, when I see it . . . smoking
And he wants to face the international situation . . .
Lunatic rages! Blackness! Suffocation!

– All this sitting about in cafés to calm down
Simply wears me out. And their idea of literature!
The idiotic cut of the stanzas; the novels, full up, gross.

I have lived it, and I know too much.
My café-nerves are breaking me
With black, exhausting information.

ROSEMARY TONKS

I Shall Vote Labour

I shall vote Labour because
  God votes Labour.
I shall vote Labour in order to protect
  the sacred institution of The Family.
I shall vote Labour because
  I am a dog.
I shall vote Labour because
  upper-class hoorays annoy me in expensive restaurants.
I shall vote Labour because
  I am on a diet.
I shall vote Labour because if I don't
  somebody else will:
  AND
I shall vote Labour because if one person does it
  everybody will be wanting to do it.
I shall vote Labour because if I do not vote Labour
  my balls will drop off.
I shall vote Labour because
  there are too few cars on the road.

I shall vote Labour because I am
   a hopeless drug addict.
I shall vote Labour because
   I failed to be a dollar millionaire aged three.
I shall vote Labour because Labour will build
   more maximum security prisons.
I shall vote Labour because I want to shop
   in an all-weather precinct stretching from Yeovil to Glasgow.
I shall vote Labour because
   the Queen's stamp collection is the best in the world.
I shall vote Labour because
   deep in my heart
I am a Conservative.

CHRISTOPHER LOGUE

Tonight at Noon

for Charles Mingus and the Clayton Squares

Tonight at noon
Supermarkets will advertise 3p EXTRA on everything
Tonight at noon
Children from happy families will be sent to live in a home
Elephants will tell each other human jokes
America will declare peace on Russia
World War I generals will sell poppies in the streets on
   November 11th
The first daffodils of autumn will appear
When the leaves fall upwards to the trees

Tonight at noon
Pigeons will hunt cats through city backyards
Hitler will tell us to fight on the beaches and on the landing
    fields
A tunnel full of water will be built under Liverpool
Pigs will be sighted flying in formation over Woolton
and Nelson will not only get his eye back but his arm as well
White Americans will demonstrate for equal rights
in front of the Black House
and the Monster has just created Dr Frankenstein

Girls in bikinis are moonbathing
Folksongs are being sung by real folk
Artgalleries are closed to people over 21
Poets get their poems in the Top 20
Politicians are elected to insane asylums
There's jobs for everyone and nobody wants them
In back alleys everywhere teenage lovers are kissing
in broad daylight
In forgotten graveyards everywhere the dead will quietly
bury the living
and
You will tell me you love me
Tonight at noon

ADRIAN HENRI

Celia, Celia

When I am sad and weary
When I think all hope has gone
When I walk along High Holborn
I think of you with nothing on

ADRIAN MITCHELL

from Briggflatts

Brag, sweet tenor bull,
descant on Rawthey's madrigal,
each pebble its part
for the fells' late spring.
Dance tiptoe, bull,
black against may.
Ridiculous and lovely
chase hurdling shadows
morning into noon.
May on the bull's hide
and through the dale
furrows fill with may,
paving the slowworm's way.

A mason times his mallet
to a lark's twitter,
listening while the marble rests,
lays his rule
at a letter's edge,

fingertips checking,
till the stone spells a name
naming none,
a man abolished.
Painful lark, labouring to rise!
The solemn mallet says:
In the grave's slot
he lies. We rot.

Decay thrusts the blade,
wheat stands in excrement
trembling. Rawthey trembles.
Tongue stumbles, ears err
for fear of spring.
Rub the stone with sand,
wet sandstone rending
roughness away. Fingers
ache on the rubbing stone.
The mason says: Rocks
happen by chance.
No one here bolts the door,
love is so sore.

Stone smooth as skin,
cold as the dead they load
on a low lorry by night.
The moon sits on the fell
but it will rain.
Under sacks on the stone
two children lie,
hear the horse stale,
the mason whistle,
harness mutter to shaft,

felloe to axle squeak,
rut thud the rim,
crushed grit.

Stocking to stocking, jersey to jersey,
head to a hard arm,
they kiss under the rain,
bruised by their marble bed.
In Garsdale, dawn;
at Hawes, tea from the can.
Rain stops, sacks
steam in the sun, they sit up.
Copper-wire moustache,
sea-reflecting eyes
and Baltic plainsong speech
declare: By such rocks
men killed Bloodaxe.

Fierce blood throbs in his tongue,
lean words.
Skulls cropped for steel caps
huddle round Stainmore.
Their becks ring on limestone,
whisper to peat.
The clogged cart pushes the horse downhill.
In such soft air
they trudge and sing,
laying the tune frankly on the air.
All sounds fall still,
fellside bleat,
hide-and-seek peewit.

Her pulse their pace,
palm countering palm,
till a trench is filled,
stone white as cheese
jeers at the dale.
Knotty wood, hard to rive,
smoulders to ash;
smell of October apples.
The road again,
at a trot.
Wetter, warmed, they watch
the mason meditate
on name and date.

Rain rinses the road,
the bull streams and laments.
Sour rye porridge from the hob
with cream and black tea,
meat, crust and crumb.
Her parents in bed
the children dry their clothes.
He has untied the tape
of her striped flannel drawers
before the range. Naked
on the pricked rag mat
his fingers comb
thatch of his manhood's home.

Gentle generous voices weave
over bare night
words to confirm and delight
till bird dawn.
Rainwater from the butt

she fetches and flannel
to wash him inch by inch,
kissing the pebbles.
Shining slowworm part of the marvel.
The mason stirs:
Words!
Pens are too light.
Take a chisel to write.

Every birth a crime,
every sentence life.
Wiped of mould and mites
would the ball run true?
No hope of going back.
Hounds falter and stray,
shame deflects the pen.
Love murdered neither bleeds nor stifles
but jogs the draftsman's elbow.
What can he, changed, tell
her, changed, perhaps dead?
Delight dwindles. Blame
stays the same.

Brief words are hard to find,
shapes to carve and discard:
Bloodaxe, king of York,
king of Dublin, king of Orkney.
Take no notice of tears;
letter the stone to stand
over love laid aside lest
insufferable happiness impede
flight to Stainmore,
to trace

lark, mallet,
becks, flocks
and axe knocks.

Dung will not soil the slowworm's
mosaic. Breathless lark
drops to nest in sodden trash;
Rawthey truculent, dingy.
Drudge at the mallet, the may is down,
fog on fells. Guilty of spring
and spring's ending
amputated years ache after
the bull is beef, love a convenience.
It is easier to die than to remember.
Name and date
split in soft slate
a few months obliterate.

BASIL BUNTING

XI

1970–2000

THE SHADOWS, THE MEADOWS, I THE LANES, THE GUILDHALLS, THE CARVED choirs...

To My Wife at Midnight

Are you to say goodnight
And turn away under
The blanket of your delight?

Are you to let me go
Alone to sleep beside you
Into the drifting snow?

Where we each reach,
Sleeping alone together,
Nobody can touch.

Is the cat's window open?
Shall I turn into your back?
And what is to happen?

What is to happen to us
And what is to happen to each
Of us asleep in our places?

I mean us both going
Into sleep at our ages
To sleep and get our fairing.

They have all gone home.
Night beasts are coming out.
The black wood of Madron

Is just waking up.
I hear the rain outside
To help me to go to sleep.

Nessie, dont let my soul
Skip and miss a beat
And cause me to fall.

III

Are you asleep I say
Into the back of your neck
For you not to hear me.

Are you asleep? I hear
Your heart under the pillow
Saying my dear my dear

My dear for all it's worth.
Where is the dun's moor
Which began your breath?

IV

Ness, to tell you the truth
I am drifting away
Down to fish for the saithe.

Is the cat's window open?
The weather is on my shoulder
And I am drifting down

Into O can you hear me
Among your Dunsmuir Clan?
Are you coming out to play?

V

Did I behave badly
On the field at Culloden?
I lie sore-wounded now

By all activities, and
The terrible acts of my time
Are only a distant sound.

With responsibility
I am drifting off
Breathing regularly

Into my younger days
To play the games of Greenock
Beside the sugar-house quays.

VI

Nessie Dunsmuir, I say
Wheesht wheesht to myself
To help me now to go

Under into somewhere
In the redcoat rain.
Buckle me for the war.

Are you to say goodnight
And kiss me and fasten
My drowsy armour tight?

My dear camp-follower,
Hap the blanket round me
And tuck in a flower.

Maybe from my sleep
In the stoure at Culloden
I'll see you here asleep

In your lonely place.

W. S. GRAHAM

Greenock at Night I Find You

I

As for you loud Greenock long ropeworking
Hide and seeking rivetting town of my child
Hood, I know we think of us often mostly
At night. Have you ever desired me back
Into the set-in bed at the top of the land
In One Hope Street? I am myself lying
Half-asleep hearing the rivetting yards
And smelling the bone-works with no home
Work done for Cartsburn School in the morning.

At night. And here I am descending and
The welding lights in the shipyards flower blue
Under my hopeless eyelids as I lie
Sleeping conditioned to hide from happy.

II

So what did I do? I walked from Hope Street
Down Lyndoch Street between the night's words
To Cartsburn Street and got to the Cartsburn Vaults
With half an hour to go. See, I am back.

III

See, I am back. My father turned and I saw
He had the stick he cut in Sheelhill Glen.
Brigit was there and Hugh and double-breasted
Sam and Malcolm Mooney and Alastair Graham.
They all were there in the Cartsburn Vaults shining
To meet me but I was only remembered.

W. S. GRAHAM

Loch Thom

I

Just for the sake of recovering
I walked backward from fifty-six
Quick years of age wanting to see,
And managed not to trip or stumble
To find Loch Thorn and turned round

To see the stretch of my childhood
Before me. Here is the loch. The same
Long-beaked cry curls across
The heather-edges of the water held
Between the hills a boyhood's walk
Up from Greenock. It is the morning.

And I am here with my mammy's
Bramble jam scones in my pocket.
The Firth is miles and I have come
Back to find Loch Thom maybe
In this light does not recognise me.

This is a lonely freshwater loch.
No farms on the edge. Only
Heather grouse-moor stretching
Down to Greenock and One Hope
Street or stretching away across
Into the blue moors of Ayrshire.

II

And almost I am back again
Wading the heather down to the edge
To sit. The minnows go by in shoals
Like iron-filings in the shallows.
My mother is dead. My father is dead
And all the trout I used to know
Leaping from their sad rings are dead.

I drop my crumbs into the shallow
Weed for the minnows and pinheads.
You see that I will have to rise
And turn round and get back where
My running age will slow for a moment
To let me on. It is a colder
Stretch of water than I remember.

The curlew's cry travelling still
Kills me fairly. In front of me
The grouse flurry and settle. GOBACK
GOBACK GOBACK FAREWELL LOCH THOM.

W. S. GRAHAM

Feeding Ducks

One duck stood on my toes.
The others made watery rushes after bread
Thrown by my momentary hand; instead,
She stood duck-still and got far more than those.

An invisible drone boomed by
With a beetle in it; the ne®ighbour's yearning bull
Bugled across five fields. And an evening full
Of other evenings quietly began to die.

And my everlasting hand
Dropped on my hypocrite duck her grace of bread.
And I thought, 'The first to be fattened, the first to be dead',
Till my gestures enlarged, wide over the darkening land.

NORMAN MACCAIG

Toad

Stop looking like a purse. How could a purse
squeeze under the rickety door and sit,
full of satisfaction, in a man's house?

You clamber towards me on your four corners –
right hand, left foot, left hand, right foot.

I love you for being a toad,
for crawling like a Japanese wrestler,
and for not being frightened.

I put you in my purse hand, not shutting it,
and set you down outside directly under
every star.

A jewel in your head? Toad,
you've put one in mine,
a tiny radiance in a dark place.

NORMAN MACCAIG

Deceptions?

To hear a dripping water tap in a house
That has no tap in it, in the dead of night.
To hear footsteps come naturally to the door
And stop there forever. In bed in an empty room
To hear a voice on the pillow say *Hello.*

A wheatstalk dances lasciviously in the fire.
My hand drags its plough across this white field.
My head from a sort of radiance watches a chair
Continually completing its meaning. A picture
Tries to plunge from its nail to the centre of the earth.

Immense tides wash through everything. My knuckles
Are tiny whirlpools in it. I stream sideways.
The room's roots are straining. Sounds of the fire
Unmuffle themselves from black coal, are a theatre.
My foot rocks because my heart says so.

How could things stop? And three plump cheers for distance . . .
To shake a hand and be left with it. To see
Sight cramming itself into an eye and wheat
A harrow of fire: and all a correspondence
Shielding the truth and giving birth to it.

NORMAN MACCAIG

The Bright Field

I have seen the sun break through
to illuminate a small field
for a while, and gone my way
and forgotten it. But that was the pearl
of great price, the one field that had
the treasure in it. I realise now
that I must give all that I have
to possess it. Life is not hurrying

on to a receding future, nor hankering after
an imagined past. It is the turning
aside like Moses to the miracle
of the lit bush, to a brightness
that seemed as transitory as your youth
once, but is the eternity that awaits you.

R. S. THOMAS

The Moon in Lleyn

The last quarter of the moon
of Jesus gives way
to the dark; the serpent
digests the egg. Here
on my knees in this stone
church, that is full only
of the silent congregation
of shadows and the sea's

sound, it is easy to believe
Yeats was right. Just as though
choirs had not sung, shells
have swallowed them; the tide laps
at the Bible; the bell fetches
no people to the brittle miracle
of the bread. The sand is waiting
for the running back of the grains
in the wall into its blond
glass. Religion is over, and
what will emerge from the body
of the new moon, no one
can say.
           But a voice sounds
in my ear: Why so fast,
mortal? These very seas
are baptised. The parish
has a saint's name time cannot
unfrock. In cities that
have outgrown their promise people
are becoming pilgrims
again, if not to this place,
then to the recreation of it
in their own spirits. You must remain
kneeling. Even as this moon
making its way through the earth's
cumbersome shadow, prayer, too,
has its phases.

R. S. THOMAS

Zero

What time is it?
       Is it the hour when the servant
of Pharaoh's daughter went down
       and found the abandoned baby
in the bulrushes ? The hour
       when Dido woke and knew Aeneas
gone from her ? When Caesar
       looked at the entrails and took
their signal for the crossing
       of the dividing river ?
                    Is it
that time when Aneirin
       fetched the poem out of his side
and laid it upon the year's altar
       for the appeasement of envious
gods?
       It is no time
at all. The shadow falls
       on the bright land and men
launder their minds in it, as
       they have done century by
century to prepare themselves for the crass deed.

R. S. THOMAS

The Elm Decline

The crags crash to the tarn; slow—
motion corrosion of scree.
From scooped corries,
bare as slag,
black sykes ooze
through quarries of broken boulders.
The sump of the tarn
slumps into its mosses – bog
asphodel, sundew, sedges –
a perpetual
sour October
yellowing the moor.

                    Seven
thousand years ago
trees grew
high as this tarn. The pikes
were stacks and skerries
spiking the green,
the tidal surge
of oak, birch, elm,
ebbing to ochre
and the wrackwood of backend.

                      Then
round the year Three
Thousand BC,
the proportion of elm pollen

preserved in peat
declined from twenty
per cent to four.

                    Stone axes,
chipped clean from the crag-face,
ripped the hide off the fells.
Spade and plough
scriated the bared flesh,
skewered down to the bone.
The rake flaked into fragments
and kettlehole tarns
were shovelled chock-full
of a rubble of rotting rocks.

                    Today
electric landslips
crack the rock;
drills tunnel it;
valleys go under the tap.
Dynamited runnels
channel a poisoned rain,
and the fractured ledges
are scoured and emery'd
by wind-to-wind rubbings
of nuclear dust.

                    Soon
the pikes, the old
bottlestops of lava,
will stand scraped bare,
nothing but air round stone

and stone in air,
ground-down stumps
of a skeleton jaw –

                              Until
under the scree,
under the riddled rake,
beside the outflow of the reedless lake,
no human eye remains to see
a landscape man
helped nature make.

NORMAN NICHOLSON

Eden Rock

They are waiting for me somewhere beyond Eden Rock:
My father, twenty-five, in the same suit
Of Genuine Irish Tweed, his terrier Jack
Still two years old and trembling at his feet.

My mother, twenty-three, in a sprigged dress
Drawn at the waist, ribbon in her straw hat,
Has spread the stiff white cloth over the grass.
Her hair, the colour of wheat, takes on the light.

She pours tea from a Thermos, the milk straight
From an old H.P. sauce bottle, a screw
Of paper for a cork; slowly sets out
The same three plates, the tin cups painted blue.

The sky whitens as if lit by three suns.
My mother shades her eyes and looks my way
Over the drifted stream. My father spins
A stone along the water. Leisurely,

They beckon to me from the other bank.
I hear them call, 'See where the stream-path is!
Crossing is not as hard as you might think.'

I had not thought that it would be like this.

CHARLES CAUSLEY

The Green Man's Last Will and Testament

In a ragged spinney (scheduled
For prompt development as a bijou housing estate)
I saw the green daemon of England's wood
As he wrote his testament. The grey goose
Had given him one of her quills for a pen;
The robin's breast was a crimson seal;
The long yellow centipede held a candle.

He seemed like a hollow oak-trunk, smothered with ivy:
At his feet or roots clustered the witnesses,
Like hectic toadstools, or pallid as broom-rape:
Wood-elves – goodfellows, hobs and lobs,
Black Anis, the child-devouring hag,
From her cave in the Dane Hills, saucer-eyed
Phantom dogs, Black Shuck and Barghest, with the cruel
  nymphs

Of the northern streams, Peg Powler of the Tees
And Jenny Greenteeth of the Ribble,
Sisters of Bellisama, the very fair one.

'I am sick, I must die,' he said. 'Poisoned like Lord Randal
From hedges and ditches. My ditches run with pollution,
My hedgerows are gone, and the hedgerow singers.
The rooks, disconsolate, have lost their rookery:
The elms are all dead of the Dutch pox.
No longer the nightjar churns in the twilit glade,
Nor the owl, like a white phantom, silent-feathered
Glides to the barn. The red-beaked chough,
Enclosing Arthur's soul, is seen no more
Wheeling and calling over the Cornish cliffs.
Old Tod has vacated his deep-dug earth;
He has gone to rummage in the city dustbins.
Tiggy is squashed flat on the M1.

'My delicate deer are culled, and on offshore islands
My sleek silkies, where puffin and guillemot
Smother and drown in oil and tar.
The mechanical reaper has guillotined
Ortygometra, though she was no traitor,
Crouching over her cradle – no longer resounds
Crek-crek, crek-crek, among the wheatfields,
Where the scarlet cockle is missing and the blue cornflower.

My orchids and wild hyacinths are raped and torn,
My lenten lilies and my fritillaries.
Less frequent now the debate
Of cuckoo and nightingale – and where is the cuckoo's maid,
The snake-necked bird sacred to Venus,
Her mysteries and the amber twirling wheel?

In no brightness of air dance now the butterflies –
Their hairy mallyshags are slaughtered among the nettles.
The innocent bats are evicted from the belfries,
The death-watch remains, and masticates history.

'I'll leave to the people of England
All that remains:
Rags and patches – a few old tales
And bawdy jokes, snatches of song and galumphing dance-steps.
Above all my obstinacy – obstinacy of flintstones
That breed in the soil, and pertinacity
Of unlovely weeds – chickweed and groundsel,
Plantain, shepherd's purse and Jack-by-the-hedge.
Let them keep it as they wander in the inhuman towns.

'And the little children, imprisoned in ogrish towers, enchanted
By a one-eyed troll in front of a joyless fire –
I would have them remember the old games and the old dances:
Sir Roger is dead, Sir Roger is dead,
She raised him up under the apple tree;
Poor Mary is a-weeping, weeping like Ariadne,
Weeping for her husband on a bright summer's day.'

JOHN HEATH-STUBBS

Thoughts after Ruskin

Women reminded him of lilies and roses.
Me they remind rather of blood and soap,
Armed with a warm rag, assaulting noses,
Ears, neck, mouth and all the secret places:

Armed with a sharp knife, cutting up liver,
Holding hearts to bleed under a running tap,
Gutting and stuffing, pickling and preserving,
Scalding, blanching, broiling, pulverising,
– All the terrible chemistry of their kitchens.

Their distant husbands lean across mahogany
And delicately manipulate the market,
While safe at home, the tender and the gentle
Are killing tiny mice, dead snap by the neck,
Asphyxiating flies, evicting spiders,
Scrubbing, scouring aloud, disturbing cupboards,
Committing things to dustbins, twisting, wringing,
Wrists red and knuckles white and fingers puckered,
Pulpy, tepid. Steering screaming cleaners
Around the snags of furniture, they straighten
And haul out sheets from under the incontinent
And heavy old, stoop to importunate young,
Tugging, folding, tucking, zipping, buttoning,
Spooning in food, encouraging excretion,
Mopping up vomit, stabbing cloth with needles,
Contorting wool around their knitting needles,
Creating snug and comfy on their needles.

Their huge hands! their everywhere eyes! their voices
Raised to convey across the hullabaloo,
Their massive thighs and breasts dispensing comfort,
Their bloody passages and hairy crannies,
Their wombs that pocket a man upside down!

And when all's over, off with overalls,
Quickly consulting clocks, they go upstairs,
Sit and sigh a little, brushing hair,
And somehow find, in mirrors, colours, odours,
Their essences of lilies and of roses.

ELMA MITCHELL

Midge

The evening is perfect, my sisters.
The loch lies silent, the air is still.
The sun's last rays linger over the water
and there is a faint smirr, almost a smudge
of summer rain. Sisters, I smell supper,
and what is more perfect than supper?
It is emerging from the wood,
in twos and threes, a dozen in all,
making such a chatter and a clatter
as it reaches the rocky shore,
admiring the arrangements of the light.
See the innocents, my sisters,
the clumsy ones, the laughing ones,
the rolled-up sleeves and the flapping shorts,
there is even a kilt (the god of the midges,

you are good to us!). So gather your forces,
leave your tree trunks, forsake the rushes,
fly up from the sour brown mosses
to the seek flesh of face and forearm.
Think of your eggs. What does the egg need?
Blood, and blood. Blood is what the egg needs.
Our men have done their bit, they've gone,
it was all they were good for, poor dears. Now
it is up to us. The egg is quietly screaming
for supper, blood, supper, blood, supper!
Attack, my little Draculas, my Amazons!
Look at those flailing arms and stamping feet.
They're running, swatting, swearing, oh they're hopeless.
Keep at them, ladies. This is a feast,
this is a midsummer night's dream.
Soon we shall all lie down filled and rich,
and lay, and lay, and lay, and lay, and lay.

EDWIN MORGAN

Sir James Murray

I pick a daimen icker from the thrave
And chew it thoughtfully. I must be brave
And fight for this. My English colleagues frown
But words come skelpin rank and file, and down
They go, the kittle kimmers, they're well caught
And I won't give them up. Who would have thought
A gleg and gangrel Scot like me should barge
Or rather breenge, like a kelpie at large
In the Cherwell, upon the very palladium

Of anglophilia? My sleekit radium
Is smuggled through the fluttering steps. My shed,
My outhouse with it's thousand-plus well-fed
Pigeon-holes, has a northern exposure. Doon
Gaed stumpie in the ink all afternoon,
As Burns and I refreshed the dictionar
With cantrips from his dancing Carrick star!
O lovely words and lovely man! We'll caw
Before as yowes tae knowes; we'll shaw the braw
Auld baudrons by the ingle; we'll comb
Quotations to bring the wild whaup safely home.
Origin obscure? Origin uncertain? Origin unknown?
I love those eldritch pliskies that are thrown
At as from a too playful past, a store
Of splore we should never be blate to semaphore!
Oxford! here is a silent collieshangie
To spike your index-cards and keep them tangy.
Some, though not I, will jib at houghmagandy:
We'll maybe not get that past Mrs Grundy
– But evening comes. To work, to work! To words!
The ban are turning into bauckie-birds.
The light in my scriptorium flickers gamely.
Pioneers must never labour tamely.
We steam along, we crawl, we pause, we hurtle,
And stir this English porridge with a spurtle.

EDWIN MORGAN

Canedolia

an off-concrete scotch fantasia

oa! hoy! awe! ba! mey!

who saw?
rhu saw rum. garve saw smoo. nigg saw tain. lairg saw lagg.
rigg saw eigg. largs saw haggs. tongue saw luss. mull saw yell.
stoer saw strone. drem saw muck. gask saw noss. unst saw cults.
echt saw banff. weem saw wick. trool saw twatt.

how far?
from largo to lunga from joppa to skibo from ratho to shona
from ulva to minto from tinto to tolsta from soutra to marsco
from braco to barra from alva to stobo from fogo to fada from
gigha to gogo from kelso to stroma from hirta to spango.

what is it like there?
och it's freuchie, it's faifley, it's wamphray, it's frandy, it's
sliddery.

what do you do?
we foindle and fungle, we bonkle and meigle and maxpoffle. we
scotstarvit, armit, wormit, and even wifflet. we play at crosstobs,
leuchars, gorbals and finfan. we scavaig, and there's aye a bit of
tilquhilly. if it's wet, treshnish and mishnish.

what is the best of the country?
blinkbonny! airgold! thundergay!

and the worst?
scrishven, shiskine, scrabster, and snizort.

listen! what's that?
catacol and wauchope, never heed them

tell us about last night
well, we had a wee ferintosh and we lay on the quiraing. it was pure strontian!

but who was there?
petermoidart and craigenkenneth and cambusputtock and ecclemuchty and corriehulish and balladolly and altnacanny and clauchanvrechan and stronachlochan and auchenlachar and tighnacrankie and tilliebruaich and killieharra and invervannach and achnatudlem and machrishellach and inchtamurchan and auchterfechan and kinlochculter and ardnawhallie and inver- shuggle

and what was the toast?
schiehallion! schiehallion! schiehallion!

EDWIN MORGAN

Barn Owl

Ernie Morgan found him, a small
Fur mitten inexplicably upright,
And hissing like a treble kettle
Beneath the tree he'd fallen from.
His bright eye frightened Ernie,
Who popped a rusty bucket over him
And ran for us. We kept him
In a backyard shed, perched
On the rung of a broken deck-chair,
Its canvas faded to his down's biscuit.
Men from the pits, their own childhood
Spent waste in the crippling earth,
Held him gently, brought him mice
From the wealth of our riddled tenements,
Saw that we understood his tenderness,
His tiny body under its puffed quilt,
Then left us alone. We called him Snowy.

He was never clumsy. He flew
From the first like a skilled moth,
Sifting the air with feathers,
Floating it softly to the place he wanted.
At dusk he'd stir, preen, stand
At the window-ledge, fly. It was
A catching of the heart to see him go.
Six months we kept him, saw him
Grow beautiful in a way each thought
His own knowledge. One afternoon, home
With pretended illness, I watched him
Leave. It was daylight. He lifted slowly

Over the Hughes's roof, his cream face calm,
And never came back. I saw this;
And tell it for the first time,
Having wanted to keep his mystery.

And would not say it now, but that
This morning, walking in Slindon woods
Before the sun, I found a barn owl
Dead in the rusty bracken.
He was not clumsy in his death,
His wings folded decently to him,
His plumes, unruffled orange,
Bore flawlessly their delicate patterning.

With a stick I turned him, not
Wishing to touch his feathery stiffness.
There was neither blood nor wound on him,
But for the savaged foot a scavenger
Had ripped. I saw the sinews.
I could have skewered them out
Like a common fowl's. Moving away
I was oppressed by him, thinking
Confusedly that down the generations
Of air this death was Snowy's
Emblematic messsenger, that I should know
The meaning of it, the dead barn owl.

LESLIE NORRIS

Water

On hot summer mornings my aunt set glasses
On a low wall outside the farmhouse,
With some jugs of cold water.
I would sit in the dark hail, or
                  Behind the dairy window,
Waiting for children to come from the town.

They came in small groups, serious, steady,
And I could see them, black in the heat,
Long before they turned in at our gate
To march up the soft, dim road.
                They would stand by the wall,
Drinking water with an engrossed thirst. The dog

Did not bother them, knowing them responsible
Travellers. They held in quiet hands their bags
Of jam sandwiches, and bottles of yellow fizz.
Sometimes they waved a gratitude to the house,
                But they never looked at us.
Their eyes were full of the mountain, lifting

Their measuring faces above our long hedge.
When they had gone I would climb the wall,
Looking for them among the thin sheep runs.
Their heads were a resolute darkness among ferns,
              They climbed with unsteady certainty.
I wondered what it was they knew the mountain had.

They would pass the last house, Lambert's, where
A violent gander, too old by many a Christmas,
Blared evil warning from his bitten moor,
Then it was open world, too high and clear
                        For clouds even, where over heather
The free hare cleanly ran and the summer sheep.

I knew this; and I knew all summer long
Those visionary gangs passed through our lanes,
Coming down at evening, their arms full
Of cowslips, moon daisies, whinberries, nuts,
                        All fruits of the sliding seasons,
And the enormous experience of the mountain

That I who loved it did not understand.
In the summer, dust filled our winter ruts
With a level softness, and children walked
At evening through golden curtains scuffed
                        From the road by their trailing feet.
They would drink tiredly at our wall, talking

Softly, leaning, their sleepy faces warm for home.
We would see them murmur slowly through our stiff
Gate, their shy heads gilded by the last sun.
One by one we would gather up the used jugs,
                        The glasses. We would pour away
A little water. It would lie on the thick dust, gleaming.

LESLIE NORRIS

Butter

Where has my butter gone? The
vanman, he took seven pounds
and a basket of warm eggs, for
jam, sugar, tea, paraffin. I
gave the tinkers a lump, to keep
this away, the black word from our
byre. I put some in the damp peats,
to coax a flame. I swear the cat
has a yellow tongue. There was only
a scrape for the fisherman's bannock
like a bit of sun on a dull day. The
old cow is giving me a mad look.

GEORGE MACKAY BROWN

Hamnavoe Market

They drove to the Market with ringing pockets.

Folster found a girl
Who put wounds on his face and throat,
Small and diagonal, like red doves.

Johnston stood beside the barrel.
All day he stood there.
He woke in a ditch, his mouth full of ashes.

Grieve bought a balloon and a goldfish.
He swung through the air,
He fired shotguns, rolled pennies, ate sweet fog from a stick.

Heddle was at the Market also.
I know nothing of his activities,
He is and always was a quiet man.

Garson fought three rounds with a negro boxer,
And received thirty shillings,
Much applause, and an eye loaded with thunder.

Where did they find Flett?
They found him in a brazen circle,
All flame and blood, a new Salvationist.

A gypsy saw in the hand of Halcro
Great strolling herds, harvests, a proud woman.
He wintered in the poorhouse.

They drove home from the Market under the stars
Except for Johnston
Who lay in a ditch, his mouth full of dying fires.

GEORGE MACKAY BROWN

Haddock Fishermen

Midnight. The wind yawing nor-east.
A low blunt moon.
Unquiet beside quiet wives we rest.

A spit of rain and a gull
In the open door.
The lit fire. A quick mouthful of ale.

We push the *Merle* at a sea of cold flame.
The oars drip honey.
Hook by hook uncoils under The Kame.

Our line breaks the trek of sudden thousands.
Twelve nobbled jaws,
Grey cowls, gape in our hands.

Twelve cold mouths scream without sound.
The sea is empty again.
Like tinkers the bright ones endlessly shift their ground.

We probe emptiness all the afternoon,
Then pause and fill our teeth
With dependable food, beef and barley scone.

Sunset drags its butcher blade
From the day's throat.
We turn through an ebb salt and sticky as blood.

More stars than fish. Women, cats, a gull
Mewl at the rock.
The valley divides the meagre miracle.

GEORGE MACKAY BROWN

Money

Quarterly, is it, money reproaches me:
   'Why do you let me lie here wastefully?
I am all you never had of goods and sex.
   You could get them still by writing a few cheques.'

So I look at others, what they do with theirs:
   They certainly don't keep it upstairs.
By now they've a second house and car and wife:
   Clearly money has something to do with life

– In fact, they've a lot in common, if you enquire:
   You can't put off being young until you retire,
And however you bank your screw, the money you save
   Won't in the end buy you more than a shave.

I listen to money singing. It's like looking down
   From long french windows at a provincial town,
The slums, the canal, the churches ornate and mad
   In the evening sun. It is intensely sad.

PHILIP LARKIN

Water

If I were called in
To construct a religion
I should make use of water.

Going to church
Would entail a fording
To dry, different clothes;

My liturgy would employ
Images of sousing,
A furious devout drench,

And I should raise in the east
A glass of water
Where any-angled light
Would congregate endlessly.

PHILIP LARKIN

Going, Going

I thought it would last my time –
The sense that, beyond the town,
There would always be fields and farms,
Where the village louts could climb
Such trees as were not cut down;
I knew there'd be false alarms

In the papers about old streets
And split-level shopping, but some
Have always been left so far;
And when the old part retreats
As the bleak high-risers come
We can always escape in the car.

Things are tougher than we are, just
As earth will always respond
However we mess it about;
Chuck filth in the sea, if you must:
The tides will be clean beyond.
– But what do I feel now? Doubt?

Or age, simply? The crowd
Is young in the M1 café;
Their kids are screaming for more –
More houses, more parking allowed,
More caravan sites, more pay.
On the Business Page, a score

Of spectacled grins approve
Some takeover bid that entails
Five per cent profit (and ten
Per cent more in the estuaries): move
Your works to the unspoilt dales
(Grey area grants)! And when

You try to get near the sea
In summer . . .
                    It seems, just now,
To be happening so very fast;
Despite all the land left free
For the first time I feel somehow
That it isn't going to last,

That before I snuff it, the whole
Boiling will be bricked in
Except for the tourist parts –
First slum of Europe: a role
It won't be so hard to win,
With a cast of crooks and tarts.

And that will be England gone,
The shadows, the meadows, the lanes,
The guildhalls, the carved choirs.
There'll be books; it will linger on
In galleries; but all that remains
For us will be concrete and tyres.

Most things are never meant.
This won't be, most likely: but greeds
And garbage are too thick-strewn
To be swept up now, or invent
Excuses that make them all needs.
I just think it will happen, soon.

PHILIP LARKIN

I Was Not There

The morning they set out from home
I was not there to comfort them
the dawn was innocent with snow
in mockery – it is not true
the dawn was neutral was immune
their shadows threaded it too soon
they were relieved that it had come
I was not there to comfort them

One told me that my father spent
a day in prison long ago
he did not tell me that he went
what difference does it make now
when he set out when he came home
I was not there to comfort him
and now I have no means to know
of what I was kept ignorant

Both my parents died in camps
I was not there to comfort them
I was not there they were alone
my mind refuses to conceive
the life the death they must have known
I must atone because I live
I could not have saved them from death
the ground is neutral underneath

Every child must leave its home
time gathers life impartially
I could have spared them nothing since
I was too young – it is not true
they might have lived to succour me
and none shall say in my defence
had I been there to comfort them
it would have made no difference

KAREN GERSHON

The Boasts of Hywel ab Owain Gwynedd

Sunday, skilled in zealous verse I praise the Lord.
Monday, I sing in bed to my busty Nest,
'Such whiteness you are, pear blossom must be jealous.'
Tuesday, scholar Gwladus. Not to love her is a sin.
My couplets she pigeon-coos when I thrust to woo her
till her pale cheeks flush like rosy apple skin.
Wednesday, Generys. Dry old hymns I steal to please her.
Then with passion fruit in season I kneel to ease her.
Thursday, Hunydd, no hesitating lady, she.
One small cherry-englyn and she's my devotee.
Friday, worried Hawis, my epic regular.
She wants no baby, she's gooseberry vehement
till sugared by my poetry of endearment.
Saturday, I score and score. One tidy eulogy
and I'm away – I can't brake – through an orchard
I adore. O sweet riot of efflorescence,
let her name be secret for her husband's sake,
my peach of a woman, my vegetarian diet.

O tongue, lick up juices of the fruit. O teeth
– I've all of mine – be sure my busy tongue keeps quiet.

DANNIE ABSE

Epithalamion

Singing, today I married my white girl
beautiful in a barley field.
Green on thy finger a grass blade curled,
so with this ring I thee wed, I thee wed,
and send our love to the loveless world
of all the living and all the dead.

Now, no more than vulnerable human,
we more than one, less than two,
are nearly ourselves in a barley field –
and only love is the rent that's due
though the bailiffs of time return anew
to all the living but not the dead.

Shipwrecked, the sun sinks down harbours
of a sky, unloads its liquid cargoes
of marigolds, and I and my white girl
lie still in the barley – who else wishes
to speak, what more can be said
by all the living against all the dead?

Come then all you wedding guests:
green ghost of trees, gold of barley,
you blackbird priests in the field,

you wind that shakes the pansy head
fluttering on a stalk like a butterfly;
come the living and come the dead.

Listen flowers, birds, winds, worlds,
tell all today that I married
more than a white girl in the barley –
for today I took to my human bed
flower and bird and wind and world
and all the living and all the dead.

DANNIE ABSE

The Lost Woman

My mother went with no more warning
Than a bright voice and a bad pain.
Home from school on a June morning
And where the brook goes under the lane
I saw the back of a shocking white
Ambulance drawing away from the gate.

She never returned and I never saw
Her buried. So a romance began.
The ivy-mother turned into a tree
That still hops away like a rainbow down
The avenue as I approach.
My tendrils are the ones that clutch.

I made a life for her over the years.
Frustrated no more by a dull marriage
She ran a canteen through several wars.
The wit of a cliché-ridden village
She met her match at an extra-mural
Class and the OU summer school.

Many a hero in his time
And every poet has acquired
A lost woman to haunt the home,
To be compensated and desired,
Who will not alter, who will not grow,
A corpse they need never get to know.

She is nearly always benign. Her habit
Is not to stride at dead of night.
Soft and crepuscular in rabbit–
Light she comes out. Hear how they hate
Themselves for losing her as they did.
Her country is bland and she does not chide.

But my lost woman evermore snaps
From somewhere else: 'You did not love me.
I sacrificed too much perhaps,
I showed you the way to rise above me
And you took it. You are the ghost
With the bat-voice, my dear. *I* am not lost.'

PATRICIA BEER

Scotland

It was a day peculiar to this piece of the planet,
when larks rose on long thin strings of singing
and the air shifted with the shimmer of actual angels.
Greenness entered the body. The grasses
shivered with presences, and sunlight
stayed like a halo on hair and heather and hills.
Walking into town, I saw, in a radiant raincoat,
the woman from the fish-shop. 'What a day it is!'
cried I, like a sunstruck madman.
And what did she have to say for it?
Her brow grew bleak, her ancestors raged in their graves
as she spoke with their ancient misery:
'We'll pay for it, we'll pay for it, we'll pay for it!'

ALASTAIR REID

The Child's Story

When I was small and they talked about love I laughed
But I ran away and I hid in a tall tree
Or I lay in asparagus beds
But I still listened.
The blue dome sang with the wildest birds
And the new sun sang in the idle noon
But then I heard love, love, rung from the steeples, each belfry,
And I was afraid and I watched the cypress trees
Join the deciduous chestnuts and oaks in a crowd of shadows
And then I shivered and ran and ran to the tall

[531]

White house with the green shutters and dark red door
And I cried 'Let me in even if you must love me'
And they came and lifted me up and told me the name
Of the near and the far stars,
And so my first love was.

ELIZABETH JENNINGS

My Grandmother

She kept an antique shop – or it kept her.
Among Apostle spoons and Bristol glass,
The faded silks, the heavy furniture,
She watched her own reflection in the brass
Salvers and silver bowls, as if to prove
Polish was all, there was no need of love.

And I remember how I once refused
To go out with her, since I was afraid.
It was perhaps a wish not to be used
Like antique objects. Though she never said
That she was hurt, I still could feel the guilt
Of that refusal, guessing how she felt.

Later, too frail to keep a shop, she put
All her best things in one long narrow room.
The place smelt old, of things too long kept shut,
The smell of absences where shadows come
That can't be polished. There was nothing then
To give her own reflection back again.

And when she died I felt no grief at all,
Only the guilt of what I once refused.
I walked into her room among the tall
Sideboards and cupboards – things she never used
But needed: and no finger-marks were there,
Only the new dust falling through the air.

ELIZABETH JENNINGS

A Bird in the House

It was a yellow voice, a high, shrill treble in the nursery
White always and high, I remember it so,
White cupboard, off-white table, mugs, dolls' faces
And I was four or five. The garden could have been
Miles away. We were taken down to the green
Asparagus beds, the cut lawn, and the smell of it
Comes each summer after rain when white returns. Our bird,
A canary called Peter, sang behind bars. The black and white cat
Curled and snoozed by the fire and danger was far away.

Far away for us. Safety was life and only now do I know
That white walls and lit leaves knocking windows
Are a good prison but always you have
To escape, fly off from love not felt as love,
But our bird died in his yellow feathers. The quick
Cat caught him, tore him through bars when we were out
And I do not remember tears or sadness, I only
Remember the ritual, the warm yellow feathers we put
In a cardboard egg. What a sense of fitness. How far, I know
   now,

Ritual goes back, egg to egg, birth to burial and we went
Down the garden softly, two in a small procession,
And the high clouds bent down, the sky pulled aside
Its blue curtains. Death was there or else
Where the wise cat had hidden. That day we buried our bird
With a sense of fitness, not knowing death would be hard
Later, dark, without form or purpose.
After my first true grief I wept, was sad, was dark, but today,
Clear of terror and agony,
The yellow bird sings in my mind and I say
That the child is callous but wise, knows the purpose of play.
And the grief of ten years ago
Now has an ancient rite,
A walk down the garden carrying death in an egg
And the sky singing, the trees still waving farewell
When dying was nothing to know.

ELIZABETH JENNINGS

When I am Reading

When I am reading
the literature of my people
I think,
We have no Homer

no poet as great as that,
at all as great as that,
in that way
in that marvellous way.

But now and again I read
about a particular girl
who died of love
in a ragged dress

or an eagle will rise
crying, I was eating
noble dead soldiers
who were lying on a battlefield.

And now and again there will sail
on the sea towards Canada
ships with salt sails,
songs that are white with pain.

IAIN CRICHTON SMITH

Owl and Mouse

The owl wafts home with a mouse in its beak.
The moon is stunningly bright in the high sky.

Such a gold stone, such a brilliant hard light.
Such large round eyes of the owl among the trees.

All seems immortal but for the dangling mouse,
an old hurt string among the harmony

of the masterful and jewelled orchestra
which shows no waste soundlessly playing on.

IAIN CRICHTON SMITH

You Are at the Bottom of My Mind

from the Gaelic

Without my knowing it you are at the bottom of my mind
like a visitor to the bottom of the sea
with his helmet and his two large eyes,
and I do not rightly know your appearance or your manner
after five years of showers
of time pouring between me and you:

nameless mountains of water pouring
between me hauling you on board
and your appearance and manner in my weak hands.
You went astray
among the mysterious plants of the sea-bed
in the green half-light without love,

and you will never rise to the surface
though my hands are hauling ceaselessly,
and I do not know your way at all,
you in the half-light of your sleep
haunting the bed of the sea without ceasing
and I hauling and hauling on the surface.

IAIN CRICHTON SMITH

Some Poetry

Poetry is a loose term and only
A fool would offer a definition.
Those not concerned with the form
At all usually refer to some
Beautiful manifestation or the other.

Chopin, dying in hellish foggy London,
Wrote to say he was leaving for
Paris to finish the ultimate act,
Begging Grzymala to make his room ready
And not to forget a bunch of violets
So that he would have a little poetry
Around him when he returned.

I like to think the violets were
Easily obtainable and that the poetry
Was there, on the table, breathing
Wordless volumes for one too tired
To turn pages while moving swiftly
Towards an inevitable incomprehensible form.

FREDA DOWNIE

Hampstead: the Horse Chestnut Trees

At the top of a low hill
two stand together, green
bobbings contained within
the general sway. They
must be about my age.
My brother and I
rode between them and
down the hill and the impetus
took us on without pedalling
to be finally braked by
a bit of sullen marsh
(no longer there) where the mud
was coloured by the red-brown
oozings of iron. It
was autumn
          or was it?

Nothing to keep it there, the
smell of leaf in May
sweet and powerful as rutting
confuses me now, it's all
getting lost, I started
forgetting it even as I wrote.

Forms remain, not the life
of detail or hue
then the forms are lost and
only a few dates stay with you.

But the trees have no sentiments
their hearts are wood
and preserve nothing
                    their
boles get great, they are
embraced by the wind they
rushingly embrace,
they spread outward
and upward
                    without regret
hardening tender green
to insensate lumber.

THOM GUNN

Father in the Railway Buffet

What are you doing here, ghost, among these urns,
These film-wrapped sandwiches and help-yourself biscuits,
Upright and grand, with your stick, hat and gloves,
Your breath of eau-de-cologne?

What have you to say to these head-scarfed tea-ladies,
For whom your expensive vowels are exotic as Japan?
Stay, ghost, in your proper haunts, the clubland smoke-rooms,
Where you know the waiters by name.

You have no place among these damp and nameless.
Why do you walk here? *I came to say goodbye.*
You were ashamed of me for being different.
It didn't matter.

You who never even learned to queue?

U. A. FANTHORPE

Football at Slack

Between plunging valleys, on a bareback of hill
Men in bunting colours
Bounced, and their blown ball bounced.

The blown ball jumped, and the merry-coloured men
Spouted like water to head it.
The ball blew away downwind –

The rubbery men bounced after it.
The ball jumped up and out and hung on the wind
Over a gulf of treetops.
Then they all shouted together, and the ball blew back.

Winds from fiery holes in heaven
Piled the hills darkening around them
To awe them. The glare light
Mixed its mad oils and threw glooms.
Then the rain lowered a steel press.

Hair plastered, they all just trod water
To puddle glitter. And their shouts bobbed up
Coming fine and thin, washed and happy

While the humped world sank foundering
And the valleys blued unthinkable
Under depth of Atlantic depression –

But the wingers leapt, they bicycled in air
And the goalie flew horizontal

And once again a golden holocaust
Lifted the cloud's edge, to watch them.

TED HUGHES

Wind

This house has been far out at sea all night,
The woods crashing through darkness, the booming hills,
Winds stampeding the fields under the window
Floundering black astride and blinding wet

Till day rose; then under an orange sky
The hills had new places, and wind wielded
Blade-light, luminous and emerald,
Flexing like the lens of a mad eye.

At noon I scaled along the house-side as far as
The coal-house door. I dared once to look up –
Through the brunt wind that dented the balls of my eyes
The tent of the hills drummed and strained its guyrope,

The fields quivering, the skyline a grimace,
At any second to bang and vanish with a flap:
The wind flung a magpie away and a black–
Back gull bent like an iron bar slowly. The house

Rang like some fine green goblet in the note
That any second would shatter it. Now deep
In chairs, in front of the great fire, we grip
Our hearts and cannot entertain book, thought,

Or each other. We watch the fire blazing,
And feel the roots of the house move, but sit on,
Seeing the window tremble to come in,
Hearing the stones cry out under the horizons.

TED HUGHES

Epiphany

London. The grimy lilac softness
Of an April evening. Me
Walking over Chalk Farm Bridge
On my way to the tube station.
A new father – slightly light-headed
With the lack of sleep and the novelty.
Next, this young fellow coming towards me.

I glanced at him for the first time as I passed him
Because I noticed (I couldn't believe it)
What I'd been ignoring.

Not the bulge of a small animal
Buttoned into the top of his jacket
The way colliers used to wear their whippets –
But its actual face. Eyes reaching out
Trying to catch my eyes – so familiar!
The huge ears, the pinched, urchin expression –
The wild confronting stare, pushed through fear,
Between the jacket lapels.
                              'It's a fox-cub!'
I heard my own surprise as I stopped.
He stopped. 'Where did you get it? What
Are you going to do with it?'
                              A fox-cub
On the hump of Chalk Farm Bridge!

'You can have him for a pound.' 'But
Where did you find it? What will you do with it?'
'Oh, somebody'll buy him. Cheap enough
At a pound.' And a grin.
                              What I was thinking
Was – what would you think? How would we fit it
Into our crate of space? With the baby?
What would you make of its old smell
And its mannerless energy?
And as it grew up and began to enjoy itself
What would we do with an unpredictable,
Powerful, bounding fox?
The long-mouthed, flashing temperament?
That necessary nightly twenty miles

And that vast hunger for everything beyond us?
How would we cope with its cosmic derangements
Whenever we moved?

The little fox peered past me at other folks,
At this one and at that one, then at me.
Good luck was all it needed.
Already past the kittenish
But the eyes still small,
Round, orphaned-looking, woebegone
As if with weeping. Bereft
Of the blue milk, the toys of feather and fur,
The den life's happy dark. And the huge whisper
Of the constellations

Out of which Mother had always returned.
My thoughts felt like big, ignorant hounds
Circling and sniffing around him.
                              Then I walked on
As if out of my own life.
I let that fox-cub go. I tossed it back
Into the future
Of a fox-cub in London and I hurried
Straight on and dived as if escaping
Into the Underground. If I had paid,
If I had paid that pound and turned back
To you, with that armful of fox –

If I had grasped that whatever comes with a fox
Is what tests a marriage and proves it a marriage –
I would not have failed the test. Would you have failed it?
But I failed. Our marriage had failed.

TED HUGHES

Elegy for the Welsh Dead,
in the Falkland Islands, 1982

Gwŷr a aeth Gatraeth oedd ffraeth eu llu;
Glasfedd eu hancwyn, a gwenwyn fu.
                    – Y Gododdin (6th century)

Men went to Catraeth, keen was their company.
They were fed on fresh mead, and it proved poison.

Men went to Catraeth. The luxury liner
For three weeks feasted them.
They remembered easy ovations,
Our boys, splendid in courage.
For three weeks the albatross roads,
Passwords of dolphin and petrel,
Practised their obedience
Where the killer whales gathered,
Where the monotonous seas yelped.
Though they went to church with their standards
Raw death has them garnished.

Men went to Catraeth. The Malvinas
Of their destiny greeted them strangely.
Instead of affection there was coldness,
Splintering iron and the icy sea,
Mud and the wind's malevolent satire.
They stood nonplussed in the bomb's indictment.

Malcolm Wigley of Connah's Quay. Did his helm
Ride high in the war-line?
Did he drink enough mead for that journey?
The desolated shores of Tegeingl,
Did they pig this steel that destroyed him?
The Dee runs silent beside empty foundries.
The way of the wind and the rain is adamant.

Clifford Elley of Pontypridd. Doubtless he feasted.
He went to Catraeth with a bold heart.
He was used to valleys. The shadow held him.
The staff and the fasces of tribunes betrayed him.
With the oil of our virtue we have anointed
His head, in the presence of foes.

A lad in Tredegar or Maerdy. Was he shy before girls?
He exposes himself now to the hags, the glance
Of the loose-fleshed whores, the deaths
That congregate like gulls on garbage.
His sword flashed in the wastes of nightmare.

Russell Carlisle of Rhuthun. Men of the North
Mourn Rheged's son in the castellated Vale.
His nodding charger neighed for the battle.
Uplifted hooves pawed at the lightning.
Now he lies down. Under the air he is dead.

Men went to Catraeth. Of the forty-three
Certainly Tony Jones of Carmarthen was brave.
What did it matter, steel in the heart?
Shrapnel is faithful now. His shroud is frost.
With the dawn men went. Those forty-three,
Gentlemen all, from the streets and byways of Wales,
Dragons of Aberdare, Denbigh and Neath –
Figment of empire, whore's honour, held them.
Forty-three at Catraeth died for our dregs.

ANTHONY CONRAN

from Mercian Hymns

I

King of the perennial holly-groves, the riven sandstone:
overlord of the M5: architect of the historic rampart
and ditch, the citadel at Tamworth, the summer
hermitage in Holy Cross: guardian of the Welsh Bridge
and the Iron Bridge: contractor to the desirable new
estates: saltmaster: money-changer: commissioner for
oaths: martyrologist; the friend of Charlemagne.

'I liked that', said Offa, 'sing it again.'

XIV

Dismissing reports and men, he put pressure on the wax,
blistered it to a crest. He threatened malefactors with
ash from his noon cigar.

When the sky cleared above Malvern, he lingered in his orchard;
by the quiet hammer-pond. Trout-fry simmered there,
translucent, as though forming the water's underskin.
He had a care for natural minutiae. What his gaze
touched was his tenderness. Woodlice sat pellet-like in
the cracked bark and a snail sugared its new stone.

At dinner, he relished the mockery of drinking his family's
health. He did this whenever it suited him, which was
not often.

XXI

Cohorts of charabancs fanfared Offa's province and his
concern, negotiating the by-ways from Teme to Trent.
Their windshields dripped butterflies. Stranded on
hilltops they signalled with plumes of steam. Twilight
menaced the land. The young women wept and
surrendered.

Still, everyone was cheerful, heedless in such days: at summer
weekends dipping into valleys beyond Mercia's dyke. Tea
was enjoyed, by lakesides where all might fancy carillons
of real Camelot vibrating through the silent water.

Gradually, during the years, deciduous velvet peeled from
evergreen albums and during the years more treasures
were mislaid: the harp-shaped brooches, the nuggets of
fool's gold.

XXII

We ran across the meadow scabbed with cow-dung, past the
crab-apple trees and camouflaged nissen hut. It was
curfew-time for our war-band.

At home the curtains were drawn. The wireless boomed its
commands. I loved the battle-anthems and the greg-
arious news.

Then, in the earthy shelter, warmed by a blue-glassed storm-
lantern, I huddled with stories of dragon-tailed airships
and warriors who took wing immortal as phantoms.

XXVII

'Now when King Offa was alive and dead', they were all there,
the funereal gleemen: papal legate and rural dean;
Merovingian car-dealers, Welsh mercenaries; a shuffle
of house-carls.

He was defunct. They were perfunctory. The ceremony stood
acclaimed. The mob received memorial vouchers and
signs.

After that shadowy, thrashing midsummer hail-storm, Earth
lay for a while, the ghost-bride of livid Thor, butcher of
strawberries, and the shire-tree dripped red in the arena
of its uprooting.

GEOFFREY HILL

Punishment

I can feel the tug
of the halter at the nape
of her neck, the wind
on her naked front.

It blows her nipples
to amber beads,
it shakes the frail rigging
of her ribs.

I can see her drowned
body in the bog,
the weighing stone,
the floating rods and boughs.

Under which at first
she was a barked sapling
that is dug up
oak-bone, brain-firkin:

her shaved head
like a stubble of black corn,
her blindfold a soiled bandage,
her noose a ring

to store
the memories of love.
Little adulteress,
before they punished you

you were flaxen-haired,
undernourished, and your
tar-black face was beautiful.
My poor scapegoat,

I almost love you
but would have cast, I know,
the stones of silence.
I am the artful voyeur

of your brain's exposed
and darkened combs,
your muscles' webbing
and all your numbered bones:

I who have stood dumb
when your betraying sisters,
cauled in tar,
wept by the railings,

who would connive
in civilised outrage
yet understand the exact
and tribal, intimate revenge.

SEAMUS HEANEY

The Harvest Bow

As you plaited the harvest bow
You implicated the mellowed silence in you
In wheat that does not rust
But brightens as it tightens twist by twist
Into a knowable corona,
A throwaway love-knot of straw.

Hands that aged round ashplants and cane sticks
And lapped the spurs on a lifetime of gamecocks
Harked to their gift and worked with fine intent
Until your fingers moved somnambulant:
I tell and finger it like braille,
Gleaning the unsaid off the palpable,

And if I spy into its golden loops
I see us walk between the railway slopes
Into an evening of long grass and midges,
Blue smoke straight up, old beds and ploughs in hedges,
An auction notice on an outhouse wall –
You with a harvest bow in your lapel,

Me with the fishing rod, already homesick
For the big lift of these evenings, as your stick
Whacking the tips off weeds and bushes
Beats out of time, and beats, but flushes
Nothing: that original townland
Still tongue-tied in the straw tied by your hand.

The end of art is peace
Could be the motto of this frail device
That I have pinned up on our deal dresser –
Like a drawn snare
Slipped lately by the spirit of the corn
Yet burnished by its passage, and still warm.

SEAMUS HEANEY

The Guttural Muse

Late summer, and at midnight
I smelt the heat of the day:
At my window over the hotel car park
I breathed the muddied night airs off the lake
And watched a young crowd leave the discotheque.

Their voices rose up thick and comforting
As oily bubbles the feeding tench sent up
That evening at dusk – the slimy tench
Once called the 'doctor fish' because his slime
Was said to heal the wounds of fish that touched it.

A girl in a white dress
Was being courted out among the cars:
As her voice swarmed and puddled into laughs
I felt like some old pike all badged with sores
Wanting to swim in touch with soft-mouthed life.

SEAMUS HEANEY

A Keen for the Coins

O henny penny! Oh horsed half-crown!
O florin salmon! O sixpence hound!
O woodcock! Piglets! Hare and bull!
O mint of field and flood, farewell!
Be Ireland's lost ark, gone to ground,
And where the rainbow ends, be found.

SEAMUS HEANEY

The Blackbird of Glanmore

On the grass when I arrive,
Filling the stillness with life,
But ready to scare off
At the very first wrong move.
In the ivy when I leave.

It's you, blackbird, I love.

I park, pause, take heed.
Breathe. Just breathe and sit
And lines I once translated
Come back: 'I want away
To the house of death, to my father

Under the low clay roof.'

And I think of one gone to him,
A little stillness dancer –
Haunter-son, lost brother –
Cavorting through the yard,
So glad to see me home,

My homesick first term over.

And think of a neighbour's words
Long after the accident:
'Yon bird on the shed roof,
Up on the ridge for weeks –
I said nothing at the time

Bur I never liked yon bird.'

The automatic lock
Clunks shut, the blackbird's panic
Is shortlived, for a second
I've a bird's eye view of myself,
A shadow on raked gravel

In front of my house of life.

Hedge-hop, I am absolute
For you, your ready talkback,
Your each stand-offish comeback,
Your picky, nervy goldbeak –
On the grass when I arrive,

In the ivy when I leave.

SEAMUS HEANEY

XII

2000–

IF A
TOKTABOOT
thi Trooth Lik
WANNA yoo
Scruff yi
widny thingk
it wuz
tROO...

Englan Voice

I prepare – an prepare well – fe Englan.
Me decide, and done leave behine
all the voice of ol slave-estate bushman.

None of that distric bad-talk in Englan,
that bush talk of ol slave-estate man.

Hear me speak in Englan, an see
you dohn think I a Englan native.

Me nah go say
'Bwoy, how you du?'
me a-go say 'How are you old man?'

Me nah go say
'Wha yu nyam las night?'
me a-go say 'What did you have for supper?'

Patois talk is bushman talk –
people who talk patois them dam lazy.

Because mi bush voice so settle in me
an might let me down in-a Englan
me a-practise.

Me a-practise talk like teacher
till mi Englan voice come out-a me
like water from hillside rock.

Even if you fellows here
dohn hear mi Englan voice
I have it – an hear it in mi head!

JAMES BERRY

The Nation

The national day
had dawned. Everywhere
the national tree was opening its blossoms
to the sun's first rays, and from all quarters
young and old in national costume
were making their way to the original National
Building, where the national standard already
fluttered against the sky. Some breakfasted
on the national dish as they walked, frequently
pausing to greet acquaintances with a heartfelt
exchange of the national gesture. Many
were leading the national animal; others carried it
in their arms. The national bird
flew overhead; and on every side
could be heard the keen strains
of the national anthem, played on
the national instrument.

Where enough were gathered together,
national feeling ran high, and concerted cries of
'Death to the national foe!' were raised.
The national weapon was brandished. Though
festivities were constrained by the size of

the national debt, the national sport was
vigorously played all day
and the national drink drunk.
And from midday till late in the evening
there arose continually from the rear
of the national prison the sounds of the national
method of execution, dealing out rapid
justice to those who had given way
– on this day of all days –
to the national vice.

ROY FISHER

Handbag

My mother's old leather handbag,
crowded with letters she carried
all through the war. The smell
of my mother's handbag: mints
and lipstick and Coty powder.
The look of those letters, softened
and worn at the edges, opened,
read, and refolded so often.
Letters from my father. Odour
of leather and powder, which ever
since then has meant womanliness,
and love, and anguish, and war.

RUTH FAINLIGHT

Willow Song

I went down to the railway
But the railway wasn't there.
A long scar lay across the waste
Bound up with vetch and maidenhair
And birdsfoot trefoils everywhere.
But the clover and the sweet hay,
The cranesbill and the yarrow
Were as nothing to the rose bay
    the rose bay, the rose bay,
As nothing to the rose bay willow.

I went down to the river
But the river wasn't there.
A hill of slag lay in its course
With pennycress and cocklebur
And thistles bristling with fur.
But ragweed, dock and bitter may
And hawkbit in the hollow
Were as nothing to the rose bay,
    the rose bay, the rose bay
As nothing to the rose bay willow.

I went down to find my love.
My sweet love wasn't there.
A shadow stole into her place
And spoiled the loosestrife of her hair
And counselled me to pick despair.
Old elder and young honesty
Turned ashen, but their sorrow

Was as nothing to the rose bay
      the rose bay, the rose bay,
As nothing to the rose bay willow.

O I remember summer
When the hemlock was in leaf.
The sudden poppies by the path
Were little pools of crimson grief.
Sick henbane cowered like a thief.
But self-heal sprang up in her way,
And mignonette's light yellow,
To flourish with the rose bay,
      the rose bay, the rose bay,
To flourish with the rose bay willow.

Its flames took all the wasteland
And all the river's silt,
But as my dear grew thin and grey
They turned as white as salt or milk.
Great purples withered out of guilt,
And bright weeds blew away
In cloudy wreaths of summer snow.
And the first one was the rose bay,
      the rose bay, the rose bay,
The first one was the rose bay willow.

ANNE STEVENSON

Immigrant

November '63: eight months in London.
I pause on the low bridge to watch the pelicans:
they float swanlike, arching their white necks
over only slightly ruffled bundles of wings,
burying awkward beaks in the lake's water.

I clench cold fists in my Marks and Spencer's jacket
and secretly test my accent once again:
St James's Park; St James's Park; St James's Park.

FLEUR ADCOCK

Begin

Begin again to the summoning birds
to the sight of light at the window,
begin to the roar of morning traffic
all along Pembroke Road.
Every beginning is a promise
born in light and dying in dark
determination and exaltation of springtime
flowering the way to work.
Begin to the pageant of queuing girls
the arrogant loneliness of swans in the canal
bridges linking the past and future
old friends passing though with us still.
Begin to the loneliness that cannot end
since it perhaps is what makes us begin,

begin to wonder at unknown faces
at crying birds in the sudden rain
at branches stark in the willing sunlight
at seagulls foraging for bread
at couples sharing a sunny secret
alone together while making good.
Though we live in a world that dreams of ending
that always seems about to give in
something that will not acknowledge conclusion
insists that we forever begin.

BRENDAN KENNELLY

River & Fountain

I

I am walking backwards into the future like a Greek.
I have nothing to say. There is nothing I would describe.
It was always thus: as if snow has fallen on Front
Square, and, feeling the downy silence of the snowflakes
That cover cobbles and each other, white erasing white,
I read shadow and snow-drift under the Campanile.

II

'It fits on to the back of a postage stamp,' Robert said
As he scribbled out in tiny symbols the equation,
His silhouette a frost-flower on the window of my last
Year, his page the sky between chimney-stacks, his head
And my head at the city's centre aching for giddy
Limits, mathematics, poetry, squeaky nibs at all hours.

III

Top of the staircase, Number Sixteen in Botany Bay,
Slum-dwellers, we survived gas-rings that popped, slop-
Buckets in the bedrooms, changeable 'wives', and toasted
Doughy doorsteps, Freshmen turning into Sophisters
In front of the higgledy flames: our still-life, crusts
And buttery books, the half-empty marmalade jar.

IV

My Dansette record player bottled up like genies
Sibelius, Shostakovich, Bruckner, dusty sleeves
Accumulating next to Liddell and Scott's *Greek–English
Lexicon* voices the fluffy needle set almost free.
I was the culture vulture from Ulster, Vincent's joke
Who heard *The Rite of Spring* and contemplated suicide.

V

Adam was first to read the maroon-covered notebooks
I filled with innocent outpourings, Adam the scholar
Whose stammer could stop him christening this and that,
Whose Eden was annotation and vocabulary lists
In a precise classicist's hand, the love of words as words.
My first and best review was Adam's 'I like these – I – I –'

VI

'College poet? Village idiot you mean!' (Vincent again).
In neither profession could I settle comfortably
Once Derek arrived reciting Rimbaud, giving names
To the constellations over the Examination Hall.
'Are you Longley? Can I borrow your typewriter? Soon?'
His was the first snow party I attended. I felt the cold.

VII

We were from the North, hitch-hikers on the Newry Road,
Faces that vanished from a hundred driving-mirrors
Down that warren of reflections – O'Neill's Bar, Nesbitt's –
And through Front Gate to Connemara and Inishere,
The raw experience of market towns and clachans, then
Back to Rooms, village of minds, poetry's townland.

VIII

Though College Square in Belfast and the Linen Hall
Had been our patch, nobody mentioned William Drennan.
In Dublin what dreams of liberty, the Index, the Ban:
Etonians on Commons cut our accents with a knife.
When Brendan from Ballylongford defied the Bishop, we
Flapped our wings together and were melted in the sun.

IX

A bath-house lotus-eater – fags, sodden *Irish Times* –
I tagged along with the Fabians, to embarrass Church
And State our grand design. Would-be class-warriors
We raised, for a moment, the Red Flag at the Rubrics,
Then joined the Civil Service and talked of Civil Rights
Was Trinity a Trojan Horse? Were we Greeks at all?

X

'The Golden Mean is a tension, Ladies, Gentlemen,
And not a dead level': the Homeric head of Stanford
Who would nearly sing the first lines of the *Odyssey*.
That year I should have failed, but, teaching the *Poetics*,
He asked us for definitions, and accepted mine:
'Sir, if prose is a river, then poetry's a fountain.'

XI

Someone has skipped the seminar. Imagine his face,
The children's faces, my wife's: she sat beside me then
And they were waiting to be born, ghosts from a future
Without Tom: he fell in love just once and died of it.
Oh, to have turned away from everything to one face,
Eros and Thanatos your gods, icicle and dew.

XII

Walking forwards into the past with more of an idea
I want to say to my friends of thirty years ago
And to daughters and a son that Belfast is our home,
Prose a river still – the Liffey, the Lagan – and poetry
A fountain that plays in an imaginary Front Square.
When snow falls it is feathers from the wings of Icarus.

MICHAEL LONGLEY

Dreams of a Summer Night

The girls are quiet now in the house upstairs.
Still bright at ten with no need of music
on local habitations, tile and brick,
as the moon rises like a magic lamp
hung in a thorn bush and the sun retires
beyond the Bandon River; but I put on
young Mozart's Oboe Concerto, K.314,
the opening bit, in search of a nice tune –
and find it straight away, quick and exact,
the broken silence of the creative act.

Strangely, after the gold rush and the slump,
what remains is a great sense of relief.
Can we relax now and get on with life?
Step out and take a deep breath of night air
in peace, not always having to defer
to market forces, to the great hegemony,
the global hurricane, the rule of money?
High over Innishannon a single star
on the woods of this unthickly wooded shore.
Can we turn now to the important things
like visible scents, how even silence sings ?
How we grew frolicsome one sunny June
some sixty years ago at Cushendun
in our young lives of clover, clock and cloud,
the first awakenings under a northern sky
heartbreaking in its extremity? 'One day
the old grow young,' as the old rock star said.

    The first movement – *aperto*, open, frank –
declares its candour with a lively run
of oboe riffs; *adagio*, and we think
of the proactive soul in wind and wood
before revisiting the original mood
though more maturely, having lived meanwhile.
It's far from what Said meant by late style
since it was written by a twenty-year-old;
but I'm late listening, taking it all in
like a dreamt 'gentle concord' in the world.
Drilling for oil and war we seldom register
the resilient silence strewn about our toes
and under our very noses: thyme and sage,
mushroom and violet, briony, briar rose
and other elfin species. Soppy, I sniff

inchoate presences in the dim, substantive
trance of a summer night, its peace and quiet,
remembering poetry is a *real* mirage
in an unreal world of cash and babble,
ringtone and car alarm, and remains 'a point of
departure not from reality but to it' –
wherein lies one function of the poet,
to be instrumental in the soul's increase.
During the May rising they used to say
«*Prenez vos désirs pour la réalité*;
l'imagination au pouvoir!» These very reasonable
demands are even more urgent for us today
trying to save ourselves from corporate space,
from virtuality with its image crime,
and Mozart from the ubiquitous pop sound:
fiddle and flute, soft oboe and clarinet,
the next best thing to silence in the mind,
that scarce but still renewable resource.
The young produce the liveliest work of course
but soon enough it's *Wild Strawberries* time,
age and experience, the lost summer house,
girls on a jetty, 'the old sunlit face'.

There was a week of dreams for some reason,
some Kafkaesque and some more seasonable:
a concrete labyrinth with no obvious exit,
a maze of corridors, little natural light,
gruff notices prohibiting this and that,
no eating, drinking, smoking, and don't laugh,
surly administrative and security staff.
Alarms went off at intervals. Doors were shut
and windows, where there were windows, unopenable;
from secret offices a mysterious mumble

qualifying the air-conditioned silence:
Genetics, Human Resources, Behavioural Sciences.
Someone had proved the soul doesn't exist
and wiped out any traces of the past;
all were in danger but it faded fast
at the last minute, only to be replaced
by animations, eyes in a twitchy forest,
oak limbs outgrabbing, knuckles whitening, rock
speaking, Rackham *púcas* at face and neck.
These vanished too; then an erotic bower
snowed in by a warm leaf-and-petal shower
around the long ears and the bristling back.
She lay there in soft focus, her bright eye
moist with provocation; but just as I . . .

So many quiet shores 'bleared, smeared with toil',
there's nowhere for a sticky duck to hide
from the unchecked invasion of crude oil
dumped on the sand by a once friendly tide;
and if they drill here what else do we gain
but a bonanza for an acquisitive crowd
of blow-hard types, determined, garish, loud?
Would we ever get our old lives back again?
Gossip is history, history is gossip –
the locals talking in a hardware shop
about Tom Barry, James II, Marlborough
or that torpedo from a German sub,
the opening wine bar and the closing pub,
the pharmaceutical giant at Dunderrow,
its ethics, working conditions and so on,
a proposal to dig the whole town up again
for fibre optics and more 'information'
now on the table at the Kinsale borough

council and more than likely to go through.
'All politics is local', right where you are.
Communities are the real vehicles of power
not merely its last points of application
or they should be, says Amit Chaudhuri;
water and gas have first consideration
as every pre-Socratic thinker knew.
You hear a different music of the spheres
depending where you sit in the concert space,
so this is the centre of the whole creation:
important or trivial, it all finishes here
on your own starlit doorstep. It could be worse.

A boreal sun, white nights of Petersburg!
The never fading gleam of Tír na nÓg!
But you can have too much of shiny things.
The dark has its own wisdom, its own owl wings,
for this is when the spirits come out to play
and the grim ghosts we daren't admit by day.
Nacht und Träume: geese dreaming of maize,
old Siggi's youngest crying out for 'stwawbewwies'
the entrepreneur with his elaborate schemes,
love dreams, exam dreams and anxiety dreams
'over-interpreted as they need to be.
I had a patient once . . .' But even he
granted the mystery of autonomous art,
those strange impulses circuiting the brain,
the plays of Shakespeare, symphonies of Mozart.

Eleven and still light. No more music now
except for night and silence round the place.
Gazing into the past I hear once more
fathers and uncles back from a won war

and see 'the ice-cream on the pier', the rain
and windy picnics laid out under the brow
of the Cave Hill, Belfast laid out below –
then jump-cut to the dreams, vivid but short,
scaring us as they did when we were ten:
child murder in *Macbeth*, wolves at the door,
the dizzying height and the obscure disgrace,
indictments for a guilt we seldom face.
Sometimes you're hauled before a midnight court,
women presiding, to face charges of
failure in generosity, patience, love
and finer feeling. Often the chief judge
condemns you roundly to a change of heart
and sends you down abruptly for an age
of solitary. Read me the riot act again
in the grave, measured tone you used to restrain
my frantic idiocies. The least *I* can do
is praise your qualities the one way I know
now that I mourn, as here, your grace and poise,
your pungent wit, the laughter in your eyes,
the buoyant upbeat, the interior light
and those odd melancholy moments when
your head would close down with fastidious pain
at a world too coarse and tragic to be borne.
Aspiring spirit, late in finding rest
and harmony, may you have peace at last.
Today in a freak of thought I wondered if
the conservation-of-energy law applies
to souls and promises us eternal life.
At times like this we let ourselves imagine
some substance in the old claim of religion
that we don't die, not really. Don't light residues
commingle with the other starry dead

when our cold ashes in the earth are laid
or scattered on the waves at Port na Spaniagh
and the mad particles begin to spin
like sand grains in the night? Our contribution:
a few good books and a few words of caution.
You the unborn, the bright ones who come later,
remember we too sparkled in the sun,
burst on the shingle, perished underwater,
revolved our secrets in the vast oceans
of time, and live on in our transmigrations.

    And you, old friend, Brancusi's 'Sleeping Muse',
who saved me when I'd nothing left to lose,
I can still wish for what you wish for too:
'the amazing truth 'tis no witchcraft to see',
refreshed tradition, lateral thought, a new
world politics and a disabused serenity.
These summer mornings I get up at five,
biro in hand, surprised to be still alive,
grateful for all the clichés and beguiled
by the first birdsong, the first light, the wild
relationship of water and cloud kingdoms
shaping our wishes and our waking dreams.
It's late, so lights out even as a last glow
still lingers on the gardens, on roof and rock:
mid-June now and it's never completely dark
but vague, ambrosial, metamorphic, slow
as if some happy mischief is at work
in the mist-pearly undergrowth below,
transfiguring the earth from dusk to dawn.

The moon floats from a cloud and two dogs bark;
the anthropomorphic trees are trees again,
the human forms recover their wood-grain
and the prehensile skins of hand and groin
revert, the limbs to branches, hair to leaves
as they resume their old arboreal lives.
The girls are fast asleep in the rooms above.
Back here from dreamland with a dewy leaf
to keep me right and ward off disbelief,
I await the daylight we were born to love:
birds at a window, boats on a rising wave,
light dancing on dawn water, the lives we live.

DEREK MAHON

Extra Helpings

In our primary school
Set lunch was the rule
Though in Scotland we call that meal 'dinner'.
We tucked in like starvelings,
Inchinnan's wee darlings,
And it didn't make thin children thinner.

But what I liked best
Was disliked by the rest,
Rice pudding with raisins and bloated sultanas,
Stewed fruit and dumplings
In big extra helpings
And hooray for first post-War bananas!

It was very good scoff
So I polished it off
A very dab hand with a spoon,
a spoon,
A very dab hand with my spoon.

Detested mashed turnip
Gave most kids the pip
While cabbage was much the same tale.
No shortage of roots, and no hardship of greens –
After mine I ate Harry's, then Elspeth's, then Jean's,
O a glutton for turnips and kail.
It was very good scoff
So I polished it off
A very dab hand with a fork,
a fork,
A very dab hand with my fork.

I used to be slim.
I used to be *slim*!
'Look!' they say now. 'There's at least *three* of him!'
To which I reply
With a daggerly eye,
'Well, that's better than three-quarters *you*!'
But my clothes don't fit
I'm fed up with it
And the sylph in me's guilty and blue.
Semolina and sago with jam,
with jam,
Oh dear, what a pudding I am,
I am,
Oh dear, what a pudding I am.

But I'm longing for lunch
And something to munch
Though I wish it was back in that school
When the dinner-bell rings
And all good things
Await to be guzzled until I am happy and full.
Dear God, I'd die
For Shepherd's Pie
In 1949 or 1950
When the dinner-bell rings
And all good things
Draw children on the sniff and make then nifty.
    It was very good scoff
    So I polished it off –
        Oh dear, what a pudding I am,
            I am,
    Oh dear, what a pudding I am,
    But a very dab hand with a spoon,
      a spoon,
    And a very dab hand with a fork.

DOUGLAS DUNN

Swineherd

When all this is over, said the swineherd,
I mean to retire, where
Nobody will have heard about my special skills
And conversation is mainly about the weather.

I intend to learn how to make coffee, at least as well
As the Portuguese lay-sister in the kitchen
And polish the brass fenders every day.
I want to lie awake at night
Listening to cream crawling to the top of the jug
And the water lying soft in the cistern.

I want to see an orchard where the trees grow in straight lines
And the yellow fox finds shelter between the navy-blue trunks,
Where it gets dark early in summer
And the apple-blossom is allowed to wither on the bough.

EILÉAN NÍ CHUILLEANÁIN

gaelic is alive

in memoriam caitlín maude

let's put aside
today's work
and dance to
the wind's port-à-beul

'gaelic is alive'
despite all arrows
she climbs the hillside
sapling of oak in her arms
her defiant eyes
reaching the far-off horizon
she aims for the far-off horizon
a bright lasting star in her breast

defend her from too bold a leap

but be dancing be dancing
it is work to be dancing

AONGHAS MACNEACAIL
translated from the Scots Gaelic by the author

When I Grow Up

When I grow up I want to have a bad leg.
I want to limp down the street I live in
without knowing where I am. I want the disease
where you put your hand on your hip
and lean forward slightly, groaning to yourself.

If a little boy asks me the way
I'll try and touch him between the legs.
What a dirty old man I'm going to be when I grow up!
What shall we do with me?

I promise I'll be good
if you let me fall over in the street
and lie there calling like a baby bird. Please,
nobody come. I'm perfectly all right. I like it here.

I wonder would it be possible
to get me into a National Health Hospice
somewhere in Manchester?
I'll stand in the middle of my cubicle
holding onto a piece of string for safety,
shaking like a leaf at the thought of my suitcase.

I'd certainly like to have a nervous tic
so I can purse my lips up all the time
like Cecil Beaton. Can I be completely bald, please?
I love the smell of old pee.
Why can't I smell like that?

When I grow up I want a thin piece of steel
inserted into my penis for some reason.
Nobody's to tell me why it's there. I want to guess!
Tell me, is that a bottle of old Burgundy
under my bed? I never can tell
if I feel randy any more, can you?

I think it's only fair that I should be allowed
to cough up a bit of blood when I feel like it.
My daughter will bring me a special air cushion
to hold me upright and I'll watch
in baffled admiration as she blows it up for me.

Here's my list: nappies, story books, munchies,
something else. What was the other thing?
I can't remember exactly,
but when I grow up I'll know. When I grow up
I'll pluck at my bedclothes to collect lost thoughts.
I'll roll them into balls and swallow them.

HUGO WILLIAMS

New Year Behind the Asylum

There was the noise like when the men in droves
Are hurrying to the match only this noise was
Everybody hurrying to see the New Year in
In town under the clock but we, that once,

He said would I come our usual Saturday walk
And see it in out there in the open fields
Behind the asylum. Even on sunny days
How it troubled me more and more the nearer we got

And he went quiet and as if he was ashamed
For what he must always do, which was
Go and grip the bars of the iron gates and stand
Staring into the garden until they saw him.

They were like the animals, so glad and shy
Like overgrown children dressed in things
Handed down too big or small and they came in a crowd
And said hello with funny chunnering noises

And through the bars, looking so serious,
He put his empty hand out. But that night
We crept past quickly and only stopped
In the middle of the empty fields and there

While the clock in the square where the normal people stood
And all the clocks in England were striking twelve
We heard the rejoicings for the New Year
From works and churches and the big ships in the docks

So faint I wished we were hearing nothing at all
We were so far away in our black fields
I felt we might not ever get back again
Where the people were and it was warm, and then

Came up their sort of rejoicing out of the asylum,
Singing or sobbing I don't know what it was
Like nothing on earth, their sort of welcoming in
Another New Year and it was only then

When the bells and the cheerful hooters couldn't be heard
But only the inmates, only the poor mad people
Singing or sobbing their hearts out for the New Year
That he gripped me fast and kissed my hair

And held me in against him and clung on tight to me
Under a terrible number of bare stars
So far from town and the lights and house and home
And shut my ears against the big children crying

But listened himself, listened and listened
That one time. And I've thought since and now
He's dead I'm sure that what he meant was this:
That I should know how much love would be needed.

DAVID CONSTANTINE

Tullynoe: Tête-à-Tête in the Parish Priest's Parlour

'Ah, he was a grand man.'
'He was: he fell out of the train going to Sligo.'
'He did: he thought he was going to the lavatory.'
'He did: in fact he stepped out the rear door of the train.'
'He did: God, he must have got an awful fright.'
'He did: he saw that it wasn't the lavatory at all.'
'He did: he saw that it was the railway tracks going away
    from him.'
'He did: I wonder if. . . but he was a grand man.'
'He was: he had the most expensive Toyota you can buy.'
'He had: well, it was only beautiful.'
'It was: he used to have an Audi.'
'He had: as a matter of fact he used to have two Audis.'
'He had: and then he had an Avenger.'
'He had: and then he had a Volvo.'
'He had: in the beginning he had a lot of Volkses.'
'He had: he was a great man for the Volkses.'
'He was: did he once have Escort?'
'He had not: he had a son a doctor.'
'He had: he had a Morris Minor too.'
'He had: and he had a sister a hairdresser in Kilmallock.'
'He had: he had another sister a hairdresser in Ballybunion.'

[583]

'He had: he was put in a coffin which was put in his father's
    cart.'
'He was: his lady wife sat on top of the coffin driving the
    donkey.'
'She did: Ah, but he was a grand man.'
'He was: he was a grand man . . .'
'Good night, Father.'
'Good night, Mary.'

PAUL DURCAN

The Achill Woman

She came up the hill carrying water.
She wore a half-buttoned, wool cardigan,
a tea-towel round her waist.

She pushed the hair out of her eyes with
her free hand and put the bucket down.

The zinc-music of the handle on the rim
tuned the evening. An Easter moon rose.
In the next-door field a stream was
a fluid sunset; and then, stars.

I remember the cold rosiness of her hands.
She bent down and blew on them like broth.
And round her waist, on a white background,
in coarse, woven letters, the words 'glass cloth.'

And she was nearly finished for the day.
And I was all talk, raw from college-
week-ending at a friend's cottage
with one suitcase and the set text
of the Court poets of the Silver Age.

We stayed putting down time until
the evening turned cold without warning.
She said goodnight and started down the hill.

The grass changed from lavender to black.
The trees turned back to cold outlines.
You could taste frost

but nothing now can change the way I went
indoors, chilled by the wind
and made a fire
and took down my book
and opened it and failed to comprehend

the harmonies of servitude,
the grace music gives to flattery
and language borrows from ambition –

and how I fell asleep

oblivious to
the planets clouding over in the skies,
the slow decline of the Spring moon,
the songs crying out their ironies.

EAVAN BOLAND

How the Wild South East was Lost

for Robert Maclean

See, I was raised on the wild side, border country,
Kent 'n' Surrey, a spit from the country line,
An' they bring me up in a prep school over the canyon:
Weren't no irregular verb I couldn't call mine.

Them days, I seen oldtimers set in the ranch-house
(Talkin' 'bout J. 'Boy' Hobbs and Pat C. Hendren)
Blow a man clean away with a Greek optative.
Scripture test, or a sprig o' that rho-do-dendron.

Hard pedallin' country, stranger, flint 'n' chalkface,
Evergreen needles, acorns an' beechmast shells,
But stop that old lone pine you could squint clean over
To the dome o' the Chamber o' Commerce in Tunbridge Wells.

Yep, I was raised in them changeable weather conditions:
I seen 'em, afternoon of a sunny dawn,
Clack up the deck chairs, bolt for the back French windows
When they bin drinkin' that strong tea on the lawn.

In a cloud o' pipesmoke rollin' there over the canyon,
Book-larned me up that Minor Scholarship stuff:
Bent my back to that in-between innings light roller
And life weren't easy. And that's why I'm so tough.

KIT WRIGHT

'Unrelated Incidents' – No. 3

this is thi
six a clock
news thi
man said n
thi reason
a talk wia
BBC accent
iz coz yi
widny wahnt
mi ti talk
aboot thi
trooth wia
voice lik
wanna yoo
scruff. if
a toktaboot
thi trooth
lik wanna yoo
scruff yi
widny thingk
it wuz troo.
jist wanna yoo
scruff tokn.
thirza right
way ti spell
ana right way
ti tok it. this
is me tokn yir
right way a
spellin. this

is ma trooth.
yooz doant no
thi trooth
yirsellz cawz
yi canny talk
right. this is
the six a clock
nyooz. belt up.

TOM LEONARD

Shakespeare at School

Forty boys on benches with their quills,
Six days a week through almost all the year,
Long hours of Latin with relentless drills
And repetition, all enforced by fear.
I picture Shakespeare sitting near the back,
Indulging in a risky bit of fun
By exercising his prodigious knack
Of thinking up an idiotic pun,
And whispering his gem to other boys,
Some of whom could not suppress their mirth –
Behaviour that unfailingly annoys
Any teacher anywhere on earth.
   The fun was over when the master spoke:
   Will Shakespeare, come up here and share the joke.

WENDY COPE

Bagpipe Muzak, Glasgow 1990

When A. and R. men hit the street
To sign up every second band they meet
Then marketing men will spill out spiel
About how us Glesca folk are really real
(Where once they used to fear and pity
These days they glamorise and patronise our city –
Accentwise once they could hear bugger all
That was not low, glottal or guttural,
Now we've 'kudos' incident'ly
And the Patter's street-smart, strictly state-of-the-art
And our oaths are user-friendly).

It's all go the sandblaster, it's all go Tutti Frutti,
All we want is a wally close with Rennie Mackintosh putti

Malkie Machismo invented a gismo for making whisky oot
    o' girders
He tasted it, came back for mair, and soon he was on to his
    thirders.
Rabbie Burns turned in his grave and dunted Hugh
    MacDiarmid,
Said: It's oor National Thorn, John Barleycorn, but I doot
    we'll ever learn it . . .

It's all go the Rotary Club, it's all go 'The Toast Tae The Lassies',
It's all go Holy Willie's Prayer and plunging your dirk in the
    haggis.

Robbie Coltrane flew Caledonian MacBrayne
To Lewis . . . on a Sunday!
Protesting Wee Frees fed him antifreeze
(Why God knows) till he was comatose
And didnae wake up till the Monday.

Aye it's Retro Time for Northern Soul and the whoop and the
    skirl o' the saxes.
All they'll score's more groundglass heroin and venison filofaxes.
The rent-boys preen on Buchanan Street, their boas are made
    of vulture,
It's all go the January sales in the Metropolis of Culture.

It's all go the PR campaign and a radical change of image –
Write Saatchi and Saatchi a blank cheque to pay them for the
    damage.

Tam o'Shanter fell asleep
To the sound of fairy laughter
Woke up on the cold-heather hillside
To find it was ten years after
And it's all go (again) the Devolution Debate and pro . . .
    pro . . . proportional representation.
Over pasta and pesto in a Byres Road bistro, Scotland
    declares hersel' a nation.

Margo McDonald spruced up her spouse for thon Govan
    By-Election
The voters they selectit him in a sideyways *left* defection,
The Labour man was awfy hurt, he'd dependit on the
    X-fillers
And the so-and-sos had betrayed him for thirty pieces of Sillars!

Once it was no go the SNP, they were sneered at as 'Tory' and
   tartan
And thought to be very little to do with the price of Spam in
   Dumbarton.
Now it's all go to the Nationalists, the toast of the folk and
   the famous
– Of Billy Connolly, Muriel Gray and the Auchtermuchty
   Proclaimers.

It's all go L.A. lager, it's all go the Campaign for an Assembly
It's all go Suas Alba and winning ten–nil at Wembley.
Are there separatist dreams in the glens and the schemes?
Well . . . it doesny take Taggart to detect it!
Or to jalouse we hate the Government
And we patently didnae elect it.
So – watch out Margaret Thatcher, and tak' tent Neil Kinnock
Or we'll tak' the United Kingdom and brekk it like a bannock.

LIZ LOCHHEAD

Belfast Confetti

Suddenly as the riot squad moved in, it was raining
    exclamation marks,
Nuts, bolts, nails, car-keys. A fount of broken type. And the
    explosion
Itself – an asterisk on the map. This hyphenated line, a burst
    of rapid fire . . .
I was trying to complete a sentence in my head, but it kept
    stuttering,
All the alleyways and side-streets blocked with stops and colons.

I know this labyrinth so well – Balaclava, Raglan, Inkerman,
    Odessa Street –
Why can't I escape? Every move is punctuated. Crimea Street.
    Dead end again.
A Saracen, Kremlin-2 mesh. Makrolon face-shields. Walkie-
    talkies. What is
My name? Where am I coming from? Where am I going? A
    fusillade of question-marks.

CIARAN CARSON

Poor Snow

The violet
light of snow falling.

Its tiny darts
make eye stripes.

Dark flakes
rapid, upwards.

It's restless, it can't
find whiteness.

Its grey and violet
trillion souls.

DENISE RILEY

Listen Mr Oxford Don

Me not no Oxford don
me a simple immigrant
from Clapham Common
I didn't graduate
I immigrate

But listen Mr Oxford don
I'm a man on de run
and a man on de run

is a dangerous one

I ent have no gun
I ent have no knife
but mugging de Queen's English
is the story of my life

I dont need no axe
to split/ up yu syntax
I dont need no hammer
to mash/ up yu grammar

I warning you Mr Oxford don
I'm a wanted man
and a wanted man
is a dangerous one

Dem accuse me of assault
on de Oxford dictionary/
imagine a concise peaceful man like me/
dem want me serve time
for inciting rhyme to riot
but I tekking it quiet
down here in Clapham Common

I'm not a violent man Mr Oxford don
I only armed wit mih human breath
but human breath
is a dangerous weapon

So mek dem send one big word after me
I ent serving no jail sentence
I slashing suffix in self-defence

I bashing future wit present tense
and if necessary

I making de Queen's English accessory/to my offence

JOHN AGARD

Alien

... as a woman I have no country.
— VIRGINIA WOOLF

I have never returned
wounded, to the white cliffs
of Dover, knowing I rule –
though a bit of shrapnel
is my heart –
over and over singing
Elizabeth and England
in the bottom of
a gunboat.

No. I walk these streets
already beautifully paved
with bones of enemies
and women. I am subject
to a proud succession,
brave and noble sons
in mufti, bowler hats.

Who point to our great poets
with their walking sticks
of oak. Who will not bury
my heart in Westminster Abbey,
singing God the Father God
the Son and God the Holy Ghost,
this morning the serving maid
burned the toast.

Eliza sits below stairs to mend
the linen here in England's
green and pleasant –

and this land is my land
to which I have never returned.

GILLIAN ALLNUTT

To a Cuckoo at Coolanlough

Driving the perfect length of Ireland,
Like a worn fold in a newspaper,
All my deep, country feelings
Wished I could have hypnotised myself
Into going back for the cherry-market
At Borris-in-Ossory.

But all I could think of was the fountain
Where Shelley wrote his 'Ode to the West Wind'
Nesting like a train-fever or combing jacket
Over the town.

A child will only
Sleep so long, and I wonder
If he is an artist, or have the six
Muscles around his eye forgotten colour,
And look it up, that Saturn-red, wild smudging,
In a dream-book?

And I wonder, after the three-minute
News, if you remember
The bits of road that I do?

MEDBH MCGUCKIAN

I think someone might write an elegy

I think someone might write an elegy
for the dead words: the shapely words
that have no shape to fit round now,
whose ladies have stepped out of them,
as it were, and left them in a huddle,
the words we don't have things for I think
someone might write an elegy for words
like timothy, cocksfoot, feverfew,
fennel and saffron, ginger and galingale.
For mowdewart and marmot; for furze-pig
and parmaceti; for feline
and anserine; for Lawrence the tod.
For cirrus, nimbus and stratocumulus.
For Persepolis, Hamadan, Shushan,
for Tolleshunt d'Arcy and Cirencester;
for Elizabeth Sarah Davidson,

which once seemed to me the fairest words
that ever anyone laid tongue to
For the words that mean nothing now
and whose loveliness, made as it was
by what they meant, has left them, the husks
of dragonflies, drying out . . . Things that are dead
we keep with words, but when the words die
themselves; oh then they're dead, and dead indeed.

SHEENAGH PUGH

Incantata

In memory of Mary Farl Powers

I thought of you tonight, *a leanbh,* lying there in your long
    barrow
colder and dumber than a fish by Francisco de Herrera,
as I X-Actoed from a spud the Inca
glyph for a mouth: thought of that first time I saw your pink
spotted torso, distant-near as a nautilus,
when you undid your portfolio, yes indeedy,
and held the print of what looked like a cankered potato
at arm's length – your arms being longer, it seemed, than
    Lugh's.

Even Lugh of the Long (sometimes the Silver) Arm
would have wanted some distance between himself and the
    army-worms
that so clouded the sky over St Cloud you'd have to seal
the doors and windows and steel
yourself against their nightmarish *déjeuner sur l'herbe*:
try as you might to run a foil
across their tracks, it was to no avail;
the army-worms shinnied down the stove-pipe on an army-
    worm rope.

I can hardly believe that, when we met, my idea of 'R and R'
was to get smashed, almost every night, on sickly-sweet
    Demerara
rum and Coke: as well as leaving you a grass widow
(remember how Krapp looks up 'viduity'?),
after eight or ten or twelve of those dark rums
it might be eight or ten or twelve o'clock before I'd land
back home in Landseer Street, deaf and blind
to the fact that not only was I all at sea, but in the doldrums.

Again and again you'd hold forth on your own version of
    Thomism,
your own *Summa*
Theologiae that in everything there is an order,
that the things of the world sing out in a great oratorio:
it was Thomism, though, tempered by *La Nausée*,
by His Nibs Sam Bethicket,
and by that Dublin thing, that an artist must walk down
    Baggott
Street wearing a hair-shirt under the shirt of Nessus.

'*D'éirigh me ar maidin*,' I sang, '*a tharraingt chun aoinigh mhóir*':
our first night, you just had to let slip that your secret amour
for a friend of mine was such
that you'd ended up lying with him in a ditch
under a bit of whin, or gorse, or furze,
somewhere on the border of Leitrim, perhaps, or Roscommon:
'gamine', I wanted to say, 'kimono';
even then it was clear I'd never be at the centre of your
    universe.

Nor should I have been, since you were there already, your
    own *Ding*
an sich, no less likely to take wing
than the Christ you drew for a Christmas card as a pupa
in swaddling clothes: and how resolutely you would pooh pooh
the idea I shared with Vladimir and Estragon,
with whom I'd been having a couple of jars,
that this image of the Christ-child swaddled and laid in the
    manger
could be traced directly to those army-worm dragoons.

I thought of the night Vladimir was explaining to all and
    sundry
the difference between *geantrai* and *suantrai*
and you remarked on how you used to have a crush
on Burt Lancaster as Elmer Gantry, and Vladimir went to brush
the ash off his sleeve with a legerdemain
that meant only one thing – 'Why does he put up with this
    crap?' –
and you weighed in with 'To live in a dustbin, eating scrap,
seemed to Nagg and Nell a most eminent domain.'

How little you were exercised by those tiresome literary
    intrigues,
how you urged me to have no more truck
than the Thane of Calder
with a fourth estate that professes itself to be *'égalitaire'*
but wants only blood on the sand: yet, irony of ironies,
you were the one who, in the end,
got yourself up as a *retiarius* and, armed with net and trident,
marched from Mount Street to the Merrion Square arena.

In the end, you were the one who went forth to beard the
    lion,
you who took the DART line
every day from Jane's flat in Dun Laoghaire, or Dalkey,
dreaming your dream that the subterranean Dodder and Tolka
might again be heard above the *hoi polloi*
for whom Irish 'art' means a High Cross at Carndonagh or
    Corofin
and *The Book of Kells:* not until the lion cried craven
would the poor Tolka and the poor Dodder again sing out for
    joy.

I saw you again tonight, in your jump-suit, thin as a rake,
your hand moving in such a deliberate arc
as you ground a lithographic stone
that your hand and the stone blurred to one
and your face blurred into the face of your mother, Betty Wahl,
who took your failing, ink-stained hand
in her failing, ink-stained hand
and together you ground down that stone by sheer force of will.

I remember your pooh poohing, as we sat there on the
    'Enterprise',
my theory that if your name is Powers
you grow into it or, at least,
are less inclined to tremble before the likes of this bomb-blast
further up the track: I myself was shaking like a leaf
as we wondered whether the IRA or the Red
Hand Commandos or even the Red
Brigades had brought us to a standstill worthy of Hamm and
    Clov.

Hamm and Clov; Nagg and Nell; Watt and Knott;
the fact is that we'd been at a standstill long before the night
things came to a head,
long before we'd sat for half the day in the sweltering heat
somewhere just south of Killnasaggart
and I let slip a name – her name – off my tongue
and you turned away (I see it now) the better to deliver the sting
in your own tail, to let slip your own little secret.

I thought of you again tonight, thin as a rake, as you bent
over the copper plate of 'Emblements',
its tidal wave of army-worms into which you all but
    disappeared:
I wanted to catch something of its spirit
and yours, to body out your disembodied vox
clamantis in deserto, to let this all-too-cumbersome device
of a potato-mouth in a potato-face
speak out, unencumbered, from its long, low, mould-filled box.

I wanted it to speak to what seems always true of the truly
    great,
that you had a winningly inaccurate
sense of your own worth, that you would second-guess
yourself too readily by far, that you would rally to any cause
before your own, mine even,
though you detected in me a tendency to put
on too much artificiality, both as man and poet,
which is why you called me 'Polyester' or 'Polyurethane'.

That last time in Dublin, I copied with a quill dipped in
    oak-gall
onto a sheet of vellum, or maybe a human caul,
a poem for *The Great Book of Ireland*: as I watched the low
swoop over the lawn today of a swallow
I thought of your animated talk of Camille Pissarro
and André Derain's *The Turning Road, L'Estaque*:
when I saw in that swallow's nest a face in a mud-pack
from that muddy road I was filled again with a profound sorrow.

You must have known already, as we moved from the 'Hurly
    Burly'
to McDaid's or Riley's,
that something was amiss: I think you even mentioned a
    homeopath
as you showed off the great new acid-bath
in the Graphic Studio, and again undid your portfolio
to lay out your latest works; I try to imagine the strain
you must have been under, pretending to be as right as rain
while hearing the bells of a church from some long-flooded
    valley.

From the Quabbin reservoir, maybe, where the banks and
    bakeries
of a dozen little submerged Pompeii reliquaries
still do a roaring trade: as clearly as I saw your death-mask
in that swallow's nest, you must have heard the music
rise from the muddy ground between
your breasts as a nocturne, maybe, by John Field;
to think that you thought yourself so invulnerable, so
    inviolate,
that a little cancer could be beaten.

You must have known, as we walked through the ankle-deep
    clabber
with Katherine and Jean and the long-winded Quintus
    Calaber,
that cancer had already made such a breach
that you would almost surely perish:
you must have thought, as we walked through the woods
along the edge of the Quabbin,
that rather than let some doctor cut you open
you'd rely on infusions of hardock, hemlock, all the idle weeds.

I thought again of how art may be made, as it was by André
    Derain,
of nothing more than a turn
in the road where a swallow dips into the mire
or plucks a strand of bloody wool from a strand of barbed wire
in the aftermath of Chickamauga or Culloden
and builds from pain, from misery, from a deep-seated hurt,
a monument to the human heart
that shines like a golden dome among roofs rain-glazed and
    leaden.

I wanted the mouth in this potato-cut
to be heard far beyond the leaden, rain-glazed roofs of Quito,
to be heard all the way from the southern hemisphere
to Clontarf or Clondalkin, to wherever your sweet-severe
spirit might still find a toe-hold
in this world: it struck me then how you would be aghast
at the thought of my thinking you were some kind of ghost
who might still roam the earth in search of an earthly delight.

You'd be aghast at the idea of your spirit hanging over this
    vale
of tears like a jump-suited jump-jet whose vapour-trail
unravels a sky: for there's nothing, you'd say, nothing over
and above the sky itself, nothing but cloud-cover
reflected in a thousand lakes; it seems that Minne-
sota itself means 'sky-tinted water', that the sky is a great slab
of granite or iron ore that might at any moment slip
back into the worked-our sky-quarry, into the worked-out
    sky-mines.

To use the word 'might' is to betray you once too often, to
    betray
your notion that nothing's random, nothing arbitrary:
the gelignite weeps, the hands fly by on the alarm clock,
the 'Enterprise' goes clackety-clack
as they all must; even the car hijacked that morning in the
    Cross,
that was preordained, its owner spread on the bonnet
before being gagged and bound or bound
and gagged, that was fixed like the stars in the Southern
    Cross.

The fact that you were determined to cut yourself off in your
    prime
because it was *pre*-determined has my eyes abrim:
I crouch with Belacqua
and Lucky and Pozzo in the Acacacac-
ademy of Anthropopopometry, trying to make sense of the
    '*quaquaqua*'
of that potato-mouth; that mouth as prim
and proper as it's full of self-opprobrium,
with its '*quaquaqua*', with its 'Quoiquoiquoiquoiquoiquoiquoiq'.

That's all that's left of the voice of Enrico Caruso
from all that's left of an opera-house somewhere in Matto
    Grosso,
all that's left of the hogweed and horehound and cuckoo-pint,
of the eighteen soldiers dead at Warrenpoint,
of the Black Church clique and the Graphic Studio claque,
of the many moons of glasses on a tray,
of the brewery-carts drawn by moon-booted drays,
of those jump-suits worn under your bottle-green worsted
    cloak.

Of the great big dishes of chicken lo mein and beef chow mein,
of what's mine is yours and what's yours mine,
of the oxlips and cowslips
on the banks of the Liffey at Leixlip
where the salmon breaks through the either/or neither/nor
    nether
reaches despite the temple-veil
of itself being rent and the penny left out overnight on the rail
is a sheet of copper when the mail-train has passed over.

Of the bride carried over the threshold, hey, only to alight
on the limestone slab of another threshold,
of the swarm, the cast,
the colt, the spew of bees hanging like a bottle of Lucozade
from a branch the groom must sever,
of Emily Post's ruling, in *Etiquette,*
on how best to deal with the butler being in cahoots
with the cook when they're both in cahoots with the
    chauffeur.

Of that poplar-flanked stretch of road between Leiden
and The Hague, of the road between Rathmullen and Ramelton,
where we looked so long and hard
for some trace of Spinoza or Amelia Earhart,
both of them going down with their engines on fire:
of the stretch of road somewhere near Urney
where Orpheus was again overwhelmed by that urge to turn
back and lost not only Eurydice but his steel-strung lyre.

Of the sparrows and finches in their bell of suet,
of the bitter-sweet
bottle of Calvados we felt obliged to open
somewhere near Falaise, so as to toast our new-found
    copains,
of the priest of the parish
who came enquiring about our 'status', of the hedge-clippers
I somehow had to hand, of him running like the clappers
up Landseer Street, of my subsequent self-reproach.

Of the remnants of Airey Neave, of the remnants of
    Mountbatten,
of the famous *andouilles*, of the famous *boudins*
noirs et blancs, of the barrel-vault
of the cathedral at Rouen, of the flashlight, fat and roll of felt
on each of their sledges, of the music
of Joseph Beuys's pack of huskies, of that baldy little bugger
mushing them all the way from Berncastel through Bacarrat
to Belfast, his head stuck with honey and gold-leaf like a
    mosque.

Of Benjamin Britten's *Lachrymae,* with its gut-wrenching
    viola,
of Vivaldi's *Four Seasons,* of Frankie Valli's,
of Braque's great painting *The Shower of Rain,*
of the fizzy, lemon or sherbet-green *Ranus ranus*
plonked down in Trinity like a little Naugahyde pouffe,
of eighteen soldiers dead in Oriel,
of the weakness for a little fol-de-rol-de-rolly
suggested by the gap between the front teeth of the Wife of Bath.

Of *A Sunday Afternoon on the Island of La Grande Jatte,* of
    Seurat's
piling of tesserae upon tesserae
to give us a monkey arching its back
and the smoke arching out from a smoke-stack,
of Sunday afternoons in the Botanic Gardens, going with the
    flow
of the burghers of Sandy Row and Donegal
Pass and Andersonstown and Rathcoole,
of the army Land Rover flaunt-flouncing by with its heavy
    furbelow.

Of Marlborough Park, of Notting Hill, of the Fitzroy Avenue
immortalised by Van 'His real name's Ivan'
Morrison, 'and him the dead spit
of Padraic Fiacc', of John Hewitt, the famous expat,
in whose memory they offer every year six of their best milch
    cows,
of the Bard of Ballymacarrett,
of every ungodly poet in his or her godly garret,
of Medhbh and Michael and Frank and Ciaran and 'wee'
    John Qughes.

Of the Belfast school, so called, of the school of hard knocks,
of your fervent eschewal of stockings and socks
as you set out to hunt down your foes
as implacably as the *tóraidheacht* through the Fews
of Redmond O'Hanlon, of how that 'd' and that 'c' aspirate
in *tóraidheacht* make it sound like a last gasp in an oxygen-
    tent,
of your refusal to open a vent
but to breathe in spirit of salt, the mordant salt-spirit.

Of how mordantly hydrochloric acid must have scored and
    scarred,
of the claim that boiled skirrets
can cure the spitting of blood, of that dank
flat somewhere off Morehampton Road, of the unbelievable
    stink
of valerian or feverfew simmering over a low heat,
of your sitting there, pale and gaunt,
with that great prescriber of boiled skirrets, Dr John
    Arbuthnot,
your face in a bowl of feverfew, a towel over your head.

Of the great roll of paper like a bolt of cloth
running out again and again like a road at the edge of a cliff,
of how you called a Red Admiral a Red
Admirable, of how you were never in the red
on either the first or the last
of the month, of your habit of loosing the drawstring of your
    purse
and finding one scrunched-up, obstreperous
note and smoothing it out and holding it up, pristine and
    pellucid.

Of how you spent your whole life with your back to the wall,
of your generosity when all the while
you yourself lived from hand
to mouth, of Joseph Beuys's pack of hounds
crying out from their felt and fat 'Atone, atone, atone',
of Watt remembering the '*Krak! Krek! Krik!*'
of those three frogs' karaoke
like the still, sad *basso continuo* of the great quotidian.

Of a ground bass of sadness, yes, but also a sennet of
    hautboys
as the fat and felt hounds of Beuys O'Beuys
bayed at the moon over a caravan
in Dunmore East, I'm pretty sure it was, or Dungarvan:
of my guest appearance in your self-portrait not as a hidalgo
from a long line
of hidalgos but a hound-dog, a *leanbh,*
a dog that skulks in the background, a dog that skulks and
    stalks.

Of that self-portrait, of the self-portraits by Rembrandt van
    Rijn,
of all that's revelation, all that's rune,
of all that's composed, all composed of odds and ends,
of that daft urge to make amends
when it's far too late, too late even to make sense of the clutter
of false trails and reversed horseshoe tracks
and the aniseed we took it in turn to drag
across each other's scents, when only a fish is dumber and colder.

Of your avoidance of canned goods, in the main,
on account of the exceeeeeeeeeeeeeeeeedingly high risk of
    ptomaine,
of corned beef in particular being full of crap,
of your delight, so, in eating a banana as ceremoniously as
    Krapp
but flinging the skin over your shoulder like a thrush
flinging off a shell from which it's only just managed to disinter
a snail, like a stone-faced, twelfth-century
FitzKrapp eating his banana by the mellow, yellow light of a
    rush.

Of the 'Yes, let's go' spoken by Monsieur Tarragon,
of the early-ripening jardonelle, the tumorous jardon, the
    jargon
of jays, the jars
of tomato relish and the jars
of Victoria plums, absolutely *de rigueur* for a passable plum
    baba,
of the drawers full of balls of twine and butcher's string,
of Dire Straits playing 'The Sultans of Swing',
of the horse's hock suddenly erupting in those boils and buboes.

Of the Greek figurine of a pig, of the pig on a terracotta frieze,
of the sow dropping dead from some mysterious virus,
of your predilection for gammon
served with a sauce of coriander or cumin,
of the slippery elm, of the hornbeam or witch-, or even wych-,
hazel that's good for stopping a haemor-
rhage in mid-flow, of the merest of mere
hints of elderberry curing everything from sciatica to a stitch.

Of the decree *condemnator,* the decree *absolvitor,* the decree
    nisi,
of *Aosdána,* of *an chraobh cnuais,*
of the fields of buckwheat
taken over by garget, inkberry, scoke – all names for
    pokeweed –
of *Mother Courage,* of *Arturo Ui,*
of those Sunday mornings spent picking at sesame
noodles and all sorts and conditions of dim sum,
of tea and ham sandwiches in the Nesbitt Arms hotel in
    Ardara.

Of the day your father came to call, of your leaving your
    sickroom
in what can only have been a state of delirium,
of how you simply wouldn't relent
from your vision of a blind
watch-maker, of your fatal belief that fate
governs everything from the honey-rust of your father's
    terrier's
eyebrows to the horse that rusts and rears
in the furrow, of the furrows from which we can no more
    deviate

than they can from themselves, no more than the map of
    Europe
can be redrawn, than that Hermes might make a harp from
    his *harpe*,
than that we must live in a vale
of tears on the banks of the Lagan or the Foyle,
than that what we have is a done deal,
than that the Irish Hermes,
Lugh, might have leafed through his vast herbarium
for the leaf that had it within it, Mary, to anoint and anneal,

than that Lugh of the Long Arm might have found in the
    midst of *lus*
na leac or *lus na treatha* or *Frannc-lus*,
in the midst of eyebright, or speedwell, or tansy, an antidote,
than that this *Incantata*
might have you look up from your plate of copper or zinc
on which you've etched the row upon row
of army-worms, than that you might reach out, arrah,
and take in your ink-stained hands my own hands stained
    with ink.

PAUL MULDOON

Inglan is a Bitch

w'en mi jus' come to Landan toun
mi use to work pan di andahgroun
but workin' pan di andahgroun
y'u don't get fi know your way aroun'

Inglan is a bitch
dere's no escapin' it
Inglan is a bitch
dere's no runnin' whey fram it

mi get a lickle jab in a big 'otell
an' awftah a while, mi woz doin' quite well
dem staat mi aaf as a dish-washah
but w'en mi tek a stack, mi noh tun clack-watchah!

Inglan is a bitch
dere's no escapin it
Inglan is a bitch
noh baddah try fi hide fram it

w'en dem gi' you di lickle wage packit
fus dem rab it wid dem big tax rackit
y'u haffi struggle fi mek en's meet
an' w'en y'u goh a y'u bed y'u jus' cant sleep

Inglan is a bitch
dere's no escapin' it
Inglan is a bitch fi true
a noh lie mi a tell, a true

mi use to work dig ditch w'en it cowl noh bitch
mi did strang like a mule, but, bwoy, mi did fool
den awftah a while mi jus' stap dhu ovahtime
den awftah a while mi jus' phu dung mi tool

Inglan is a bitch
dere's no escapin it
Inglan is a bitch
y'u haffi know how fi suvvive in it

well mi dhu day wok an' mi dhu nite wok
mi dhu clean wok an' mi dhu dutty wok
dem seh dat black man is very lazy
but if y'u si how mi wok y'u woulda sey mi crazy

Inglan is a bitch
dere's no escapin it
Inglan is a bitch
y'u bettah face up to it

dem have a lickle facktri up inna Brackly
inna disya facktri all dem dhu is pack crackry
fi di laas fifteen years dem get mi laybah
now awftah fifteen years mi fall out a fayvah

Inglan is a bitch
dere's no escapin' it
Inglan is a bitch
dere's no runnin' whey fram it

mi know dem have work, work in abundant
yet still, dem mek mi redundant
now, at fifty-five mi gettin' quite ol'
yet still, dem sen' mi fi goh draw dole

Inglan is a bitch
dere's no escapin' it
Inglan is a bitch fi true
is whey wi a goh dhu 'bout it?

LINTON KWESI JOHNSON

The Orchids at Cwm y Gaer

Now, disbelieving, I will go
Down a road so narrow
I must travel sideways
Though still the willows will swat me with their swags of rain
And my own sweat tighten under my arms
    As once my father's fingers did.

Step carefully
For here they are,
Newborn but already white with webs.
    Once the superstitious thought
    It was Christ's blood that mottled the leaves,
But now it's as easy to suppose
That these eruptions, under a shadow's anglepoise,
    Are uranium rods
    Broken through from the terrible core.

We build our legends;
We build our gods;
But how does a people understand its gods?
These might be such, thrusting up
Like the pillars of the reactor,
Their alpha-love kissing our skin,
Their gamma-love passing through our bones
To leave their ghosts forever hidden in our chromosomes.

We are people who worships gods
Whose mouths gasp electric,
                              whose eyes
Are a dull, totalitarian
Gold, whose commerce is strange
As a rockpool's
                pornography.

    I pause one moment
    On this narrow road
With the light tipping out of a tree's tundish
And the spiders at their riot after rain.
    Already a thread hangs from my hair
    And ties me to this place.
So I open my hands to the orchids at Cwm y Gaer
    And count each breath.
How long before the welts appear?
How soon before the cradle of nightsweats,
Or that deep, enriched delirium, dark as dew?

ROBERT MINHINNICK

Cousin Coat

You are my secret coat. You're never dry.
You wear the weight and stink of black canals.
Malodorous companion, we know why
It's taken me so long to see we're pals,
To learn why my acquaintance never sniff
Or send me notes to say I stink of stiff.

But you don't talk, historical bespoke.
You must be worn, be intimate as skin,
And though I never lived what you invoke,
At birth I was already buttoned in.
Your clammy itch became my atmosphere,
An air made half of anger, half of fear.

And what you are is what I tried to shed
In libraries with Donne and Henry James.
You're here to bear a message from the dead
Whose history's dishonoured with their names.
You mean the North, the poor, and troopers sent
To shoot down those who showed their discontent.

No comfort there for comfy meliorists
Grown weepy over Jarrow photographs.
No comfort when the poor the state enlists
Parade before their fathers' cenotaphs.
No comfort when the strikers all go back
To see which twenty thousand get the sack.

Be with me when they cauterise the facts.
Be with me to the bottom of the page,
Insisting on what history exacts.
Be memory, be conscience, will and rage,
And keep me cold and honest, cousin coat,
So if I lie, I'll know you're at my throat.

SEAN O'BRIEN

Aubade

It's all the same to morning what it dawns on –
On the bickering of jackdaws in leafy trees;
On that dandy from the wetlands, the green mallard's
Stylish glissando among reeds; on the moorhen
Whose white petticoat flickers around the boghole;
On the oystercatcher on tiptoe at low tide.

It's all the same to the sun what it rises on –
On the windows in houses in Georgian squares;
On bees swarming to blitz suburban gardens;
On young couples yawning in unison before
They do it again; on dew like sweat or tears
On lilies and roses; on your bare shoulders.

But it isn't all the same to us that night-time
Runs out; that we must make do with today's
Happenings, and stoop and somehow glue together
The silly little shards of our lives, so that
Our children can drink water from broken bowls,
Not from cupped hands. It isn't the same at all.

NUALA NÍ DHOMHNAILL
translated from the Irish by Michael Longley

From the Irish

According to Dinneen, a Gael unsurpassed
in lexicographical enterprise, the Irish
for moon means 'the white circle in a slice
of half-boiled potato or turnip'. A star
is the mark on the forehead of a beast
and the sun is the bottom of a lake, or well.

Well, if I say to you your face
is like a slice of half-boiled turnip,
your hair is the colour of a lake's bottom
and at the centre of each of your eyes
is the mark of the beast, it is because
I want to love you properly, according to Dinneen.

IAN DUHIG

Phrase Book

I'm standing here inside my skin,
which will do for a Human Remains Pouch
for the moment. Look down there (up here).
Quickly. Slowly. This is my own front room

where I'm lost in the action, live from a war,
on screen. I am an Englishwoman, I don't understand you.
What's the matter? You are right. You are wrong.
Things are going well (badly). Am I disturbing you?

TV is showing bliss as taught to pilots:
Blend, Low silhouette, Irregular shape, Small,
Secluded. (Please write it down. Please speak slowly.)
Bliss is how it was in this very room

when I raised my body to his mouth,
when he even balanced me in the air,
or at least I thought so and yes the pilots say
yes they have caught it through the Side-Looking

Airborne Radar, and through the J-Stars.
I am expecting a gentleman (a young gentleman,
two gentlemen, some gentlemen). Please send him
(them) up at once. This is really beautiful.

Yes they have seen us, the pilots, in the Kill Box
on their screens, and played the routine for
getting us Stealthed, that is, Cleansed, to you and me,
Taken Out. They know how to move into a single room

like that, to send in with Pinpoint Accuracy, a hundred Harms.
I have two cases and a cardboard box. There is another
bag there. I cannot open my case – look out,
the lock is broken. Have I done enough?

Bliss, the pilots say, is for evasion
and escape. What's love in all this debris?
Just one person pounding another into dust,
into dust. I do not know the word for it yet.

Where is the British Consulate? Please explain.
What does it mean? What must I do? Where
can I find? What have I done? I have done
nothing. Let me pass please. I am an Englishwoman.

JO SHAPCOTT

I swear

Because I turned up from Bombay
too prissy to be rude
because you arrived via Leeds and Burnley
you thought it would do me good

to learn some Language. So

you never just fell, you went arse over tits,
and you were never not bothered
you just couldn't be arsed, and when

you laughed you laughed like an effing drain
and when there was pain it was a pain
in the arse.

That was just the start: you taught me
all the Language you knew
right through the alphabet from a to z,
from first to last, from bad to worse and worser
and the very worst you could muster.

I learned the curses. I learned the curser.
So proper you looked in your nice shoes and suit
until you produced Language like magic
out of your mouth and I was impressed

and oh I fell for you arse over tits
and when I said so you laughed like a drain
and we blinded and swore like the daft buggers
we were, all the way down Clerkenwell
and all the way up on the train
to the Horseshoe Pass.

And I tell you, since you went it's a pain
in the arse, and when some days I feel like shit
or when I say that I feel flat, I swear
I hear you laugh like a drain.
*Not just flat, Mrs, Flat as a witch's tit,
that's what you say. Flat*

as a witch's tit.

IMTIAZ DHARKER

Presents from my Aunts in Pakistan

They sent me a salwar kameez
        peacock-blue,
                    and another
    glistening like an orange split open,
    embossed slippers, gold and black
            points curling.
    Candy-striped glass bangles
            snapped, drew blood.
Like at school, fashions changed
            in Pakistan –
the salwar bottoms were broad and stiff,
            then narrow.
My aunts chose an apple-green sari,
    silver-bordered
            for my teens.

I tried each satin-silken top –
    was alien in the sitting room.
I could never be as lovely
            as those clothes –
    I longed
for denim and corduroy.
    My costume clung to me
            and I was aflame,
I couldn't rise up out of its fire,
    half-English,
            unlike Aunt Jamila.

I wanted my parents' camel-skin lamp –
    switching it on in my bedroom,

to consider the cruelty
        and the transformation
from camel to shade,
    marvel at the colours
            like stained glass.

My mother cherished her jewellery –
    Indian gold, dangling, filigree,
            But it was stolen from our car.
The presents were radiant in my wardrobe.
    My aunts requested cardigans
            from Marks and Spencers.

My salwar kameez
    didn't impress the schoolfriend
who sat on my bed, asked to see
    my weekend clothes.
But often I admired the mirror-work,
    tried to glimpse myself
            in the miniature
glass circles, recall the story
    how the three of us
            sailed to England.
Prickly heat had me screaming on the way.
    I ended up in a cot
in my English grandmother's dining-room,
    found myself alone,
            playing with a tin boat.

I pictured my birthplace
    from fifties' photographs.
            When I was older
there was conflict, a fractured land

throbbing through newsprint.
Sometimes I was Lahore –
                my aunts in shaded rooms,
screened from male visitors,
    sorting presents,
                wrapping them in tissue.

Or there were beggars, sweeper-girls
    and I was there
                of no fixed nationality,
staring through fretwork
        at the Shalimar Gardens.

MONIZA ALVI

Seed

The first warm day of spring
and I step out into the garden from the gloom
of a house where hope had died
to tally the storm damage, to seek what may
have survived. And finding some forgotten
lupins I'd sown from seed last autumn
holding in their fingers a raindrop each
like a peace offering, or a promise,
I am suddenly grateful and would
offer a prayer if I believed in God.
But not believing, I bless the power of seed,
its casual, useful persistence,
and bless the power of sun,

its conspiracy with the underground,
and thank my stars the winter's ended.

PAULA MEEHAN

The Singer

A weekday haar.
                The boats are out to sea
in a radio stasis, physical and stilled
between the water and unending sky.
It's late in the afternoon; it's holiday:
they've set the fair up at the harbour's edge
amongst the lobster creels and fishing nets,
matching the reds of marker buoys and floats
with scarlet bulbs and candied apple-skins.
The rides look pale and quiet in the grey
of four o'clock, and most are stalled, or vacant,
waiting for the night and mystery.
On days like these the fair is mostly refuge:
the booths at the pier-end lit against the fog
like one of those chalk-coloured prints that Harunobu
committed to paper so fine it seems
intangible, a pop song from the sixties
working against the foghorn's steady bass
like tinselwork.
                On days like these
the one thing that never ends is the expectancy
of standing in the haar and listening
for stars on their crystal axis, or the slide
of nightfall, like the whisper in the strands

of coloured lights around the carousel.
The singer is lost in a web
of speakers and wires, and voices from the quay,
but now and then she rises through it all,
her voice like a thread I keep
losing and finding again, though I'm never quite sure
if it's love she intends, or loss, or a moment's
angry hosanna.
    At sea
the stillness thickens, charged with idle boats
and schools of fishes swimming in the blur
of memory, or joy, or what it is
to happen in the hurry of a world
that ebbs and flows like song, or given light,
against the random static of the dark.

JOHN BURNSIDE

On the Roof of the World

'Hey Jude' was the longest single, up to that time,
ever released. It sweats off, chorus like a mantra.
The times are changing. New musics divide the audience
and skirts are longer, but it's a bright London shopping day
when the traffic stops. Only a black cab moves
gingerly through the crowd, like a toy cruiser nudging weed,
and we're all craning upwards: planks and scaffolding
on the townhouse roof and the clipped, drifting music
the Beatles play. It is their last concert,
though nobody knows this. George twangs his Fender, John
hammers-off on his Epiphone, Paul stomps

with his violin-bodied fretless bass and Ringo, dreamed up
by a manager who died a long time ago, kicks the years
out of his bass drum padded with a rug. How sweet

it would have been, someone will write, to watch them
play the Marquee, this funky little rock'n'roll band.
They are so far above us, we can hardly see them.
They are playing for God. They are playing for cameras
because the show's outgrown the road. We can't believe it.
Tomorrow's papers will acclaim a British institution.
I'll read them and imagine I was there like everyone.
They are already going out of fashion. There's nothing left
but acrimony, separation, lawsuits. The last great single,
'The Ballad of John and Yoko', will be John and Paul
alone, hurrying in midsummer heat, the way it was at the start.
Nobody knows this. They have climbed too far to get back
anywhere we might be among the crowd who clap then drift
    apart
when the helmeted bobbies have the amps turned off.

LACHLAN MACKINNON

The Wife of Bath Speaks in Brixton Market

My life is my own bible
wen it come to all de woes
in married life
fah since I reach twelve,
Tanks to Eternal Gawd,
is five husban I have
                    (if dat is passible)

but all of dem was wort someting
in dem own way
doah dem say
dat troo Jesas only go to one weddin
in Canaan
we no suppose fi married
more dan once
but den again
dem say Im tell de Samaritan woman
by de well
dat doah she did have five husban
de laas one never count
   is wat Im mean by dat
   why jus de fif one lef out
   ow much she can have den
     four?
Im don't give no precise number
Well,
   people can argue it forever
   but me sure of one serious ting
   Im order we to sex an multiply
Im also say dat
   de man mus lef im madda an im fadda
   an cling to me
   but Im never say
   how many
   mi no hear no mention of bigamy
   or polygamy
   so why me or anyone
   should tink it is a crime
An wat about de wise king Soloman
look how much wife im tek, Lawd,
ah wish ah did have as much in bed as him!

God mus did give him some 'great' gif
No one alive did ever have such fun
But still
I will tank de Lawd
fah doah I have only five
I shall welcome de sixt one
wenever im choose to arrive
because I nat lacking up my foot at all
if one husban dead
anadda christian man will surely come
fah even de apostle say dat den mi free
to tek anadda man dat can please me
        betta to married dan to bun

Abraham, Joseph,
nuff adda holy man
did have nuff wife
Whey God forbid dat?
Yuh see no clear word?
Where Im ever order virginity?
        Dere is no such commandment!
is de apostle Paul come talk bout maidenhead
an him never qualify fi talk bout dat.
Im say a man may counsel a woman
but counselling is nat command
wat I do wid my body is my personal business
an if God did command virginity
nobady wouldn married
fah married woulda dead
an no more pickney wouldn born
so no new maidenhead.

How Paul him want to tek command
wen Jesas wouldn dweet
we all know pum pum is someting sweet
an nuff sword will falla it.
Whoever, jus like de apostle,
want to do widdouten sex
is free to choose dat,
but wid we, no badda vex
fah if my husban wear out an im dead
you free to marry me
dat is nat bigamy
an to enjoy good sex
is nat a frailty
nat unless yuh did decide, like Paul,
fi tek up chastity
because a man don't want pure gold pot
in im house
im want some mek wid good wood
as a spouse
an God did give we all a different gif
we choose wat we is suited for
everyone don't have to give up everyting fah Christ
Im neva aks we dat
dat is fah who want perfect peace
an you all know already
dat is nat me
I gwine mek de bes of all my years
fah dat is de joy an fruit of marriage
an why we have dese private parts so sweet
dem cyan jus mek so an don't put to use
except to piss
or tell man apart from woman
das wat you tink?

fram wat me feel already
dat could nat be so
a man mus give im wife er tings
Piss yes, an tell we apart
but wat pleasure dese instrument brings!

JEAN 'BINTA' BREEZE

From Dublin to Ramallah

for Ghassan Zaqtan

Because they would not let you ford the river Jordan
and travel here to Dublin, I stop this postcard in its tracks –
before it reaches your sealed-up letterbox, before yet another
   checkpoint,
before the next interrogation even begins.

And instead of a postcard, I post you a poem of water.
Subterranean subterfuge,
an indolent element that slides across borders,
as boundaries are eroded by the fluency of tongues.

I send you a watery bulletin from the underwater backroom
of Bewley's Oriental Café,
my hands tinted by stainedglass light as I write,
near windows thickened with rain.

I ship you the smoked astringency of Formosa Lapsang
   Souchong
and a bun with a tunnel of sweet almond paste

set out on a chipped pink marble-topped table,
from the berth of a high-backed red-plush settle.

I greet you from the ranks of the solitary souls of Dublin,
fetched up over dinner with the paper for company.
Closer to home and to exile,
the waters will rise from their source.

I give you the Liffey in spate.
Drenched, relentless, the soaked November clouds
settle a torrent of raindrops
to fatten the flood.

Puddles pool into lakes, drains burst their sides,
and each granite pavement's slick rivulet has the purpose of
    gravity.
Wet, we are soaking in order to float.
Dogs in the rain: the cream double-decker buses steam up
    and stink

of wet coats and wet shopping,
a steep river of buses plying the Liffey;
the big circumnavigations swing in from the suburbs, turn,
cluster in the centre, back off once more.

Closer to home and to exile:
I seek for this greeting the modesty of rainwater,
the wet from ordinary clouds
that darkens the soil, swells reservoirs, curls back

the leaves of open books on a damp day into rows of
    tsunami,
and, once in a while, calls for a song.

I ask for a liquid dissolution:
let borders dissolve, let words dissolve,

let English absorb the fluency of Arabic, with ease,
let us speak in wet tongues.
Look, the Liffey is full of itself. So I post it
to Ramallah, to meet up with the Jordan,

as the Irish Sea swells into the Mediterranean,
letting the Liffey
dive down beneath bedrock
swelling the limestone aquifer from Hebron to Jenin,

plumping each cool porous cell with good Irish rain.
If you answer the phone, the sea at Killiney
will sound throughout Palestine.
If you put your head out the window (avoiding the snipers,
    please)

a cloud will rain rain from the Liffey
and drench all Ramallah, drowning the curfew.
Sweet water will spring from your taps for *chai bi nana*
and not be cut off.

Ghassan, please blow up that yellow inflatable dinghy stored
in your roof,
dust off your compass,
bring all friends,
and swim through the borders from Ramallah to Dublin.

SARAH MAGUIRE

The Women of Mumbles Head

The moon is sixpence,
a pillar of salt or
a shoal of herring.
But on such a night,
wild as the wet wind,
larger than life,
she casts a long line
over the slippery sea.
And the women of Mumbles Head
are one, a long line,
over the slippery sea.
Wet clothes clog them,
heavy ropes tire them,
but the women of Mumbles Head
are one, a long line,
over the slippery sea.
And under white beams
their strong arms glisten,
like silver, like salt,
like a shoal of herring,
under the slippery sea.
And they haul
for their dear ones,
and they call
for their dear ones,
casting a long line
over the slippery sea.
But the mounting waves
draw from them,
the mountain waves

draw from them,
the bodies of their dear ones,
O, the bodies of their dear ones,
drawn under the slippery sea.
In a chain of shawls
they hook one in,
fish-wet, moonlit,
they've plucked him back
from under the slippery sea.
For the moon is sixpence,
a pillar of salt
or a shoal of herring,
and the women of Mumbles Head
are one, a long line
over the slippery sea.

MAURA DOOLEY

The Numties

The parsnip Numties: I was a teenager then,
Collecting clip-together models
Of historical windsocks, dancing the Cumbernauld bump.

Satirical pornography, plant-staplers, nostalgiaform shoes
Were brochure-fresh. It was numty-four
I first saw a neighbour laughing in a herbal shirt.

Moshtensky, Garvin, Manda Sharry –
Names as quintessentially Numties
As Hearers and Bonders, duckponding, or getting a job

In eradication. Everything so familiar and sandwiched
Between the pre-Numties and the debouche of decades after.
I keep plunging down to the wreck

Of the submerged Numties, every year
Bringing back something jubilantly pristine,
Deeper drowned, clutching my breath.

ROBERT CRAWFORD

Song of a Wire Fence

Once I loved a woman
with barbed wire dreams
and scars ploughed into her skin.
She almost slept in my arms,
she almost slept in my arms.

And I sang her *Dafydd y Garreg*
and *Bugeilio'r Gwenith Gwyn*
from the harps of Capel Curig
to the hooves of Synod Inn.

I gave her a young man's stare
the night she read my palm,
my fingers ploughed her wild hair
and she almost slept in my arms,
she almost slept in my arms.

And I sang her *Tros y Garreg*
and *Ar Hyd y Nos*
from the floods of Pencarreg
to the sands of Ynyslas.

The song of a wire fence
crossed over a thousand farms
and love, she knew no distance,
she almost slept in my arms,
she almost slept in my arms.

PAUL HENRY

Pride

When I looked up, the black man was there,
staring into my face,
as if he had always been there,
as if he and I went a long way back.
He looked into the dark pool of my eyes
as the train slid out of Euston.
For a long time this went on
the stranger and I looking at each other,
a look that was like something being given
from one to the other.

My whole childhood, I'm quite sure,
passed before him, the worst things
I've ever done, the biggest lies I've ever told.
And he was a little boy on a red dust road.
He stared into the dark depth of me,

and then he spoke:
'Ibo,' he said. 'Ibo, definitely.'
Our train rushed through the dark.
'You are an Ibo!' he said, thumping the table.
My coffee jumped and spilled.
Several sleeping people woke.
The night train boasted and whistled
through the English countryside,
past unwritten stops in the blackness.

'That nose is an Ibo nose.
Those teeth are Ibo teeth,' the stranger said,
his voice getting louder and louder.
I had no doubt, from the way he said it,
that Ibo noses are the best noses in the world,
that Ibo teeth are perfect pearls.
People were walking down the trembling aisle
to come and look
as the night rain babbled against the window.
There was a moment when
my whole face changed into a map,
and the stranger on the train
located even the name
of my village in Nigeria
in the lower part of my jaw.

I told him what I'd heard was my father's name.
Okafor. He told me what it meant,
something stunning,
something so apt and astonishing.
Tell me, I asked the black man on the train
who was himself transforming,
at roughly the same speed as the train,

and could have been
at any stop, my brother, my father as a young man,
or any member of my large clan,
Tell me about the Ibos.

His face had a look
I've seen on a MacLachlan, a MacDonnell, a MacLeod,
the most startling thing, pride,
a quality of being certain.
Now that I know you are an Ibo, we will eat.
He produced a spicy meat patty,
ripping it into two.
Tell me about the Ibos.
'The Ibos are small in stature
Not tall like the Yoruba or Hausa.
The Ibos are clever, reliable,
dependable, faithful, true.
The Ibos should be running Nigeria.
There would be none of this corruption.'

And what, I asked, are the Ibos' faults?
I smiled my newly acquired Ibo smile,
flashed my gleaming Ibo teeth.
The train grabbed at a bend,
'Faults? No faults. Not a single one.'

'If you went back,' he said brightening,
'The whole village would come out for you.
Massive celebrations. Definitely.
Definitely,' he opened his arms wide.
'The eldest grandchild – fantastic welcome.
If the grandparents are alive.'

I saw myself arriving
the hot dust, the red road,
the trees heavy with other fruits,
the bright things, the flowers.
I saw myself watching
the old people dance towards me
dressed up for me in happy prints.
And I found my feet.
I started to dance.
I danced a dance I never knew I knew.
Words and sounds fell out of my mouth like seeds.
I astonished myself.
My grandmother was like me exactly, only darker.

When I looked up, the black man had gone.
Only my own face startled me in the dark train window.

JACKIE KAY

Mappamundi

Eh've wurkt oot a poetic map o thi warld.

Vass tracts o land ur penntit reid tae shaw
Englan kens naethin aboot um. Ireland's
bin shuftit tae London, whaur
oafficis o thi Poetry Sock occupeh fehv
squerr mile. Seamus Heaney occupehs three
o thon. Th'anerly ithir bits in Britain
ur Oaxfurd an Hull. Scoatlan, Thi Pool,
an Huddersfield, ur cut ti cuttilbanes in

America, which issa grecht big burdcage wi
a tartan rug owre ut, tae shaw
Roabirt Lowell. Chile disnae exist.
Argentina's bin beat. Hungary and Russia
haena visas. Africa's editid doon ti
a column in Poetry Verruca,
whaur Okigbo's gote thi ghaist
o Roy Campbill hingin owre um. Thi Faur East's
faan aff – aa but China: thon's renemmed
Ezra Poond an pit in thi croncit cage.
France disna get a luke-in:
accoardin tae Geoffrey Hill, plucky wee
Charles Péguy is wrasslin wi
this big deid parrot caad 'Surrealism' fur
thi throne o Absinthe Sorbet.

In this scenario Eh'm a bittern stoarm aff Ulm.

W. N. HERBERT

Elevation

3.2.11

Flying over Wales, suspended
high above, is to learn
how to love her; gliding slow,
knowing her from this new angle.

Between the tease of mare-tail clouds,
her peninsula arm exposed,
sleeve eager, rolled-ready.

And look, beneath her collage of a dress,
the mystery of the mountain
elegantly stonewall-stitched.

And there, the furrows of unearthed slate
combed like the drag
of fingers through sand

and the small bright lakes
like enigmatic birth marks
glimpsed while lovers lock.

Tonight, nose pressed against the window,
your lips insist on reciting
the litany of place names,

'Dyfi Junction, Cors Fochno . . .'
your breath a sacred shuffle across her body,
'Dowlais, Penrhys, Gilfach Goch . . .'

And as she wraps her shyness with a veil of cloud,
the plane's shadow
casts a cross below,

a timeless kiss on this love letter,

a hesitant vote for her future.

IFOR AP GLYN
translated from the Welsh by Clare Potter

Flood Before and After

It reeled across the North, to the extent
that even Northerners cried 'This is North!'
and what would you have said, to see a sky

threatening the children with great change?
Extraordinary clouds! Spectaculars!
There was the Dimden family, in their barn.

And long, quite vertical rain, the three horizons
hunched, different formulations, browns
and oranges. Then the unlucky Greens

running with their sons to find their sons.
The scarecrow and the crow, they did okay,
getting dark together, but unfrightened.

Fists of clouds! Genii of glamour!
Not to mention thunders – not again!
There stand the Dimdens, safe for once and sad.

The Greens have found their sons! Now for their daughters.
But out goes the lightning, giant's fork
into a mound of chilli, steaming there

and where's it gone? Into the open mouth,
barn and all, flavours and seasonings!
Cuddle in the rain, old favourites.

There goes a Noah, borrowing a plank.
Little slow to move, we thought. It ends
with tangles, the new rivers, and the sunshine

formally requesting a rainbow. Granted.
The creaking and excusing back to work.
A valuable man was lost in it.

That was in the paper, with the picture.
All the Northern correspondents went
reading to the telephones, all cold,

which brought the dry onlookers from the South,
gaspers, whistlers, an ambassador
and leading lights to mingle with the hurt.

The clouds were diplomats of the same kind,
edging over to exonerate
and praise. And then the royal son arrived,

helicoptered down on a flat field,
glancing up at the sky through the whup of blades,
attending to the worried with a joke.

Hell, I don't know what – we were all cold.
The landscape looked an archipelago.
The Dimdens finally twigged, the Greens were found

beating the Blooms at rummy, in a cave.
All were interviewed and had lost all.
All saluted when the helicopter rose.

Only some came up the knoll with us
to check our options. Only two of those
saw, as I did, Noah's tiny boat

scarcely moving, at the edge of sight
below the line, and only I'd admit
the crow and the scarecrow were rowing it.

GLYN MAXWELL

Mr and Mrs Scotland Are Dead

On the civic amenity landfill site,
the coup, the dump beyond the cemetery
and the 30-mile-an-hour sign, her stiff
old ladies' bags, open mouthed, spew
postcards sent from small Scots towns
in 1960: Peebles, Largs, the rock-gardens
of Carnoustie, tinted in the dirt.
Mr and Mrs Scotland, here is the hand you were dealt:
fair but cool, showery but nevertheless,
Jean asks kindly; the lovely scenery;
in careful school-room script –
The Beltane Queen was crowned today.
But Mr and Mrs Scotland are dead.

Couldn't he have burned them? Released
in a grey curl of smoke
this pattern for a cable knit? Or this:
tossed between a toppled fridge
and sweet-stinking anorak: *Dictionary for Mothers*

M – Milk, *the woman who worries . . . ;*
And here, Mr Scotland's John Bull Puncture Repair Kit;
those days when he knew intimately
the thin roads of his country, hedgerows
hanged with small black brambles' hearts;
and here, for God's sake, his last few joiners' tools,
SCOTLAND, SCOTLAND, stamped on their tired handles.

Do we take them? Before the bulldozer comes
to make more room, to shove aside
his shaving brush, her button tin.
Do we save this toolbox, these old-fashioned views
addressed, after all, to Mr and Mrs Scotland?
Should we reach and take them? And then?
Forget them, till that person enters
our silent house, begins to open
to the light our kitchen drawers,
and performs for us this perfunctory rite:
the sweeping up, the turning out.

KATHLEEN JAMIE

Blackwater

Where the coastline doubles up on itself
as if punched in the gut by the god Meander,
who likes to dabble in landscapes
but, with this one, lost his grip.
He muddled salt and sweet,
bent the creeks more than double,
loaded each distinction

till it burst its banks. Picture this:
an estuary where the eye can't tell
sea from river, hill from valley,
near from far, first from last, in from out
– any one thing, in fact, from any other.

Where the stumps of Saxon fishtraps
butt up through the silt at low tide
like the rusted teeth in the wrecked head
of the god Yawn, who can't keep his mouth shut,
not here, where the land spits out
its haul of the useless,
the shapeless, tasteless, nameless.

Where there has been nothing as clear
as the winter in which the goddess Inertia
hunkered down over Maldon
– the town hemmed in with skirts of ice.
The men of the saltworks and oyster pits,
bass fishers, whelk pickers, farmers and bargees
were hamstrung. Some set off
to find the first three miles in any direction
glass, their boats sleeved in glass,
glass hobbling their horses.

Where the vague men of the Dengie Peninsula
drove their marsh lambs a fortnight's walk
to market and picked up a wife on the way:
an inland girl from a county town
whose clean lungs became damp rooms,
whose good skin leathered and would not cure,
whose blood was drunk by the god Stagnant

who came at night and took little sips
till her blackened soul left her body,
how else, but by way of water.

Where you think you've reached open sea
till something catches in your throat
– fossil fuel and fish long out of water.
Where the goddess Stasis laid a path
towards the horizon, which seems not far
till you sidle, circle, give up, settle in
like the World War One submarines
docked in the shallows near Osea.
They grew so at home
that Stasis offered them the gift of life
as mud lumps on mud banks
who honk and puff their way off shore
to zoom, reborn, to the battle zone
(where Osea keeps watch on Ostend),
drawn to the mutating warmth
of Bradwell power station's radiant pools.

Where they at last unplugged the glottal stop
in the throat of the god Moribund
and opened a wall to unravel the fields
where the borrow dyke lends itself to the polder,
mops up sticklebacks and sea lavender:
– bristling, stunted, salt and sweet.

Where the county arms are three cutlasses,
each with a bite taken out
by a bored god. Salt of earth,
they chew the matter over:
'Whatever's it all about, John?'
'Whenever is it all going to end?'

LAVINIA GREENLAW

To the Women of the Merrie England
Coffee Houses, Huddersfield

O women of the Merrie England Coffee Houses,
    Huddersfield,
when I break sweat just thinking about hard work, I think
    about you.
Nowhere to hide behind that counter, nowhere to shirk.
I'm watching you right now bumping and grinding hip to
    hip,
I'm noting your scrubbed pink hands in the cabinet of fancy
    cakes,
loose and quick among the lemon meringues and cream puffs
and custard tarts, darting and brushing like carp in a glass
    tank.

O women, the soles of your feet on fire in your sensible
    shoes,
your fingers aflame, spitting and hissing under the grill.
You, madam, by the cauldron of soup – you didn't hassle us,
just wiped the crumbs from under our genius poems,

me and the boy Smith, one toasted teacake between us,
eking it out through the dead afternoons, our early drafts
hallmarked and franked with rings of coffee and tea.

Women of the Merrie England, under those scarlet aprons are
    you naked?
Are you calendar girls? Miss July traps a swarm of steam in a
    jug
as perspiration rolls from the upper delta of her open neck
to where Christ crucified bobs and twists on a gold chain.
Miss April delivers the kiss of life to a Silk Cut by the fire
    escape.
Miss November, pass me the key to the toilets, please,
I won't violate your paintwork, desecrate the back of the door

with crude anatomical shapes or the names of speedway stars.
I'm no closet queen in search of a glory hole for gay sex,
no smackhead needing a cubbyhole to shoot up –
one glass of your phosphorescing, radioactive orange crush
was always enough for me and the boy Smith, his mother
asleep at the wheel on the long drive back from Wales,
the airbag not invented yet – just a bubble in somebody's
    dream.

Does he pay you a pittance in groats, King Henry, stuffing his
    face
with hare and swan, his beard dyed red with venison blood
and pinned with the fiddling bones of partridge and quail,
while you, O women of the Merrie England, his maids,
swab the greasy tiles with a bucket of rain and a bald mop
or check for counterfeit tenners under the sun-tanning light?
A tenner! – still two hours' graft at the minimum wage.

Don't let catering margarine ease off your eternity rings.
Don't lose your marriages down the waste-disposal pipe.
Hang on to your husbands and friends – no sugar daddies or
    lovers
or cafetières for you, O women of the Merrie England,
no camomile or Earl Grey, just take-it-or-leave-it ground or
    char
served in the time-bitten cups my grandmother sipped from,
hooking the milky membrane aside with a spoon, watching it
    reform.

I've seen you nudging and winking. Look who just dropped
    in, you say,
The Man Who Fell to Earth, wanting tea for one and the
    soup of the day.
I take the window seat and gawp at the steeplejacks: all gone –
Kaye's, the Coach House, Leeds Road, the White Lion and
    the Yards.
But you, under the mock Tudor beams, under the fake
    shields,
under the falsified coats of arms, you go on, you go on
O women of the Merrie England, O mothers of Huddersfield,
    O ladies!

                                    SIMON ARMITAGE

A Private Bottling

So I will go, then. I would rather grieve over
your absence than over you.
— ANTONIO PORCHIA

Back in the same room that an hour ago
we had led, lamp by lamp, into the darkness
I sit down and turn the radio on low
as the last girl on the planet still awake
reads a dedication to the ships
and puts on a recording of the ocean.

I carefully arrange a chain of nips
in a big fairy-ring; in each square glass
the tincture of a failed geography,
its dwindled burns and woodlands, whin-fires, heather,
the sklent of its wind and its salty rain,
the love-worn habits of its working-folk,
the waveform of their speech, and by extension
how they sing, make love, or take a joke.

So I have a good nose for this sort of thing.

Then I will suffer kiss after fierce kiss
letting their gold tongues slide along my tongue
as each gives up, in turn, its little song
of the patient years in glass and sherry-oak,
the shy negotiations with the sea,
air and earth, the trick of how the peat-smoke
was shut inside it, like a black thought.

Tonight I toast her with the extinct malts
of Ardlussa, Ladyburn and Dalintober
and an ancient pledge of passionate indifference:
Ochon o do dhóigh mé mo chlairsach ar a shon,
wishing her health, as I might wish her weather.

When the circle is closed and I have drunk myself sober
I will tilt the blinds a few degrees, and watch
the dawn grow in a glass of liver-salts,
wait for the birds, the milk-float's sweet nothings,
then slip back to the bed where she lies curled,
replace the live egg of her burning ass
gently, in the cold nest of my lap,
as dead to her as she is to the world.

*

Here we are again; it is precisely
twelve, fifteen, thirty years down the road
and one turn higher up the spiral chamber
that separates the burnt ale and dark grains
of what I know, from what I can remember.
Now each glass holds its micro-episode
in permanent suspension, like a movie-frame
on acetate, until it plays again,
revivified by a suave connoisseurship
that deepens in the silence and the dark
to something like an infinite sensitivity.
This is no romantic fantasy: my father
used to know a man who'd taste the sea,
then leave his nets strung out along the bay
because there were no fish in it that day.

Everything is in everything else. It is a matter
of attunement, as once, through the hiss and backwash,
I steered the dial into the voice of God
slightly to the left of Hilversum,
half-drowned by some big, blurry waltz
the way some stars obscure their dwarf companions
for centuries, till someone thinks to look.

In the same way, I can isolate the feints
of feminine effluvia, carrion, shite,
those rogues and toxins only introduced
to give the composition a little weight
as rough harmonics do the violin-note
or Pluto, Cheiron and the lesser saints
might do to our lives, for all you know.
(By Christ, you would recognise their absence
as anyone would testify, having sunk
a glass of *North British*, run off a patent still
in some sleet-hammered satellite of Edinburgh:
a bleak spirit no amount of caramel
could sweeten or disguise, its after-effect
somewhere between a blanket-bath and a sad wank.
There is, no doubt, a bar in Lothian
where it is sworn upon and swallowed neat
by furloughed riggers and the Special Police,
men who hate the company of women.)

O whiskies of Long Island and Provence!
This little number catches at the throat
but is all sweetness in the finish: my tongue trips
first through burning brake-fluid, then nicotine,
pastis, *Diorissimo* and wet grass;
another is silk sleeves and lip-service

with a kick like a smacked puss in a train-station;
another, the light charge and the trace of zinc
tap-water picks up at the moon's eclipse.
You will know the time I mean by this.

Because your singular absence, in your absence,
has bred hard, tonight I take the waters
with the whole clan: our faceless ushers, bridesmaids,
our four Shelties, three now ghosts of ghosts;
our douce sons and our lovely loudmouthed daughters
who will, by this late hour, be fully grown,
perhaps with unborn children of their own.
So finally, let me propose a toast:
not to love, or life, or real feeling,
but to their sentimental residue;
to your sweet memory, but not to you.

The sun will close its circle in the sky
before I close my own, and drain the purely
offertory glass that tastes of nothing
but silence, burnt dust on the valves, and whisky.

DON PATERSON

[657]

The London Eye

Through my gold-tinted Gucci sunglasses,
the sightseers. Big Ben's quarter chime
strikes the convoy of number 12 buses
that bleeds into the city's monochrome.

Through somebody's zoom lens, me shouting
to you, *Hello! . . . on . . . bridge . . . 'minster!*
The aerial view postcard, the man writing
squat words like black cabs in rush hour.

The South Bank buzzes with a rising treble.
You kiss my cheek, formal as a blind date.
We enter Cupid's capsule, a thought bubble
where I think, 'Space age!' you think, 'She was late.'

Big Ben strikes six. My SKIN .Beat™ blinks, replies
18·02. We're moving anticlockwise.

PATIENCE AGBABI

from The Electric Poly-Olbion

Godspeed our flashy myths that last five minutes.
Godspeed the 'Devil's Christmas Tree' at Widnes
where the river widens, turns to brainy channels,
Godspeed the Childe of Hale, whose famous long bones
lie in the churchyard children still walk miles
to see, escaping the estates in summer,

Godspeed the all night burn-off flame at Stanlow
and those who watched it from the opposite bank
claiming it was eternal, Godspeed men
who, six-foot-nine, could walk it at low tide,
Godspeed Runcorn and Legoland, Godspeed
the Weaver Navigation and a sky
the colour of a sandbank fat with water,
Godspeed the heavy metals, been and gone,
the fish ladders, the runs of river lymph,
Godspeed the pop and soul, the punk and glam
all been and gone and still the river runs,
the iron and limpet, cadmium and starfish,
the mighty waste, the flags flying at half-mast
in mourning for the North Atlantic Gulf Stream,
the mercury and medusae, zinc and winkles,
the sediment a tide file stretching back
to when records began, the paint-stripped, bleached out
afternoons of wanks and toxic dog-walks,
and somewhere out to sea the cold miracle,
the strange comportment of wind and saltwater
that cleans and lifts and moves back in to bless
hill sources once again, against the grain
of by-product and irony. Godspeed
the steady state that waits once men have left
the estuary to silvery skies and starlight
and skeins of waterfowl, and silent bridges.

PAUL FARLEY

Our Town with the Whole of India!

Our town in England with the whole of India sundering
out of its temples, mandirs and mosques for the customised
streets. Our parade, clad in cloak-orange with banners
and tridents, chanting from station to station for Vaisakhi
over Easter. Our full-moon madness for Eidh with free
pavement tandooris and legless dancing to boostered
cars. Our Guy Fawkes' Diwali – a kingdom of rockets
for the Odysseus-trials of Rama who arrowed the jungle
foe to re-palace the Penelope-faith of his Sita.

Our Sunrise Radio with its lip sync of Bollywood lovers
pumping through the rows of emporium cubby holes
whilst bhangra beats slam where the hagglers roar
at the pulled-up back-of-the-lorry cut-price stalls.
Sitar shimmerings drip down the furbishly columned
gold store. Askance is the peaceful Pizza Hut . . .
A Somali cab joint, been there for ever, with smiley
guitar licks where reggae played before Caribbeans
disappeared, where years before Teddy Boys jived.

Our cafés with the brickwork trays of saffron sweets,
brass woks frying flamingo-pink syrup-tunnelled
jalebis networking crustily into their familied clumps.
Reveries of incense scent the beefless counter where
bloodied men sling out skinned legs and breasts
into thin bags topped with the proof of giblets.
Stepped road displays – chock-full of ripe karela,
okra, aubergine – sunshined with mango, pineapple,
lychee. Factory walkers prayer-toss the river of

sponging swans with chapattis. A posse brightens
on park-shots of Bacardi – waxing for the bronze
eyeful of girls. The girls slim their skirts after college
blowing dreams into pink bubble gums at neck-
descending and tight-neck sari-mannequins. Their grannies
point for poled yards of silk for own-made styles.
The mother of the runaway daughter, in the marriage
bureau, weeps over the plush-back catalogues glossed
with tuxedo-boys from the whole of our India!

DALJIT NAGRA

Another Westminster Bridge

go and glimpse the lovely inattentive water
discarding the gaze of many a bored street walker

where the weather trespasses into strip-lit offices
through tiny windows into tiny thoughts and authorities

and the soft beseeching tapping of typewriters

take hold of a breath-width instant, stare
at water which is already elsewhere
in a scrapwork of flashes and glittery flutters
and regular waves of apparently motionless motion

under the teetering structures of administration

where a million shut-away eyes glance once
restlessly at the river's ruts and glints

count five, then wander swiftly
away over the stone wing-bone of the city

ALICE OSWALD

Liverpool Blues

The skyline in the moonlight, the river running thin,
my lover weeping lotus blossom for his next of kin.
The stars will tell their stories over Birkenhead and Cammell
    Laird's.

In Berry Street, in Bold Street, in Princes Park and Princess
    Street
I've seen a girl I never knew and never thought to meet.
The Liver Birds have flown away, the cathedrals' doors are
    closed.

To hospitals and factories, bars, clubs, churches, loony bins,
something is uneasy beneath the city's restless din.
A woman has been murdered, yet no one says a word.

The homeless and the helpless, the workers on the street
have nothing left to live for, can only smell defeat.
My husband's left his heart elsewhere, my love has been
    foreclosed.

We're living in a borderland, somewhere between life and
   death,
losing ourselves in the search for a self.
It's a country of our making, the cards are curiously dealt.

The helicopter spotlights buzz us, lights come flooding in,
even our bedroom's no longer safe, we're living on a pin.
We mouth our dreams in the telling dark, but nothing can be
   heard.

We mouth our dreams in the telling dark, but nothing can be
   heard.

We mouth our dreams in the telling dark, and only words are
   lost.

We mouth our dreams in the telling dark, still nothing can be
   heard.

DERYN REES-JONES

And They Call It Lovely Derry

And so, strangely enough, to Florida.
Twenty from our side of the River
Foyle and twenty more from the other,
lifted out of a 'war-torn community'
to mix three weeks in a normal society.
That was the general idea.

When we arrived we were paired
and placed with a host couple, good
church people, settled and stable.
She was the first Prod I had ever met;
a small girl, pale and introvert, who wept
for home, then sniffed, and smiled.

The husband sat at the head of the table
holding forth, hot and bothered.
He couldn't decide on the right word,
hmmed and hawed between Blacks and Coloured,
whatever, his point? They were bone idle,
wouldn't accept the jobs they were offered.

The woman dreamed of having a child,
I took to the role of living doll
and would tolerate each morning's session
under the rug of curling tongs.
I had never even heard of Racism.
We gave a concert on the last night,

forty of us, rigid with stage fright.
My whistle shrieked on a high note.
We harmonised on all the songs
but fell apart with the grand finale,
the well-rehearsed 'O I know a wee spot . . .'
as the group split between London and Lovely.

COLETTE BRYCE

10th February: Queen

I keep the queen, she is long in my hand,
her legs slightly pliant;
folded, dropped down, wings flat
that flew her mating flight
to the sun and back, full of spermatozoa, dronesong.
She was made mechanically ecstatic.
I magnify what she is, magnify her skews and centres.
How downy she is, fur like a fox's greyness, like a thistle's mane.
Wings perfect, abdomen subtle in shades of brittle;
her rear legs are big in the lens;
feet like hung anchors are hooks for staying on cell-rims.
Veins in her wings are a rootwork of rivers,
all echo and interlace. This is her face, compound eye.
I look at the slope of her head, the mouth's proboscis;
her thin tongue piercing is pink as cut flesh, flash glass.
Some hairs feather and split below the head.
Those eyes are like castanets, cast nets;
woman all feral and ironwork, I slip
under the framework, into the subtle.
The wing is jointed at the black leather shoulder.
I wear it, I am soft to stroke, the lower blade fans.
Third generation queen of our stock,
you fall as I turn. I hold your hunchback;
a carcase of lightness, no grief, part animal, part flower.

SEAN BORODALE

In Belfast

I

Here the seagulls stay in off the Lough all day.
Victoria Regina steering the ship of the City Hall
in this the first and last of her intense provinces,
a ballast of copper and gravitas.

The inhaling shop-fronts exhale the length
and breadth of Royal Avenue, pause,
inhale again. The city is making money
on a weather-mangled Tuesday.

While the house for the Transport Workers' Union
fights the weight of the sky and manages
to stay up, under the Albert Bridge the river
is simmering at low tide and sheeted with silt.

II

I have returned after ten years to a corner
and tell myself it is as real to sleep here
as the twenty other corners I have slept in.
More real, even, with this history's dent and fracture

splitting the atmosphere. And what I have been given
is a delicate unravelling of wishes
that leaves the future unspoken and the past
unencountered and unaccounted for.

This city weaves itself so intimately
it is hard to see, despite the tenacity of the river
and the iron sky; and in its downpour and its vapour I am
as much at home here as I will ever be.

SINÉAD MORRISSEY

Already someone's set their dogs among the swans

The loch looks away, up at the crags
of Holyrood Park, as the landscape
turns witness to all that, one day,
I'd be surprised to think of as myself.
My tongue slumps in my mouth again,
a bastard feather. The moon, wearing
her off-the-shoulder number, slips

her bare shadows down to my feet –
my ghost preceding me, like a magnet.
The swans begin to nest, or, snorting water,
turn like hefty lanterns
gazing around themselves
as headlights of late traffic, brash crescendos,
rally for expiring destinations.

For nothing withstands this coolness
closing in, so constantly remote.
I'd live the night out
on the dark hymnal lake, to hear it talking
towards the edges of itself – that voice of the waters
so completely unbothered,
syllabic and out for the count.

RACHAEL BOAST

Us

If you ask me, *us* takes in *undulations* –
each wave in the sea, all insides compressed –
as if, from one coast, you could reach out to

the next; and maybe it's a Midlands thing
but when I was young, *us* equally meant *me*,
says the one, 'Oi, you, tell us where yer from';

and the way supporters share the one fate –
I, being one, am *Liverpool* no less –
cresting the Mexican wave of *we* or *us*,

a shore-like state, two places at once, God
knows what's in it; and, at opposite ends
my heart's sunk at separations of *us*.

When it comes to us, colour me unsure.
Something in me, or it, has failed the course.
I'd love to think I could stretch to it – us –

but the waves therein are too wide for words.
I hope you get, here, where I'm coming from.
I hope you're with me on this – between love

and loss – where I'd give myself away, stranded
as if the universe is a matter of one stress.
Us. I hope, from here on, I can say it

and though far-fetched, it won't be too far wrong.

ZAFFAR KUNIAL

ACKNOWLEDEGEMENTS

The publisher gratefully acknowledges permission to reprint copyright material in this book as follows:

ABSE, DANNIE: 'Epithalamion' from *New & Collected Poems* (Hutchinson 2003) © Dannie Abse 2003; 'The Boasts of Hywel ab Owain Gwynedd' © Dannie Abse; both poems reproduced by permission of the Estate through United Agents

ADCOCK, FLEUR: 'Immigrant' © Fleur Adcock reprinted by kind permission of Bloodaxe Books

AGARD, JOHN: 'Listen, Mr Oxford Don' © John Agard reprinted by kind permission of Bloodaxe Books from *Alternative Anthem: Selected Poems,* with Live DVD (Bloodaxe Books 2009)

AGBABI, PATIENCE: 'The London Eye', from *Bloodshot Monochrome* (Canongate 2008), reprinted by permission of the publisher

ALLNUTT, GILLIAN: 'Alien' © Gillian Allnut reprinted by kind permission of Bloodaxe Books from *How the Bicycle Shone: New & Selected Poems* (Bloodaxe 2007)

ALVI, MONIZA: 'Presents from my Aunts in Pakistan' © Moniza Alvi reprinted by kind permission of Bloodaxe Books from *Split World: Poems 1990–2005* (Bloodaxe Books 2005)

ARMITAGE, SIMON: 'To the Women of Merrie England Coffee Houses, Huddersfield', Taken from *Paper Aeroplane: Selected Poems 1988–2014* © Simon Armitage and reprinted with permission of Faber & Faber; translation © Simon Armitage and reprinted with permission of Faber & Faber

AUDEN, W. H.: 'Refugee Blues'; 'Night Mail'; 'In Memory of W. B. Yeats' © the Estate of W. H. Auden by kind permission of the Estate through its agents Curtis Brown

BECKETT, SAMUEL: 'Cascando', taken from *Collected Poems of Samuel Beckett* © Estate of Samuel Beckett and reprinted with permission of Faber & Faber

BEER, PATRICIA: 'The Lost Woman' © the Estate of Patricia Beer reprinted by kind permission of Carcanet Press Ltd, Manchester, UK

BELLERBY, FRANCES: 'Lovers are Separate'; 'Ends Meet', from *Selected Poems* (Enitharmon)

[671]

[672]

EDGAR, MARRIOTT: 'The Lion and Albert' © the Estate of Marriott Edgar

ELIOT, T. S.: 'The Love Song of Alfred J. Prufrock' taken from *The Poems of T. S . Eliot: Volume I* © the Estate of T. S. Eliot and reprinted with permission of Faber & Faber; 'A Game of Chess' taken from *The Waste Land* © the Estate of T. S. Eliot and reprinted with permission of Faber & Faber

EVANS, MARGIAD: 'To my sister Sian' © the Estate of Margiad Evans

FAINLIGHT, RUTH: 'Handbag' © Ruth Fainlight reprinted by kind permission of Bloodaxe Books from *New & Collected Poems* (Bloodaxe Books 2011)

FANTHORPE, U. A.: 'Father in the Railway Buffet' from *New and Collected Poems,* Enitharmon Press 2010

FARLEY, PAUL: '*from* The Electric Poly-Olbion' © Paul Farley reproduced by permission of Rogers Coleridge and White

FISHER, ROY: 'The Nation' © Roy Fisher reprinted by kind permission of Bloodaxe Books from *The Long & the Short of It: Poems 1955–2010* (Bloodaxe Books 2012)

FRANCIS, MATTHEW: '*from* The Mabinogian' © Matthew Francis and Faber & Faber

GARIOCH, ROBERT: 'Brither Worm'; 'I'm Neutral'; 'Ghaisties' © The Estate of Robert Garioch

GASCOYNE, DAVID: 'A Wartime Dawn' © The Estate of David Gascoyne

GERSHON, KAREN: 'I Was Not There' © The Estate of Karen Gershon

GLYN, IFOR AP: 'Elevation' © Ifor ap Glyn

GRAHAM, W. S.: 'To My Wife at Midnight'; 'Greenock at Night I Find You'; 'Loch Thom' reproduced by permission of Rosalind Mudaliar, the Estate of W. S. Graham

GRAVES, ROBERT: 'Tilth'; 'The Christmas Robin' © Estate of Robert Graves reprinted by kind permission of Carcanet Press Ltd, Manchester, UK

GREENLAW, LAVINIA: 'Blackwater' taken from *Minsk* © Lavinia Greenlaw and reprinted with permission of Faber & Faber

GWENALLT JONES, D.: 'Sin' © The Estate of D. Gwenallt Jones

GUNN, THOM: 'Hampstead: Horse Chestnut Trees' taken from *Collected Poems* © Estate of Thom Gunn and reprinted with permission of Faber & Faber

HAMER, RICHARD: translations © Richard Hamer reprinted by permission of Faber & Faber

[675]

[677]

Pharoah's Daughter (1990)

NICHOLSON, NORMAN: 'The Elm Decline' from *Collected Poems* reprinted by permission of Faber & Faber

NORRIS, LESLIE: 'Barn Owl'; 'Water' © Meic Stephens

O'BRIEN, SEAN: 'Cousin Coat' © Sean O'Brien reproduced by kind permission of Picador

O'CONNOR, FRANK: translations © the Estate of Frank O'Connor reproduced by kind permission of Peters Fraser and Dunlop

O'DONOGHUE, BERNARD: translation © Bernard O'Donoghue reproduced by permission of the author and Faber & Faber

OSWALD, ALICE: 'Another Westminster Bridge' taken from *Woods etc* © Alice Oswald and reprinted with permission of Faber & Faber

PARRY, ROBERT: 'The Fox' © The Estate of Robert Williams Parry

PATERSON, DON: 'A Private Bottling' taken from *God's Gift to Women* © Don Paterson and reprinted with permission of Faber & Faber

PITTER, RUTH: 'An Old Woman Speaks of the Moon'; 'Wild Honey' © The Estate of Ruth Pitter

PLATH, SYLVIA: 'The Bee Meeting'; 'Blackberrying' taken from *Collected Poems* © Estate of Sylvia Plath and reprinted with permission of Faber & Faber

POTTER, CLARE: translation © Clare Potter

PUGH, SHEENAGH: 'I think someone might write an elegy' © Sheenagh Pugh from *Selected Poems* (Seren 1990)

RAINE, KATHLEEN: 'Northumbrian Sequence: IV' © The Literary Estate of Kathleen Raine from *Collected Poems* (2000)

READ, HERBERT: 'To a Conscript of 1940' © the Estate of Herbert Read from *Selected Poetry* (Sinclair-Stevenson)

REED, HENRY: 'Lessons of War' © Royal Literary Fund

REES-JONES, DERYN: *'Liverpool Blues',* © Deryn Rees-Jones reprinted by kind permission of Seren Books

REID, ALASTAIR: 'Scotland' © Alastair Reid reproduced with permission from *Inside Out – Selected Poetry and Translations* (Polygon 2008)

RIDLER, ANNE: 'The Child Expected' © Estate of Anne Ridler reprinted by kind permission of Carcanet Press Ltd, Manchester, UK

RILEY, DENISE: 'Poor Snow' © Denise Riley reproduced from *No Fee* (Street Editions, 1977)

RIORDAN, MAURICE: translation © Maurice Riordan reproduced with

INDEX OF POETS AND TRANSLATORS

INDEX OF TITLES AND FIRST LINES

[689]

[691]

[693]